Peripheral Nerve Injuries

Principles of Diagnosis

WEBB HAYMAKER, M.D.

CHIEF, NEUROPATHOLOGY SECTION
ARMED FORCES INSTITUTE OF PATHOLOGY
WASHINGTON, D.C.

BARNES WOODHALL, M.D.

PROFESSOR OF NEUROSURGERY
DUKE UNIVERSITY SCHOOL OF MEDICINE
DURHAM, NORTH CAROLINA

Second Edition   *272 Illustrations*

W. B. SAUNDERS COMPANY

Philadelphia & London

W. B. Saunders Company: West Washington Square
Philadelphia, Pa.   19105

12 Dyott Street
London, WCIA   1DB

833 Oxford Street
Toronto 18, Ontario

Peripheral Nerve Injuries   ISBN   0-7216-4590-9

Print No.:   12   11   10   9   8   7

To

E. V. H. *and* F. C. W.

Foreword

SINCE PERIPHERAL NERVE INJURIES are frequently encountered among battle casualties, and since the recuperative period is long and tedious, the problem of these injuries is an exceedingly important one to the Armed Services. The expertness with which these peripheral nerve injuries are treated by the neurosurgeon, the orthopedic surgeon and the physical therapist, all working together as a team, continues to be gratifying, but nonetheless many soldiers, because of the seriousness of their injuries, are returned to civil life with crippled limbs.

The success of our efforts to reduce the disability period and the incidence of unsatisfactory end results will in large measure be contingent on earlier recognition of such injuries. In this connection the second edition of Haymaker and Woodhall's monograph, which has undergone extensive revision, is particularly welcome, for it deals in a terse manner with the fundamentals of diagnosis.

The end results of various neurosurgical procedures carried out on injured peripheral nerves during Word War II are still being analyzed. Evaluation has sometimes been difficult because of the diverse ways in which the sensory changes have been recorded. This is apparent in some of the illustrations of the present monograph selected from the collection of peripheral nerve injuries in the files of the Armed Forces Institute of Pathology. In an effort to encourage uniformity of documentation and thus to make available the basic data needed for scientific inquiry, the authors have provided a simple method for the recording of sensory changes (Fig. 138, page 142).

In examining this monograph one cannot but be impressed with the richness of the illustrative material. Virtually all the photographs were obtained from the enormous collection assembled at the Armed Forces Institute of Pathology during World War II and in the course of the recent Korean conflict. The wisdom of the policy of making available in one central institution all this vast material, a policy initiated by Colonel James E. Ash, Medical Corp, previous Director of the Armed Forces Institute of Pathology, and ably carried on and amplified by the present Director, General Elbert DeCoursey, is illustrated in this monograph.

Many individuals have contributed to the present work unselfishly and often unknowingly. Their contributions in the conversion of war experience to the interests of general medical knowledge have, however, been acknowledged in the text wherever possible.

GEORGE E. ARMSTRONG
Major General, MC, USA
The Surgeon General

Preface to the Second Edition

In the Korean conflict, as in former ones, many medical officers not previously trained in the recognition of peripheral nerve injuries have been brought face-to-face with problems of diagnosis, the solution of which has not always been apparent. It is for these officers, as well as for medical students and civilian physicians who will be required to treat such patients, that this volume is intended.

The text is divided into four Sections: The *first* deals with the principles of innervation, the *second* with examination of the patient, the *third* with a clinicopathological classification of peripheral nerve injuries and causes and the general symptomatology of such injuries, and the *fourth* with the clinical features of individual plexus and peripheral nerve injuries. At the beginning of each Section there are brief remarks intended to indicate the highlights of the subject matter.

Most of the photographs included in this volume were selected from the collection at the Armed Forces Institute of Pathology made available to us through the courtesy of the Director, General Elbert De Coursey. The source of each is indicated by initials in legends, as follows: *A.G.H.*, Ashford General Hospital; *B.G.H.*, Bushnell General Hospital; *C.H.*, Camp Haan; *DUH*, Duke University Hospital; *E.G.H.*, England General Hospital; *F.A.H.*, Fitzsimons Army Hospital; *F.G.H.*, Finney General Hospital; *H.H.*, Halloran General Hospital; *H.G.H.*, Hammond General Hospital; *N.D.B.*, Newton D. Baker Army Hospital; *R.G.H.*, Ream General Hospital; *Rh.G.H.*, Rhodes General Hospital; *P.J.H.*, Percy Jones Army Hospital; *V.A.*, Veterans Administration Hospital; *W.G.H.*, Wakeman General Hospital; *W.R.*, Walter Reed Army Hospital; *20th G.H.*, 20th General Hospital.

Credit for most of the drawings goes to Sgt. Frederic Stiner, Sgt. Frederick Toelle, Cpl. A. Manfredi, and Nancy Weyl. Considerable help was also rendered by Pfc. N. B. Raum and Mr. Paul Peck. All were stationed at the Armed Forces Institute of Pathology either during World War II or subsequently. The painstaking lettering is the work of Mr. Rudolph Stuven.

Certain standard works have been consulted in the preparation of the text: particularly, Cunningham on anatomy, and Foerster, Tinel, Pollock and Davis, Benisty and Kinnier Wilson on the clinical features of peripheral nerve injuries. Although valuable data were obtained from these sources it was felt that in the interests of brevity, acknowledgment in the text of each source of information was impracticable. *Aids to Investigation of Peripheral Nerve Injuries,* prepared at the beginning of World War II by the Nerve Injuries Committee of the Medical Research Council, England, under the direction of Sir James Learmonth, has been especially valuable to the authors in their selection of tests for motor power. The chapter on this subject has also benefited from the collaboration of Dr. John B. deC. M. Saunders of the University of California, San Francisco and Berkeley.

In the present edition the text has been thoroughly reworked and more abundantly supported by references to literature. Greater emphasis has been given to such topics as pain, trick movements, contracture, electromyographic studies, and Hoffmann-Tinel's sign. A new chapter on the different degrees of nerve injury in terms of pathological changes has been introduced, for it is felt that diagnosis can be more easily reached and therapy more intelligently pursued when the nature of the nerve injury is understood. Forty-seven new illustrations have been added and numerous others have been modified. Many of the changes and additions were in response to criticisms of the previous edition. Those who thus favored us, to whom we wish to express our deep appreciation, include Sir James Learmonth, of Edinburgh, Dr. Sydney Sunderland and Dr. Keith C. Bradley, of Melbourne, Australia, Dr. Robert Wartenberg, of San Francisco, Dr. H. Gaylis, of Johannesburg, South Africa, and Dr. Robert Hodes, of New Orleans. Dr. Curt Richter, of Baltimore, did us the great service of rewriting the paragraphs on skin resistance (in Chap. 9), and Dr. Keith C. Bradley provided a description of the pain in amputees (in Chap. 8), for which we are very grateful.

A source of great satisfaction in the preparation of this edition was the cooperative spirit of the staff of the W. B. Saunders Company. To Mrs. Helen Knight Steward and Miss Jessie Clare Tomlinson—of the Armed Forces Institute of Pathology—for their aid in preparing the manuscript also go the authors' sincere thanks.

WEBB HAYMAKER
BARNES WOODHALL

October, 1953

Contents

SECTION II

Examination of the Peripheral Nervous System

SECTION III

Classification, Causes and Symptomatology of Peripheral Nerve Injuries

SECTION IV

Injuries of Plexuses and Peripheral Nerves

Chapter 12

An Analysis of the Segmental and the Peripheral Nerve Supply of Skin, Muscles and Skeleton

THE OPENING section is intended to provide a background for the diagnosis of peripheral nerve injuries. The first chapter, in dealing with the principles of innervation of dermatomes, myotomes, and peripheral nerve fields, emphasizes the structural characteristics of the simplest segmental nerve, an intercostal. It then indicates wherein such a nerve differs from those that traverse plexuses to course distally in the limbs. Consideration is given also to the routes traveled by sympathetic neurons.

Succeeding chapters deal mainly with the distribution of segmental and peripheral nerves and to a certain extent with clinical application. The discussion of segmental innervation brings out the importance of the mode of migration of the limb buds and the development of the head and face in determining the position of dermatomes. The chapter on peripheral nerve fields reiterates the distinction between anterior and posterior primary rami and emphasizes certain structural features of a limb plexus. The concluding chapter is concerned principally with anatomical aspects of segmental and peripheral nerve supply of the skeleton.

CHAPTER 1

General Principles of the Composition of Segmental Nerves, Plexuses and Peripheral Nerves

THE ARRANGEMENT of the neural pathways from spinal cord to periphery provides the basis for distinguishing clinically the site of a given lesion—whether it be in a peripheral nerve, a plexus, a mixed spinal nerve, a spinal root, or the spinal cord. Although neural patterns vary, there are certain features of the arrangement which are common to all spinal nerves. These may be observed most readily in the simplest of spinal nerves, the intercostals, which still retain their metameric features.

The Gross Pattern of a Segmental Nerve

The pattern of an intercostal nerve is illustrated in Figure 1. It may be divided into three parts: the mixed spinal nerve* (formed by the union of anterior and posterior roots), the posterior primary ramus, and the anterior primary ramus.

On emergence from its intervertebral foramen, the mixed spinal nerve almost immediately divides into two rami, posterior and anterior. The *posterior primary ramus* is distributed to the dorsal part of the trunk where it innervates the skin and the longitudinal muscles of the axial skeleton. The *anterior primary ramus* circles the trunk, giving off twigs to muscles. On reaching the lateral aspect of the body, the anterior primary ramus divides into a *lateral cutaneous branch*, which, as the term indicates, is distributed to the skin of the lateral part of the body, and an *anterior cutaneous branch*, which reaches the anterior surface of the body.

Characteristic of a segmental nerve is the presence of two sympathetic rami, which are the means of communication between the anterior primary ramus and sympathetic ganglia. The more lateral of these is the *white ramus communicans*, extending to the sympathetic

---

* This component frequently is referred to as the "trunk of the spinal nerve" but in order to avoid confusion with trunks of plexuses, the term *mixed spinal nerve* generally is employed. "Mixed" refers to the presence of sensory, motor, and sympathetic elements in this part of the nerve.

ganglion; the other is the *grey ramus communicans,* which conveys fibers away from the sympathetic ganglion.

Variations in the Pattern of the Segmental Nerve

The patterns of individual posterior and anterior primary rami are subject to considerable variation. In Figure 1, which represents an inter-

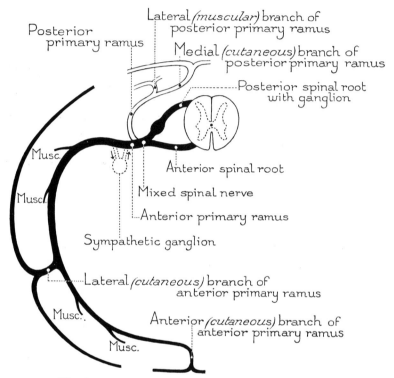

FIGURE 1.   *The Components of a Segmental Nerve.* For purposes of clarity the posterior primary ramus is indicated in outline. *Musc.* refers to the muscular branches given off by the anterior primary ramus.

costal nerve, it will be noted that the lateral branch of the *posterior primary ramus* is muscular in distribution, and that the medial branch is cutaneous. This arrangement is characteristic of the upper part of the body. In the lower part of the body the reverse obtains, the lateral branches reaching the skin, and the medial ones, the muscles.

In regard to distribution, the posterior primary rami innervate (1) the longitudinal muscles of the back (i.e., only those associated with the axial skeleton), and (2) the skin of the dorsal part of the trunk and the neck as well as the scalp of the back of the head (the region bounded by broken lines in Figs. 27 and 28; pp. 39 and 40).

Anterior primary rami supply the nonaxial skeletal muscles in addition to the skin of the lateral and anterior aspects of the trunk and neck. The formation of limb plexuses by anterior primary rami is described on pages 209–210, 273–274 and 286–287.

As to the *sympathetic rami communicantes*, each anterior primary ramus from T1 to L2 inclusive is in communication with a sympathetic ganglion in a manner identical with that shown in Figure 1: each sends a white ramus communicans to a sympathetic ganglion and each receives a grey ramus communicans from the same ganglion. In other regions the arrangement differs in that each anterior primary ramus receives a grey ramus communicans but has no white one. In all, there are 14 pairs of *white* rami communicans and 31 pairs of *grey*.

The Component Fibers of a Segmental Nerve

The trunk of a segmental nerve, like that of any other nerve, contains fibers of three categories: motor, sensory and sympathetic.

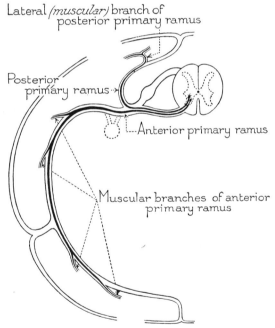

Lateral *(muscular)* branch of posterior primary ramus

Posterior primary ramus

Anterior primary ramus

Muscular branches of anterior primary ramus

FIGURE 2.   *A Segmental Nerve, Illustrating the Routes Traveled by Efferent Fibers to Muscles.*

MOTOR COMPONENTS

The motor components extend from anterior horns of the spinal cord to skeletal muscles (Fig. 2). They arise in the anterior horn cells of a given spinal segment, course in the converging filaments of the anterior root, then gain the mixed spinal nerve where they divide into two groups: one of these enters the posterior primary ramus and proceeds distally to reach the lateral (muscular) branch of the ramus while the other group takes its course through the anterior primary ramus to be distributed at various intervals to muscles.

Sensory Components

The sensory components of a segmental nerve arise from nerve endings in a variety of somatic structures: cutaneous and subcutaneous

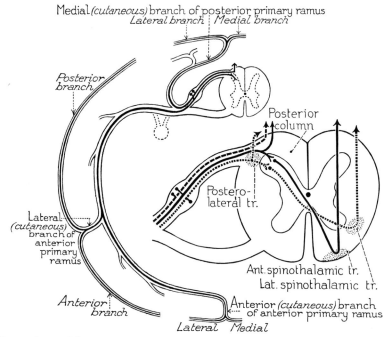

Medial *(cutaneous)* branch of posterior primary ramus
Lateral branch | *Medial branch*

Posterior branch

Posterior column

Postero-lateral tr.

Lateral (cutaneous) branch of anterior primary ramus

Ant. spinothalamic tr.
Lat. spinothalamic tr.

Anterior branch

Anterior *(cutaneous)* branch of anterior primary ramus

Lateral   Medial

Figure 3.   *A Segmental Nerve, Showing the Course of Sensory Neurons from the Periphery to the Spinal Cord.* The fibers indicated by the *broken line* convey deep sensibility; those in *solid black,* touch; those shown as *dotted lines,* pain and thermal sensibility.

tissues, tendons, joint tissues, periosteum, and skeletal muscle (Fig. 3). They extend proximally in the anterior and posterior primary rami, traverse the mixed spinal nerve with the motor fibers, and then enter the diverging filaments of the posterior root. After making connections with their respective ganglion cells, they gain and ascend the spinal cord, taking various routes in accordance with the type of sensibility they transmit (Fig. 3):

TYPE OF SENSIBILITY	COURSE IN SPINAL CORD
Muscle and joint sensibility (appreciation of position and movement)	Direct ascent in homolateral posterior column, with first synapse in nuclei gracilis and cuneatus.
Tactile sensibility	A minority of the fibers take the same course as just indicated. The others synapse in the posterior horn about cells, the fibers of which decussate and ascend in the anterior spinothalamic tract.
Pain and thermal sensibility	The incoming fibers synapse in the substantia gelatinosa of the corresponding segment and, after ascending the posterolateral tract, they end in the substantia gelatinosa of the two or three (or possibly more) successively higher segments. Secondary fibers decussate and ascend the spinal cord in the lateral spinothalamic tract.

Sympathetic Components

The sympathetic pathway from the spinal cord to the periphery consists of two groups of neurons: preganglionic and postganglionic (Fig. 4). In every segment from T1 to L2, the *preganglionic fibers* take origin from intermediolateral horn cells and traverse the anterior spinal root and the mixed spinal nerve to gain the anterior primary ramus. They split off en masse from the proximal part of this ramus to enter the white ramus communicans ("white" because the fibers are myelinated) and extend to the respective sympathetic ganglion where they synapse with postganglionic neurons.

The *postganglionic fibers* (nonmyelinated and therefore grey) make up the emergent grey ramus communicans. The fibers, on reaching the anterior primary ramus, split into two groups, one extending into the posterior primary ramus, the other pursuing its course through the branches of the anterior primary ramus. These fibers innervate blood vessels, sweat glands, and erector muscles of the hairs.

The Spinal Nerves to the Limbs

The components of the spinal nerves which extend into the limbs are in some respects the same as those of the segmental nerve already described. Thus, each limb nerve has an anterior and a posterior spinal root, a mixed spinal nerve, an anterior primary ramus and, with certain exceptions, a posterior primary ramus. Here the analogy ends. Limb nerves differ in that the fibers of their anterior primary rami form plexuses in which the fibers destined for ventral and dorsal parts of the limb are segregated. The rearrangement in plexuses is such that each of the emergent peripheral nerves receives fibers from more than one spinal segment.

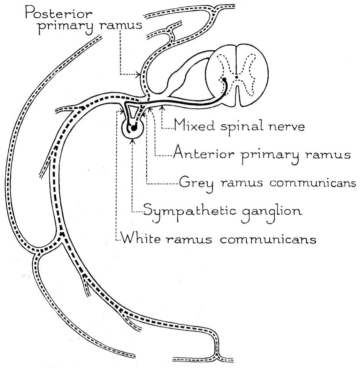

Posterior primary ramus

Mixed spinal nerve

Anterior primary ramus

Grey ramus communicans

Sympathetic ganglion

White ramus communicans

FIGURE 4.   *The Course of Sympathetic Fibers in a Segmental Nerve.* Preganglionic fibers are indicated by solid line, postganglionic by broken lines.

THE PATTERN OF THE MOTOR ELEMENTS

As in the segmental nerve, the motor fibers extending to the limbs pass distally in anterior spinal roots and mixed spinal nerves. The motor fibers then divide into two groups, one entering the posterior primary ramus, the other the anterior primary ramus. Those reaching the posterior primary rami are relatively few in number; none of them reaches the limb muscles.

The Means by Which Myotomes Are Innervated

Motor elements arising in a given segment pursue their course through certain components of a plexus and through certain peripheral nerves to reach a number of muscles. The group of muscles supplied from a single spinal segment is known as a *myotome*. To cite a specific example: the motor fibers from spinal segment C5 extend through the corresponding anterior root, mixed spinal nerve, and undivided anterior primary ramus; they then traverse the upper trunk of the brachial plexus and its anterior and posterior divisions and, subsequently, the lateral and the posterior cords (Fig. 5; see also Fig. 180 for trunks, divi-

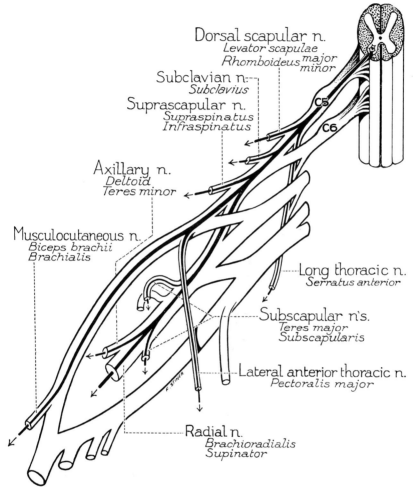

Dorsal scapular n.
Levator scapulae
Rhomboideus major
minor

Subclavian n.
Subclavius

Suprascapular n.
Supraspinatus
Infraspinatus

C5

C6

Axillary n.
Deltoid
Teres minor

Musculocutaneous n.
Biceps brachii
Brachialis

Long thoracic n.
Serratus anterior

Subscapular n's.
Teres major
Subscapularis

Lateral anterior thoracic n.
Pectoralis major

Radial n.
Brachioradialis
Supinator

FIGURE 5.   *The Distribution of Motor Fibers of the Fifth Cervical Spinal Segment.* The muscles supplied by this spinal segment constitute a *myotome.* The components of the brachial plexus and the peripheral nerves traversed by the fibers in reaching the myotome are indicated.

sions and cords). En route, the fibers enter several peripheral nerves, each of which supplies muscles of the shoulder or the arm.

If the upper trunk is interrupted distal to the point where the long thoracic, dorsal scapular, and suprascapular nerves are given off, only a part of the myotome will be affected; when the lateral cord is interrupted at a point just beyond the emergence of the lateral anterior thoracic nerve the disability in the myotome will be even less widespread (Fig. 5). Thus, the more distal the lesion in the plexus, the smaller the compass of myotomic derangement.

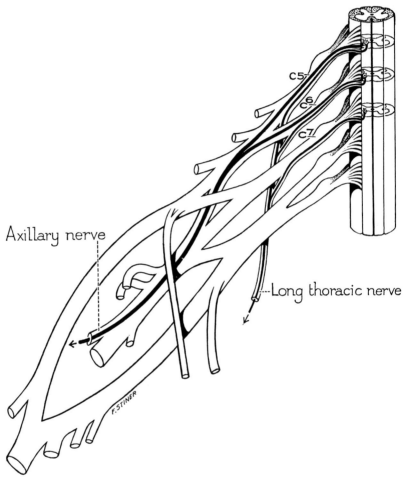

FIGURE 6.   *The Origin and Course of Fibers Extending via the Axillary Nerve to the Deltoid Muscle and via the Long Thoracic Nerve to the Serratus Anterior.* The components of the brachial plexus and peripheral nerves traversed are indicated (cf. Fig. 180, p. 210.)

The Innervation of Individual Limb Muscles

The fact that a certain muscle receives innervation from a given spinal segment does not imply that the same muscle cannot receive a supply from other segments as well. Indeed, all the limb muscles receive fibers from more than one spinal segment, as a glance at Tables I to IV (pp. 34 to 37) will illustrate. The deltoid muscle, for instance, in addition

to being innervated by segment C5, receives fibers from C6; the serratus anterior gets its supply from spinal segments C5, C6 and C7 (Fig.
6). Most muscles receive their innervation from a single nerve while
others, owing to fusion, have a double nerve supply. Examples of
doubly innervated muscles are the pectoralis major, the subscapularis,
the flexor digitorum profundus, the soleus, the biceps femoris, and the
adductor magnus.

The innervation of a single limb muscle by more than one segment or by
more than one nerve has clinical significance: complete paralysis of a given
muscle, with subsequent total atrophy, results only if the fibers from each
of the participating spinal segments are destroyed. If the muscle is com-
posite, atrophy will be complete only if the fibers of both its nerves are
interrupted.

The Pattern of the Sensory Elements

The pattern of sensory elements of the spinal nerves is similar to that
of motor elements in that the sensory fibers coursing proximally in the
peripheral nerves regroup in the plexuses and then gain their respective
posterior roots and spinal segments.

Each of the peripheral nerve fields is innervated by fibers which
enter more than one spinal segment. The course of the fibers of the
radial nerve will serve as an example (Fig. 7). By way of contrast the
fibers from dermatomes usually traverse a combination of peripheral
nerves and plexus components to gain their spinal segment.

Lesions of sensory elements can be localized with a reasonable degree of
accuracy. Interruption of a peripheral nerve leads to sensory deficit, variable
in extent, within the region of distribution of the nerve. In lesions of the
distal part of a plexus, the pattern of sensory loss tends to simulate that of a
combined peripheral nerve palsy. When the most proximal part of a plexus
is affected, the pattern of altered sensibility is segmental in character. The
more distal the damage in the plexus, the less the tendency toward segmental
arrangement of the sensory deficit.

The Pattern of the Sympathetic Elements

Every nerve trunk contains sympathetic fibers which reach the
plexuses and peripheral nerves by certain well defined routes.

The Origin and Distribution of Sympathetic Fibers Gaining the Brachial Plexus

The preganglionic fibers arise in the intermediolateral horn cells of
spinal segments T3 to T6 inclusive; probably also those of T2 (Smithwick, 1936) and T7 (Foerster, 1939) (Fig. 8). They emerge from the
spinal cord through the corresponding anterior roots, traverse the proximal part of the anterior primary rami and, in turn, the white rami communicantes, to gain the sympathetic chain. They then proceed upward

in the chain to the stellate and the middle cervical sympathetic ganglia where they synapse with postganglionic neurons. As separate bundles, the postganglionic fibers extend to the undivided anterior primary rami of the brachial plexus. Sunderland and Bedbrook (1949) have observed

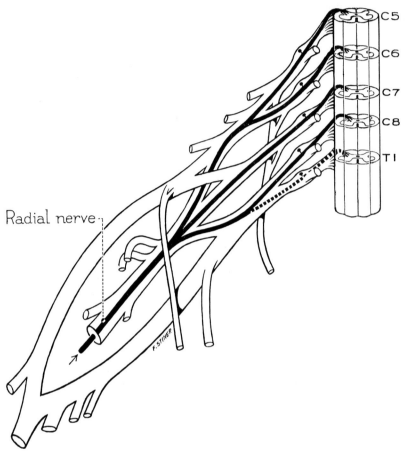

FIGURE 7.   *The Pathways Followed by Fibers of the Radial Nerve in Reaching the Spinal Cord.* The fibers of the radial nerve traverse, in turn, the posterior cord of the brachial plexus, the posterior divisions of the trunks, the trunks and all the undivided anterior primary rami except possibly that of segment T1 (in dotted line).

that the lowest root of the brachial plexus (T1) receives more post-ganglionic fibers than any other root, and root C5 the fewest. The postganglionic fibers pass through the plexus and the peripheral nerves to supply arterioles, sweat glands, and pilo-erector muscles. The fibers destined for arterioles take two routes: (1) down the peripheral nerves as just indicated, branching at intervals to gain larger vessels or continuing into distal ramifications of the nerve to reach smaller ones; (2) from the stellate and upper thoracic sympathetic ganglia, as a group of nerves extending to the subclavian artery to reach arterioles of the upper arm.

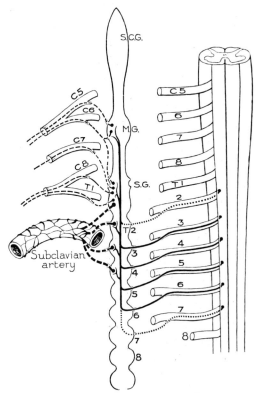

FIGURE 8.   *Diagram of the Sympathetic Supply of the Upper Limb.* Preganglionic fibers take origin from spinal segments T3 to T6 (*solid lines*) and perhaps from T2 and T7 (*dotted lines*). At the point of emergence from anterior primary rami they form white rami communicates. Postganglionic neurons (indicated by *broken lines*) extend to components of the brachial plexus and to the subclavian artery as grey rami communicates. *S.C.G.,* Superior cervical sympathetic ganglion; *M.G.,* middle cervical sympathetic ganglion; *S.G.,* stellate ganglion. (After Foerster, 1939.)

The Relation to the Brachial Plexus of Sympathetic Fibers Extending to Orbital Structures

The preganglionic fibers for the supply of orbital structures arise in spinal segments T1 and T2 (and perhaps also T3), traverse the corresponding anterior roots, mixed spinal nerves, and the proximal part of the anterior primary rami (Fig. 9). As white rami communicates they

reach the sympathetic chain and ascend to the superior cervical sympathetic ganglion, where they end. Postganglionic fibers, traveling via
the internal carotid and ophthalmic arteries, gain the orbit, where they

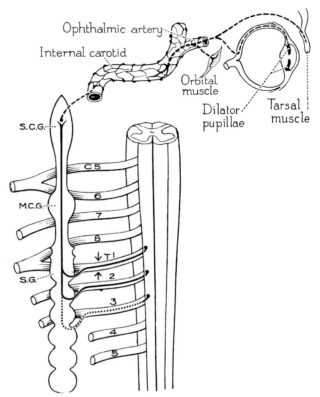

FIGURE 9.   *Diagram of the Sympathetic Innervation of Ocular Structures.* The
preganglionic fibers take origin from spinal segments T1 and T2 (in
solid lines) and possibly from T3 (in *dotted line*) (see Fulton, 1949).
They leave the anterior primary rami as white rami communicantes to
enter into and ascend in the sympathetic ganglionated chain. The postganglionic neurons (in *broken lines*) arise in the superior cervical
sympathetic ganglion. The arrows indicate the root damaged in cases
of plexus injury in which Horner's syndrome develops. *S.C.G.*, Superior cervical sympathetic ganglion; *M.C.G.*, middle cervical sympathetic ganglion; *S.G.*, stellate ganglion.

supply the dilator muscle of the pupil, the smooth muscle of the upper
eyelid, and the smooth muscle in the back of the orbit. They also innervate the arterioles of the eyeball, including those of the conjunctivae.

The Origin and Distribution of Sympathetic Fibers Reaching the Lumbosacral Plexus

The sympathetic preganglionic fibers arise in spinal segments T10
to L2 inclusive, and extend through the corresponding anterior roots,

mixed spinal nerves, and proximal part of the anterior primary rami (Foerster, 1939) (Fig. 10). Through corresponding white rami com-

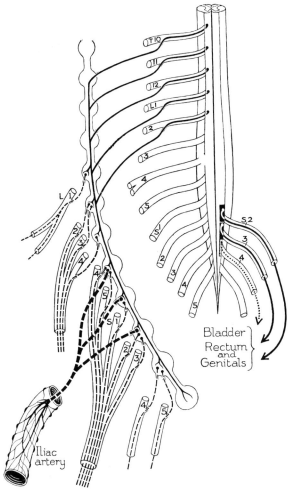

FIGURE 10.   *Diagram of the Sympathetic Supply of the Lower Limb.* Preganglionic fibers (in *solid lines*) emerge from anterior primary rami as
white rami communicantes to reach the ganglionated sympathetic
chain. Postganglionic fibers (in *broken lines*) extend to components
of the lumbosacral plexus as well as directly to the iliac artery. On
the right side is indicated the origin of parasympathetic fibers destined for pelvic viscera and organs; they arise from spinal segments
S2 and S3 (in *solid lines*) and probably from S4 (in *dotted line*).
(After Foerster, 1939).

municantes they reach the sympathetic chain, and descend to the ganglia
adjacent to vertebrae L3 to S3 inclusive. From here the postganglionic
fibers pass as grey rami communicantes to the various undivided an-

terior primary rami of the plexus. As in the upper limb, the sympathetic fibers reach blood vessels of the lower limb (1) directly from the sympathetic chain (from sympathetic ganglia at levels L5, S1 and S2), gaining the iliac artery and coursing with it a relatively short distance, and (2) via the plexus and the peripheral nerves. The fibers to sweat glands and pilo-erector muscles utilize the second route.

If any part of the neural pathway from intermediolateral horn cells to the periphery is cut off, there usually is preliminary redness (vasodilatation) of the field concerned and subsequent blanching (vasoconstriction). Sweating in the affected area no longer occurs. Moreover, the pilomotor reflex is lost and gooseflesh does not develop when the individual is exposed to a cold environment. When interruption is partial and irritative, or when adequate regeneration has occurred, vasodilatation and an increased tendency to sweat are evident.

Interruption of sympathetic fibers destined for orbital structures causes constriction of the pupil (*miosis*), drooping of the upper eyelid (*ptosis*) and, in some instances, a dilatation of the vessels of the eye, including those of the conjunctiva. Slight sinking of the eyeball into the orbit (*enophthalmos*) is generally said to be an additional feature of ocular sympathetic paralysis, but measurements of the position of the eye in the presence of sympathetic paralysis have shown that enophthalmos is only apparent, not real (Mutch, 1936); "strictly speaking, the eyeball does not sink into the orbit but gives the impression of so doing because both eyelids come together" (Learmonth, 1950). The presence of miosis, ptosis and apparent enophthalmos (*Horner's syndrome**) in injuries of the brachial plexus usually indicates that undivided primary ramus T1 (near the intervertebral foramen) has been severely damaged, for this is the sole component of the brachial plexus which contains sympathetic fibers. Occasionally, when injury exerts an irritative action, the sympathetic fibers are stimulated, as a result of which the palpebral fissure widens and the pupil dilates.

* In the case reported by Horner (1869), the patient, a woman aged 40, was aware for years of the ptosis of her right eyelid, and examination revealed miosis of that eye. The eyeball, according to Horner, had definitely sunk into the orbit, and he stated that measurements revealed that that eyeball was somewhat less resistant than the left. In this case there were also attacks of profound vasodilatation of the face (and to a less degree of the retina) of the same side. The cause of the sympathetic paralysis of the ocular structures and the trigeminal region was not determined.

CHAPTER 2

The Innervation of Skin
and Muscles by Spinal Segments

A KNOWLEDGE of segmental supply is essential in the diagnosis of lesions of peripheral nerves and limb plexuses. Frequently the first question arising in the mind of the examiner is: "Where is the lesion—in the spinal cord, a spinal root, a mixed nerve, a plexus component, or in a peripheral nerve?" In order to provide a background for differential diagnosis between peripheral nerve and plexus injuries and those more proximally located, the text deals in some detail with the pattern of innervation by spinal segments.

The Dermatomes

The cutaneous area supplied by a single posterior root and its ganglion through the intermediation of one or more peripheral nerves is known as a *dermatome*. There are as many dermatomes as there are spinal segments, with the single exception of the first cervical segment which, for practical purposes at least, has no cutaneous distribution.

THE EMBRYOLOGICAL DEVELOPMENT OF THE DERMATOMES

The Factor of Migration of the Limb Buds

During early embryonic life the spinal portion of the embryo is divided into segments called *metameres*, each of which is composed of ectoderm, mesoderm, and entoderm. This arrangement loses its uniformity when certain groups of metameres migrate into the limb buds. As the limb buds extend more and more distally the corresponding dermatomes also migrate, so that on the axial part of the trunk, dermatome C4 comes to lie next to dermatome T2 (Fig. 11), and L2 next to S3 (Fig. 12).

The Formation of the Axial Lines

The dermatomes that have migrated become grouped parallel to the long axis of the future limb, except at the periphery where they are arranged in a semicircular fashion. The dermatomes of the higher segments are grouped along the preaxial border of the limb, those of the lower segments along the postaxial border. The boundary between preaxial and postaxial dermatomes is known as an *axial line*. The distal part of each limb lacks axial lines.

As may be seen in Figure 12, the *dorsal axial line* of the upper limb may be traced from the vertebral column (in the region of spinous process T1), over the shoulder, and down the back of the arm to the middle third of the forearm. The *ventral axial line* starts in the region of the manubriosternal joint, spans the chest and extends downward on the front of the arm and forearm.

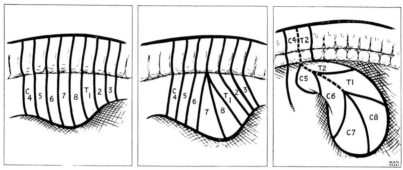

FIGURE 11.   *Diagram of Various Stages of Development of the Upper Limb, Showing the Mode of Migration of Its Dermatomes.* In the course of development, dermatomes C5, C6 and C7 come to occupy the preaxial part of the limb bud while dermatomes C8, T1 and T2 cover the postaxial portion. The migration of dermatomes is such that in the dorsal part of the trunk C4 eventually lies adjacent to T2. The extent of the dorsal axial line is indicated by a broken line. (After Bolk, 1898.)

In the lower limb, the mode of dermatomic migration is, in principle, the same, but, owing to rotation of the limb, the axial lines have assumed a semispiral course. When the factor of rotation is taken into account, the apparently confused dermatomic arrangement of the lower limb becomes clear. In the lower limb the *dorsal axial line* runs distally from the vertebral column (in the vicinity of spinous process S2), crosses the buttock and thigh, reaches the lateral aspect of the knee (where part of it winds round the knee to gain the subpatellar region), and then descends to the lateral aspect of the ankle. The *ventral axial line* may be traced from the root of the penis, round the medial aspect of the upper thigh, across the back of the thigh, then through the middle of the popliteal fossa, ultimately reaching the medial aspect of the ankle.

Although in the foregoing account the view is taken that as dermatomes migrate they become disconnected from their sources, there is evidence from

a study by Richter and Woodruff (1945) and others that all these dermatomes are continuous proximally to the midline. Thus, *dorsally*, instead of C4
lying next to T2, as shown in Figure 12, dermatomal strips from C5 through
T1 are interposed between C4 and T2, and the same arrangement applies to
the lower limb. *Ventrally*, C5 abuts against T1, and L1, L2, L3 and L4, repre-

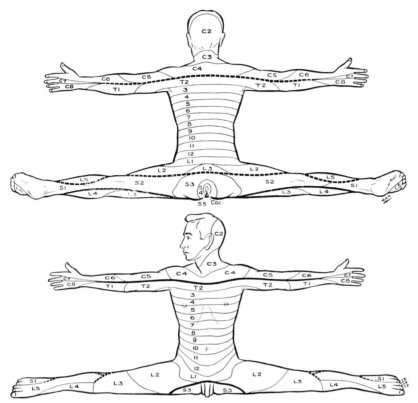

FIGURE 12.   *Diagram to Illustrate the Position of Ventral* (in solid lines) *and
              Dorsal* (in broken lines) *Axial Lines.* The axial lines of the upper
              limb extend down the middle of the corresponding surfaces. In the
              lower limb the ventral axial line starts in the region of the pubis and
              winds round the inner side of the thigh to gain the back of the thigh
              and subsequently the calf; the dorsal line, after crossing the upper
              part of the buttock, pursues a course down the more lateral part of
              the leg to the region of the ankle. (The dermatomic pattern is after
              Foerster, 1933.)

sented *seriatim* down the thigh, wind laterally round the hip to reach the
dorsal midline.

Because of overlapping, such zones can seldom be identified by the conven-
tional means of neurological examination, but can be detected by the electrical skin resistance method.

Keegan and Garrett's (1948) mapping (Fig. 13) was based on hyposensitivity to pin scratch in cases of herniated intervertebral disc. Neither they nor we have been able to obtain such an elongated dermatomic pattern by means of sharp pin-point stimulation. On the basis of the latter type of stimulus, one of us (B.W.) (1947) has found that the dermatomal field of sensory deficit resulting from pressure exerted by a herniated nucleus pulposus on a root is sometimes more extensive (Figs. 14, 15) than the fields of Foerster but never

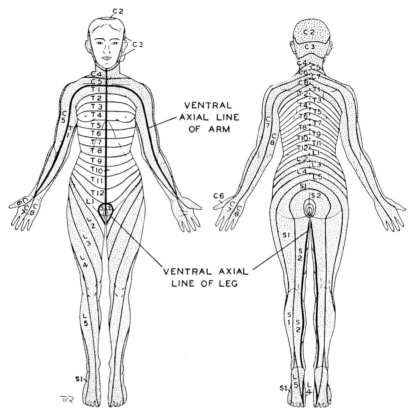

FIGURE 13.   *Dermatome Map According to Keegan and Garrett (1948).* The position of the dermatomal fields was based on hyposensitivity to pin scratch in cases of herniated intervertebral disc. (From original of Figure 2; J. J. Keegan and F. D. Garrett, Anat. Rec. *102:* 411, 1948.)

as extensive as those depicted by Keegan and Garrett. An average-sized field of sensory deficit is illustrated in Figure 16. Actually in herniated nucleus pulposus, Foerster's dermatomal map has in most cases held up day in and day out even with the pin-scratch method of examination. It seems likely that the extent of sensory change is dependent upon the degree of pressure upon the spinal root.

In Keegan and Garrett's map it will be noted that part of the great toe is in dermatome L4. Dejerine (1914), Tilney and Riley (1938), and Foerster (1933), however, have found that the great toe is supplied exclusively by dermatome L5 (Fig. 17). This is in line with our experience, except in one case in which the great toe was in field L4. Spurling also lists such an innervation as rare. Richter and Woodruff's (1945) map (Fig. 18), based on the

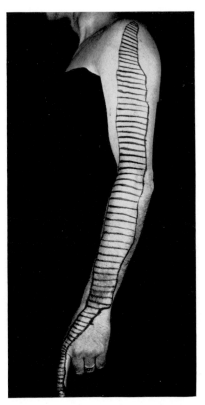

FIGURE 14. *Area of Sensory Deficit Resulting from Compression of Dorsal Spinal Root C7 by a Herniated Nucleus Pulposus.* The disc implicated was that between vertebrae C6 and C7. This photograph was taken one month after the onset of symptoms. There was no history of initiating trauma other than heavy lifting. In addition to the sensory loss the cervical spine was fixed and tilted to the right, pressure on the spinous processes of C6 and C7 caused radicular pain in the arm and paresthesias in the second finger. Also there were weakness of the triceps muscle and loss of the triceps reflex. The area of sensory deficit, obtained on the basis of sharp pin prick, extends much further proximally than the map of Foerster would indicate but not as far proximally as contended by Keegan and Garrett. Usually the area of sensory deficit is less extensive. (Case C-24265; DUH.)

skin resistance technique, differs from that of the other sources mentioned. Our experience with this method has been too limited to allow comment.

Moreover, Keegan and Garrett contended that no sensory overlap exists between dermatomes, but our experience is in accord with that stated on page 23.

THE CONFIGURATION OF THE DERMATOMES

The Dermatomes of the Neck, Body and Limbs

Of the methods devised to determine the site and extent of the various dermatomes in man, that of "remaining sensibility," employed by Foerster (1933), probably has yielded the most exact information. It

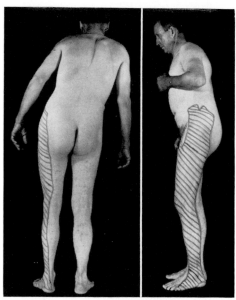

FIGURE 15.   *Area of Sensory Deficit Resulting from Compression of Dorsal Spinal Root S1 by the Herniated Intervertebral Disc Between Vertebrae L5 and S1.* The photograph was secured fifteen weeks after heavy lifting, at which time sciatic pain developed. The pain was accentuated by coughing. The alterations in the low back region are apparent. Straight leg raising on the left was restricted by pain to 15 degrees. Moreover, there was slight weakness of dorsal flexion at the left ankle, and the left ankle jerk was absent. The remarks on extent of sensory deficit in the legend of Figure 14 apply equally to this case. (Case C-11469; DUH.)

consists of severing a number of posterior roots above and below one that is left intact and then determining the boundaries of the field of unaltered sensibility. The area of skin in which sensibility is preserved was regarded as the dermatome of the intact root. For the study of those dermatomes which were not investigated in this manner, Foerster employed the "constructive method," which consists of dividing a series of contiguous posterior roots, and testing sensibility in the areas they supply. The superior border of the resulting area of anesthesia marked the lower limit of the next upper dermatome; the inferior border of the area of anesthesia indicated the upper limit of the next lower dermatome. The boundaries of virtually all the dermatomes have been traced by means of these two methods.

As may be seen in Figure 19, in which the dermatomes of three spinal segments are portrayed, there is considerable overlap of contiguous fields. The extent of overlap usually is enough so that interruption of a single posterior root of either a segmental (intercostal) or a peripheral nerve does not give rise to sensory deficit.

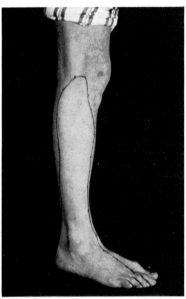

FIGURE 16.   *The Average-Sized Area of Sensory Deficit Resulting from Compression of Posterior Root S1 by an Extruded Intervertebral Disc.* The patient, a 45 year old farmer, had had low back pain and right-sided sciatica for three and one-half months previously. The dark line indicates the area of hypalgesia and hypesthesia elicited by a sharp pin and by cotton wool. (Case D-56184; DUH.)

The cutaneous maps (Figs. 20, 21, 22, 23) are designed for ready reference. It is to be understood that the lines bounding the dermatomes are only approximate—actually each dermatome extends further (in all directions) than indicated. In Figure 24, which shows the alignment of the dermatomes when the subject is in the quadruped position, most of the dermatomes are perpendicular to the ground.

Segmentation of the Skin of the Face

According to Dejerine (1914), Kraus (1935), Bing (1940), and others of the classical school of neurology, the skin of the face has segmental as well as peripheral nerve fields and thus its innervation does not differ, in principle, from that of the body. Facial dermatomes have been

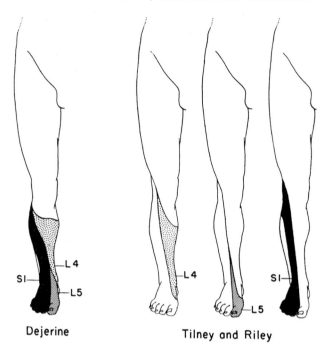

FIGURE 17.   *Dermatomes L4, L5 and S1 According to Dejerine (1914), and Tilney and Riley (1938).*

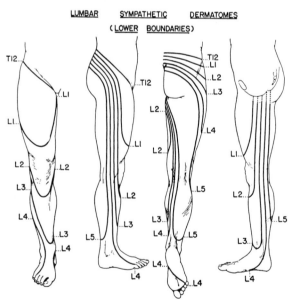

FIGURE 18.   *Dermatome Map Based on the Skin Resistance Studies of Richter and Woodruff (1945)*

depicted as having a concentric, or "onion peel," arrangement, center-
ing on the nose (Fig. 24).

The concept of facial cutaneous segmentation has been based on the
occurrence of "onion peel" analgesia and thermoanesthesia in syringobulbia and in syphilitic lesions of the medulla oblongata; and from

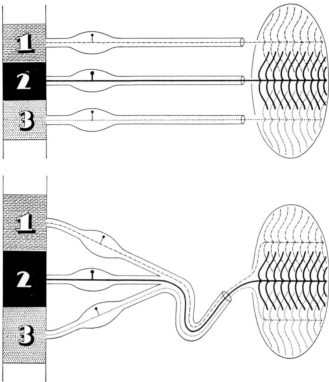

FIGURE 19.   *Diagrams Illustrating Overlap of Cutaneous Fields of Segmental and
Peripheral Nerves.* In the upper figure three intercostal nerves extending from periphery to spinal cord are represented; the lower figure
illustrates an analogous arrangement in a peripheral nerve. Because
of the overlap, interruption of any given spinal root causes little or
no change in cutaneous sensibility. (Modified after Bing, 1940.)

pathoanatomical studies of such cases it has been asserted that facial
segmentation is a reflection of lamination of the nucleus of the spinal
tract of the trigeminal nerve, the upper part of the nucleus innervating
the field nearest the nose and mouth, the intermediate part the semicircular area from forehead to chin in front of the ear, and the lower
part the most caudal area of the face.

Some recent observations have failed, however, to support this view.
From the studies of facial sensibility after tractotomy (performed for

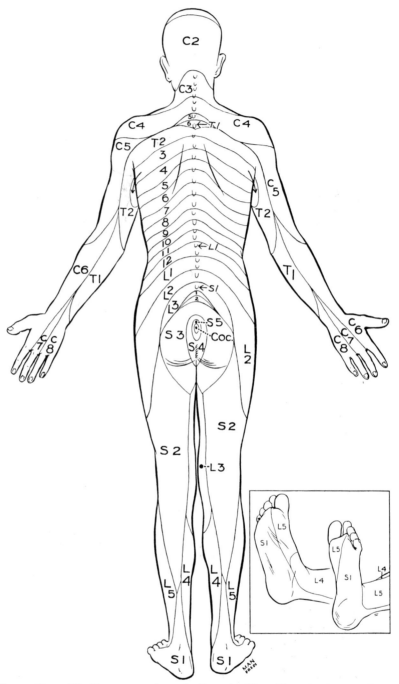

FIGURE 20. *The Dermatomes from the Posterior View.* Note the absence of cutaneous innervation by the first cervical segment. Arrows in the axillary regions indicate the lateral extent of dermatome T3; those in the region of the vertebral column point to the first thoracic, the first lumbar and the first sacral spinous processes. (After Foerster, 1933.)

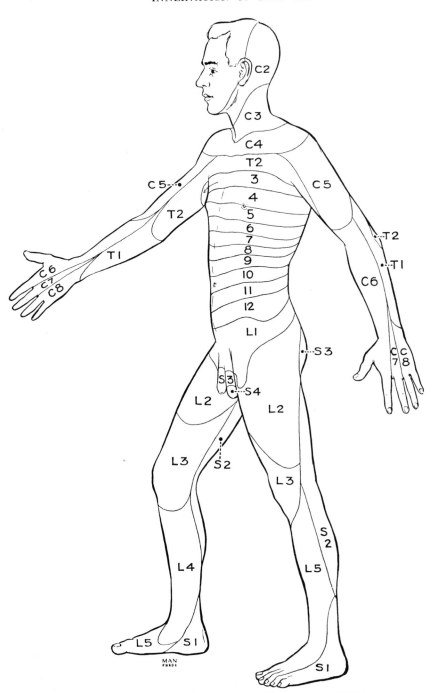

FIGURE 21. *A Side View of the Dermatomes.* (After Foerster, 1933.)

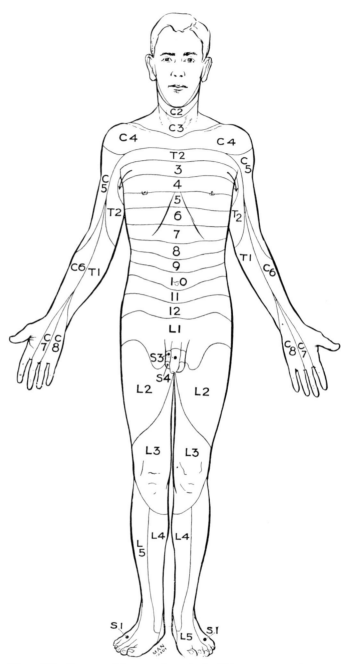

FIGURE 22.   *The Segmental Innervation of the Skin from the Anterior Aspect.*
The uppermost dermatome adjoins the cutaneous field of the mandibular division of the trigeminal nerve. The arrows indicate the lateral
extensions of dermatome T3. (After Foerster, 1933.)

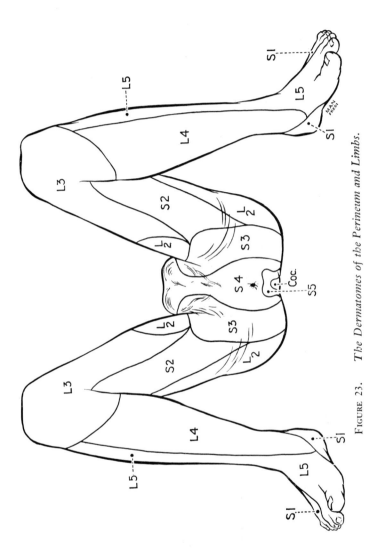

FIGURE 23.   *The Dermatomes of the Perineum and Limbs.*

the relief of facial pain), for instance, it has been concluded that only trigeminal *divisions* are represented in the nucleus of the spinal tract of the trigeminal nerve, the ophthalmic division in the lower part of the nucleus, the maxillary in an intermediate part of the nucleus, and

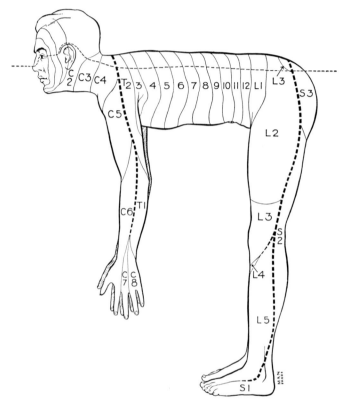

FIGURE 24.   *The Alignment of Dermatomes in the Quadruped Position.* This diagram, which is included for mnemonic purposes, emphasizes the positions of the dermatomic fields. The horizontal broken line extending from the sacral region to the tip of the nose marks the boundary between dorsal and ventral portions of trunk, neck, head and face. The vertical heavy broken lines on the limbs represent the dorsal axial lines. The facial segments (after Kraus, 1935), unlabeled because of variation of their boundaries, are the expression of lamination of the spinal nucleus of the trigeminal nerve. (The dermatomic fields are after Foerster, 1933.)

the mandibular highest of all. Richter and Woodruff (1942) have, however, convincingly demonstrated by means of the electrical skin resistance method (p. 190) that "onion-peel" type of innervation of the face exists. The patterns of low skin resistance which they observed corresponded closely with patterns of remaining pain and temperature sensibility found in patients with syringomyelia and syringobulbia.

The Topographical Relation of Spinal Segments to Vertebrae

In traumatic lesions involving spinal roots it is often necessary to explore surgically. The location of the "sensory level" will help in determining the site at which laminectomy is to be performed. In lesions of the spinal cord, by way of contrast, the upper border of the cutaneous area of sensory deficit may be two, three or possibly more segments below the level of the spinal lesion.

The relation of spinal segments and posterior roots to the vertebral column is illustrated in Figure 25. The spinal cord extends downward as far as the lower border of the first lumbar vertebra or the upper border of the second, and is therefore considerably shorter than the spinal canal. The mixed spinal nerves emerge from intervertebral foramina either at the level of the corresponding cord segment or after traversing the spinal canal for varying distances. It will be noted that the cervical roots pursue a course through intervertebral foramina *above* the respective vertebral bodies (root C8 is an exception in that it passes above vertebra T1), whereas the spinal roots of thoracic, lumbar and sacral nerves traverse intervertebral foramina *below* the respective vertebral bodies.

Using spinous processes as landmarks, most of the spinal segments may be located with a degree of accuracy by adhering to the following rule: Add 2 to the number of the spinous process and the resulting number is that of the underlying spinal segment. This applies from spinous process C2 to spinous process T10. Thus, spinous process C5 overlies spinal segment C7, and spinous process T6 covers spinal segment T8. Spinous processes T11, T12 and L1 overlie eleven spinal segments: L1–L5, S1–S5 and the 1st coccygeal.

Figure 26 is included for the purpose of identifying more precisely the relation of lumbosacral spinal roots to intervertebral foramina. In this illustration, in which the cauda equina is shown, it will be noted that the roots of each spinal segment course diagonally downward through the intervertebral space immediately below the pedicle of the corresponding vertebra. Relations are such, however, that a herniated intervertebral disc is apt to impinge on the posterior root of the next lower spinal segment: for instance, a disc which protrudes between vertebral bodies L4 and L5 is apt to compress spinal root L5.

The Myotomes

The group of muscles supplied from a single spinal segment is referred to as a *myotome*. The principles of myotomic innervation have been treated in Chapter 1. Tables 1 to 4 give lists of skeletal muscles in which the segmental supply of each is indicated. The information will aid the examiner in determining whether a given lesion is segmental in

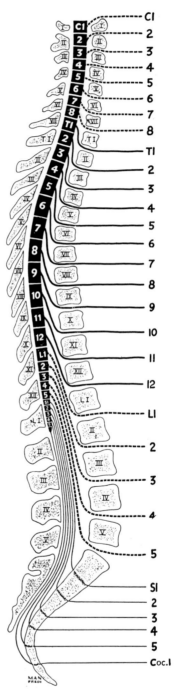

Figure 25.   *The Alignment of Spinal Segments with Vertebrae.* The bodies and spinous processes of the vertebrae are indicated by Roman numerals,

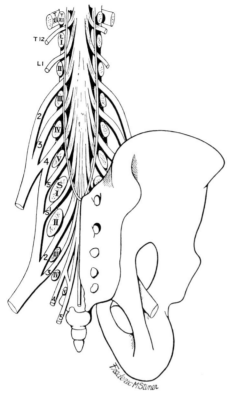

FIGURE 26.   *The Relations of the Roots of the Cauda Equina to Vertebrae.* The pedicles of vertebrae are indicated by Roman numerals, the spinal nerves by Arabic. Before extending through an intervertebral foramen a given root passes close to the next higher intervertebral disc. Landmarks of the pelvis as they pertain to the vertebral column and spinal roots also are indicated.

distribution. For a tabulation of the myotomic patterns proposed by several authors, see Kendall and Kendall (1949).

the spinal segments and their respective roots by Arabic. It will be noted that the cervical roots (except C8) take exit through intervertebral foramina *above* their respective vertebral bodies and that the other nerves issue *below* these bodies. This figure was traced from a 5-foot photograph of a sagittally-sectioned vertebral column, with spinal cord and roots *in situ.*

TABLE 1   *Segmental Innervation of Muscles of the Neck, Shoulder and Upper Arm (Modified after Bing, 1940)*

The asterisks indicate a supply also from the accessory nerve. A line bisecting a segment indicates that the muscle receives minor innervation from that segment.

SPINAL SEGMENTS								
C1	C2	C3	C4	C5	C6	C7	C8	T1
Sternomastoid*								
	Trapezius*							
		Levator scapulae						
				Teres minor				
				Supra-spinatus				
				Rhomboids				
				Infraspinatus				
				Deltoid				
				Teres major				
				Biceps				
				Brachialis				
				Serratus anterior				
				Subscapularis				
				Pectoralis major				
					Pectoralis minor			
					Coraco-brachialis			
					Latissimus dorsi			
						Anconeus		
						Triceps		

TABLE 2   *Segmental Innervation of Muscles of the Forearm and Hand (Modified after Bing, 1940)*

A line bisecting a segment indicates that the muscle receives minor innervation from that segment.

SPINAL SEGMENTS				
C5	C6	C7	C8	T1
Brachioradialis				
Supinator				
	Pronator teres			
	Ext. carpi radial. longus & brevis			
	Flexor carpi ulnaris			
	Flexor carpi radialis			
		Ext. digitorum		
		Ext. carpi ulnaris		
		Ext. indicis		
		Ext. digiti 5		
		Ext. pollic. longus		
		Ext. pollic. brevis		
		Abductor pollicis longus		
		Palmaris longus		
		Pronator quadratus		
		Flexor digitorum sublimis		
		Flexor digitorum profundus		
		Flexor pollicis longus		
			Opponens pollicis	
			Abduct. pollic. brevis	
			Flexor pollicis brevis	
			Palmaris brevis	
			Adductor pollicis	
			Flexor digiti 5	
			Abductor digiti 5	
			Opponens digiti 5	
			Interossei	
			Lumbricals	

TABLE 3   *Segmental Innervation of Muscles of the Hip and Thigh (Modified after Bing, 1940)*

A line bisecting a segment indicates that the muscle receives minor innervation from that segment.

	SPINAL SEGMENTS						
L1	**L2**	**L3**	**L4**	**L5**	**S1**	**S2**	
Iliopsoas	Iliopsoas	Iliopsoas					
	Gracilis	Gracilis	Gracilis				
	Sartorius	Sartorius	Sartorius				
	Pectineus	Pectineus	Pectineus				
	Adductor longus	Adductor longus	Adductor longus				
	Adductor brevis	Adductor brevis	Adductor brevis				
		Adductor minimus	Adductor minimus				
		Quadriceps femoris	Quadriceps femoris				
		Adductor magnus	Adductor magnus	Adductor magnus			
		Obturator externus	Obturator externus				
			Tensor fasciae latae	Tensor fasciae latae	Tensor fasciae latae		
			Gluteus medius	Gluteus medius	Gluteus medius		
			Gluteus minimus	Gluteus minimus	Gluteus minimus		
				Quadratus femoris	Quadratus femoris		
				Gemelli	Gemelli		
				Semitendinosus	Semitendinosus	Semitendinosus	
				Semimembranosus	Semimembranosus	Semimembranosus	
					Piriformis	Piriformis	
					Obturator internus	Obturator internus	
					Biceps femoris	Biceps femoris	
					Gluteus maximus	Gluteus maximus	

TABLE 4   *Segmental Innervation of Muscles of the Leg and Foot (Modified after Bing, 1940)*

A line bisecting a segment indicates that the muscle receives minor innervation from that segment.

SPINAL SEGMENTS			
L4	L5	S1	S2
Tibialis anterior			
Popliteus			
Plantaris			
	Peroneus tertius		
	Extensor digitorum longus		
	Abductor hallucis		
	Flexor digitorum brevis		
	Flexor hallucis brevis		
	Extensor hallucis brevis		
	Flexor digitorum longus		
	Peroneus longus		
	Peroneus brevis		
	Tibialis posterior		
	Flexor hallucis longus		
		Extensor hallucis longus	
		Soleus	
		Gastrocnemius	
		Extensor digitorum brevis	
		Flexor digitorum accessorius	
		Adductor hallucis	
		Abductor digiti quinti	
		Flexor digiti quinti brevis	
		Interossei	
	Lumbricals		

CHAPTER 3

The Distribution
of the Peripheral Nerves

THE TERM "peripheral nerves" generally is applied to the nerves coursing distally in the neck, the shoulder, the pelvic girdle, and the limbs. They need not actually reach the periphery in order to be designated as peripheral nerves. The intercostals customarily are not referred to as peripheral nerves since they retain their segmental arrangement; nor do the posterior primary rami come into the category of peripheral nerves. According to current usage, the peripheral nerves may be defined as those taking origin from various components of the limbplexuses: undivided anterior primary rami, trunks, divisions, and cords.

Figures 27 to 31, inclusive, illustrate virtually all the cutaneous fields, i.e., those of the trigeminal nerve, the posterior primary rami, the intercostals, and the spinal peripheral nerves.

The Relation of Trigeminal and Upper Cervical Fields

The Upper Limit of the Cervical Cutaneous Fields

Figure 27 shows the upper boundary of the area supplied by the cervical nerves. It will be noted that three cervical nerves come in contact with the trigeminal: the *great auricular*, which supplies the lower part of the cheek and much of the external ear; the *lesser occipital*, which innervates the scalp of the lateral side of the head; and the *greater occipital*, which sends fibers to the back of the head.

The Trigeminal Map

Figure 27 illustrates the fields supplied by the three divisions of the trigeminal nerve: I, ophthalmic, II, maxillary, III, mandibular, together with their subdivisions. The position of each of these fields is based on dissection. The degree of overlap between trigeminal and cervical nerves becomes evident after extirpation of the gasserian ganglion, for after this operation the caudal boundary of sensory loss is to be found in front of the ear (Fig. 27, inset). The area of sensory deficit in the inset represents the "autonomous zone" of the trigeminal nerve.

Certain Features of Distribution of the Primary Rami

Posterior Primary Rami

The distribution of the posterior primary rami is shown in Figures 27 and 28. The boundaries between posterior and anterior primary rami

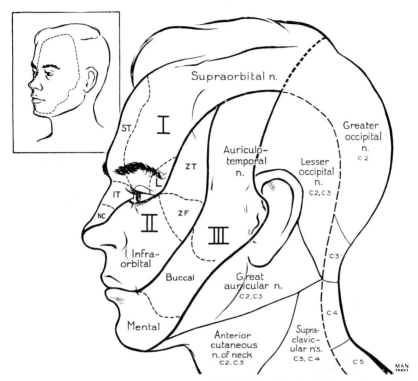

FIGURE 27.   *Diagram of the Cutaneous Fields of the Head and Upper Part of the Neck.* The fields supplied by the three divisions of the trigeminal nerve (I, ophthalmic; II, maxillary; III, mandibular) are indicated by heavy lines, and their respective subdivisions by light broken lines. The conjunctivae are innervated by the ophthalmic division. Abbreviations refer to the following nerves: *B,* buccal; *IT,* infratrochlear; *L,* lacrimal; *NC,* external nasal branch of the nasociliary; *ST,* supratrochlear; *ZF,* zygomaticofacial; *ZT,* zygomaticotemporal. The lateral and superior boundaries of the posterior primary rami are indicated by broken lines. The caudal boundary of the mandibular division is taken from a publication by Foerster (1933), as is also the the area of sensory loss in the face following resection of the trigeminal nerve (*see inset*).

are indicated by broken lines. In Figure 27 the segmental contributions to the cervical nerves are tabulated. It will be noted that none of the nerves contains elements from spinal segment C1. This lack of representation is due to the absence of direct cutaneous branches from the

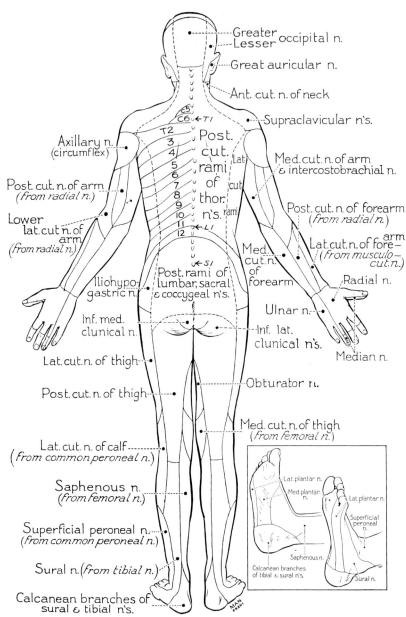

FIGURE 28.   *The Cutaneous Fields of Peripheral Nerves from the Posterior Aspect.* The boundaries of cutaneous supply of the posterior primary rami are indicated by broken lines. The designation, *Post. cut. rami of thor. n's.*, refers to the cutaneous branches of the posterior primary rami; *Lat. cut. rami* indicates the distribution from the lateral branches of the anterior primary rami. For purposes of orientation the spinous processes of the first thoracic (T1), the first lumbar (L1) and the first sacral (S1) vertebrae are indicated by arrows.

corresponding posterior and anterior primary rami. It is possible, however, that these branches reach the skin by means of a communication with the second cervical nerve.

Posterior primary rami of C7 and C8 also fail to reach the skin (Fig. 28). The same is true of L4 and L5. These gaps coincide spatially with the central parts of the regions where the limb buds (Fig. 11) are given off; they doubtless constitute regressions associated with the development of the limbs.

A feature of interest and of some importance is that of extension of cutaneous branches of certain posterior primary rami to regions considerably removed from their sites of origin. The shift is greatest at the forward end of the body and in the caudal region. Thus, the rami of C2 and C3 extend upward as the greater occipital and lesser occipital nerves to supply the back of the scalp, the ramus of T2 reaches laterally on to the shoulders, and the rami of L1, L2 and L3 spread downward, partly covering the buttock (Fig. 28). These extensions are ascribed to a drawing out of cutaneous branches of the posterior primary rami during displacement of dermatomes coincident with development of the head and outgrowth of the limb buds.

Kraus (1935) has contended that the ophthalmic division of the trigeminal is a posterior primary ramus or an equivalent of this ramus. According to this view the other two divisions of the trigeminal occupy what may be regarded as the ventral part of the face.

Anterior Primary Rami

The lateral and anterior branches of the anterior primary rami are illustrated in Figures 29, 30 and 31. The lateral branches of these rami supply the lateral side of the trunk and the axilla. In the shoulder, the pelvic girdle and the limbs, however, a distinction between the cutaneous realms of the anterior and the lateral branches of the anterior primary rami cannot be drawn, since during the development of the limbs the identity of these rami has been lost. The point that deserves most emphasis is that the plexuses and their peripheral nerves are subdivisions of anterior primary rami.

Extension of "Ventral" Nerves on to the Dorsum of Distal Parts of the Limbs

In Figure 28, it will be noted that the median and ulnar, which are ventral nerves, extend on to the dorsum of the hand and fingers. This anatomical arrangement would seem to constitute an exception to the generally accepted rule that nerve fibers traversing the medial and lateral cords of the brachial plexus supply only the ventral part of the limb, while those coursing through the posterior cord of the plexus

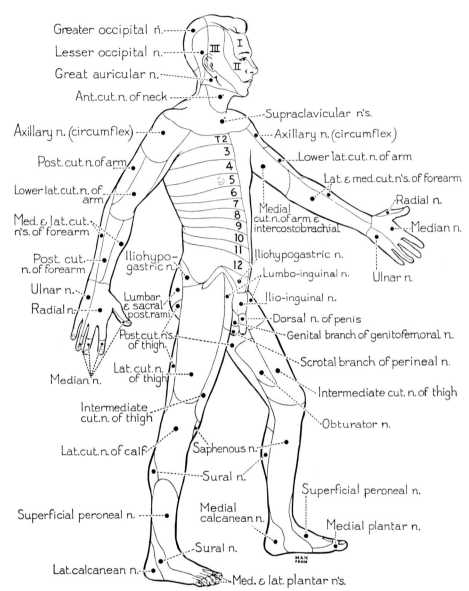

Greater occipital n.
Lesser occipital n.
Great auricular n.
Ant. cut. n. of neck
Axillary n. (circumflex)
Post. cut. n. of arm
Lower lat. cut. n. of arm
Med. & lat. cut. n's. of forearm
Post. cut. n. of forearm
Ulnar n.
Radial n.
Iliohypogastric n.
Lumbar & sacral post. rami.
Post. cut. n's. of thigh.
Median n.
Lat. cut. n. of thigh
Intermediate cut. n. of thigh
Lat. cut. n. of calf
Superficial peroneal n.
Lat. calcanean n.

Supraclavicular n's.
Axillary n. (circumflex)
Lower lat. cut. n. of arm
Lat. & med. cut. n's. of forearm
Radial n.
Medial cut. n. of arm & intercostobrachial
Median n.
Iliohypogastric n.
Lumbo-inguinal n.
Ulnar n.
Ilio-inguinal n.
Dorsal n. of penis
Genital branch of genitofemoral n.
Scrotal branch of perineal n.
Intermediate cut. n. of thigh
Obturator n.
Saphenous n.
Sural n.
Medial calcanean n.
Sural n.
Superficial peroneal n.
Medial plantar n.
Med. & lat. plantar n's.

T2 3 4 5 6 7 8 9 10 11 12

III I II

Figure 29.   *Side View of the Cutaneous Fields of Peripheral Nerves.* The face and anterior half of the head are innervated by the three divisions of the trigeminal: I, ophthalmic; II, maxillary; III, mandibular. The fields of the intercostal nerves are indicated by numerals. The unlabeled cutaneous field between great and second toe is supplied by the deep peroneal nerve.

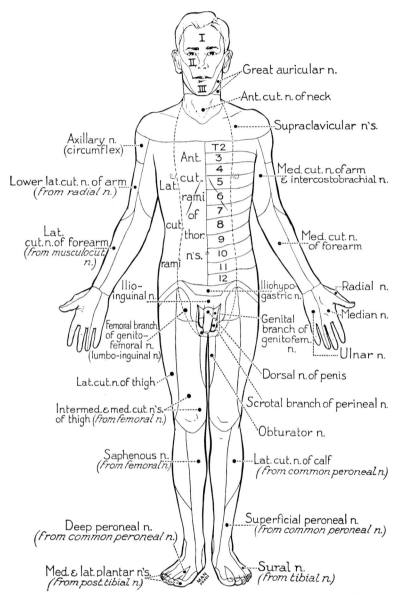

FIGURE 30. *The Cutaneous Fields of Peripheral Nerves from the Anterior Aspect.* The numbers on the left side of the trunk refer to the intercostal nerves. On the right side are shown the cutaneous fields of the lateral and medial branches of the anterior primary rami. The asterisk just beneath the scrotum is in the field of the posterior cutaneous nerve of the thigh.

remain strictly dorsal. Evidence (based on dissections of reptiles and monotremes by Harris, 1939) would seem to indicate, however, that the fibers reaching the dorsal surface of hands and fingers are, indeed, dorsal fibers which, instead of gaining the posterior cord, have continued distally in the medial cord, to be distributed with median and ulnar nerves. The same applies to the innervation of certain dorsal muscles (e.g., the dorsal interossei) by ventral nerves.

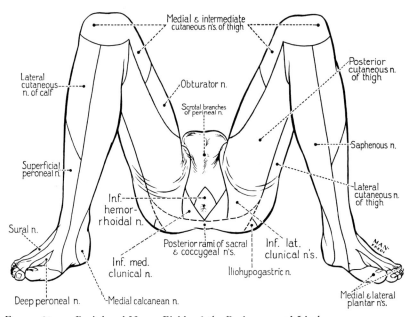

FIGURE 31.   *Peripheral Nerve Fields of the Perineum and Limbs.*

In the lower limb there is a similar extension of ventral fibers (via plantar nerves) to the dorsum of the toes, and of dorsal fibers to the ventral, or plantar, surface of the foot. The interpretation given for innervation of the dorsal aspect of the hands applies equally to the feet.

The Emergence of Individual Branches from Nerve Trunks

Individual funiculi emerge from parent nerve trunks with a considerable degree of regularity, as has been demonstrated by anatomical dissection and by the sequence with which muscles are restored by neural regeneration. This regularity in the emergence of individual nerve branches constitutes an important aid in the localization of the level of a lesion in a nerve trunk. For instance, the radial nerve constantly gives off a branch to the brachioradialis muscle at a level below that at which branches for the triceps emerge; a lesion which paralyzes the brachi-oradialis but not the triceps obviously must lie between the level of emergence of these two nerve groups. The sequence with which branches are given off from each of the peripheral nerve trunks is illustrated in Section IV, e.g., Figure 208 (p. 242).

Intraneural Topography

The ultimate distribution of nerve fibers to skin and to muscles is contingent not only on their rearrangement in the brachial and lumbo-sacral plexuses but also on their regrouping as they course in peripheral nerves. Through the intermediation of *intraneural plexuses*, the several funiculi (or bundles) which comprise the nerve trunk constantly divide and anastomose with one another, so much so that the funicular pattern differs considerably at levels only a few millimeters apart. In the region in which a nerve branch enters a nerve trunk, its fibers ascend for a distance as an independent funiculus or (for large nerve branches) as a group of funiculi, and then the funiculus or funiculi loses its iden-tity by dividing and anastomosing with other funiculi (Foerster, 1929).

On the average, the funiculus is independent of other nerve fibers in a nerve trunk for a distance of a few centimeters, but there are numerous instances in which the course of the funiculus is longer: for example, in the superficial peroneal nerve the funiculus to the peroneus longus is 7.1 cm. and in the tibial nerve that to the semimembranosus is 17.7 cm. (Sunderland and Ray, 1948). In Figure 160 (p. 175) is illus-trated a case of palsy of the radial nerve in which only the funiculus extending to the extensor pollicis longus is affected. In this case the distance traversed in the nerve trunk by this funiculus is estimated to be approximately 7 cm.

Considering a well defined funiculus at a distal level, the further proximal its course the more the funiculus will lose its identity, for its fibers progressively intermingle with those of other funiculi, until eventually they become component parts of all or nearly all the funi-culi. At a proximal level each funiculus does not, however, necessarily contain fibers from all branches distal to it. In short, the funiculi of a nerve trunk are of two types, those composed solely of fibers from one branch and those containing fibers from several branches in various combinations and proportions (Sunderland, 1952a). Thus, in funicular injury the site of sensory loss and of motor disability will vary greatly from case to case.

The number of funiculi and the percentage cross-sectional area of a nerve trunk varies considerably, though at any given level the percentage funicular area varies inversely as the number of funiculi. The poor recoveries reported after suture of the sciatic nerve in the buttock and in the proximal half of the thigh may be attributed to the low percentage funicular areas obtaining in these regions (Sunderland and Bradley, 1949).

Plexus Formation at the Periphery and Overlap of Cutaneous Fields

Redistribution of fibers during their course from the spinal cord or dorsal root ganglia to the periphery is also carried out through the intermediation of plexuses situated in the skin through which the fine terminals of neighboring nerve trunks anastomose. It is through the plexuses that all cutaneous nerves overstep their so-called anatomical boundaries to assist in the innervation of adjacent fields.

CHAPTER 4

Innervation of the Skeleton, and Disorders of Bones and Joint Tissues Resulting from Nerve Injuries

THE MODE of innervation of the skeleton and of joint tissues is the same as that of muscles and skin in that there is both segmental and peripheral nerve representation; in details, however, there are differences.

Sclerotomes

Areas of segmental innervation of bone (*sclerotomes*) are illustrated in Figures 32 and 33. These areas do not coincide spatially with those of corresponding dermatomes, as is evident in a comparison of Figures 32 and 20, and of Figures 33 and 22. In some instances, however, a dermatome may overlie a limited portion of a corresponding sclerotome. Dermatomes are arranged along preaxial and postaxial borders of a limb whereas sclerotomes extend distally for almost the entire length of a limb. In some instances the sclerotome is continuous; in others it is interrupted.

The clinical import of sclerotomal innervation is still little understood. There is reason to believe that in traumatic lesions of bones, ligaments, tendons, fasciae, and other mesodermal structures of the body, the pain may be referred to sclerotomes. For instance, the infragluteal pain associated with lesions of the L4 and L5 roots may be referred to the periosteum of the respective sclerotomal areas (Inman and Saunders, 1944). Regardless of the area affected, the pains are described as dull, aching or boring, and deep. They are characteristically difficult to localize and have a tendency to radiate either proximally or distally. Physical examination fails to reveal muscular weakness, altered reflex activity, or changes in cutaneous sensibility.

Peripheral Nerve Supply of the Skeleton

The peripheral nerve supply of skeletal parts, which is illustrated in Figures 34 and 35, is closely linked with muscle innervation. Most of the bones of the skeleton receive their innervation from nerve twigs

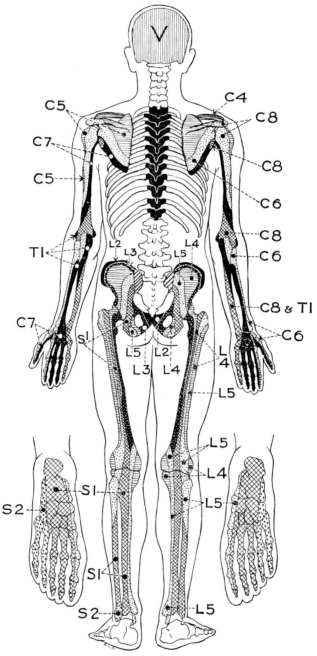

FIGURE 32.   *The Segmental Innervation of the Skeleton from the Posterior Aspect.* The various patterns indicate the fields of supply from spinal segments. The back of the skull is innervated by the trigeminal (indicated by V). The vertebrae are supplied by posterior primary rami of the respective spinal nerves, the ribs by both posterior and anterior primary rami. (Modified after Dejerine, 1914.)

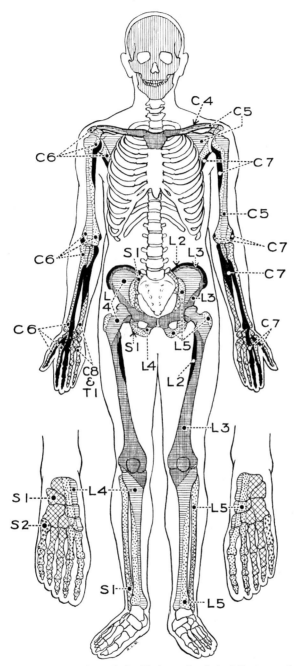

FIGURE 33.   *The Innervation of the Skeleton by Spinal Segments from the Anterior Aspect.* The various sclerotomes are indicated by the different styles of shading. The insets show sclerotomes of the dorsal aspect of the feet. (Modified after Dejerine, 1914.)

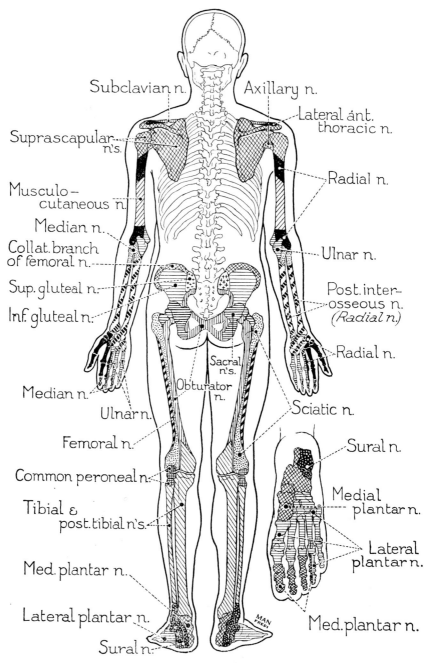

FIGURE 34. *The Peripheral Nerve Supply of the Skeleton from the Posterior Aspect.* The various fields are indicated by different patterns. (Modified after Dejerine, 1914.)

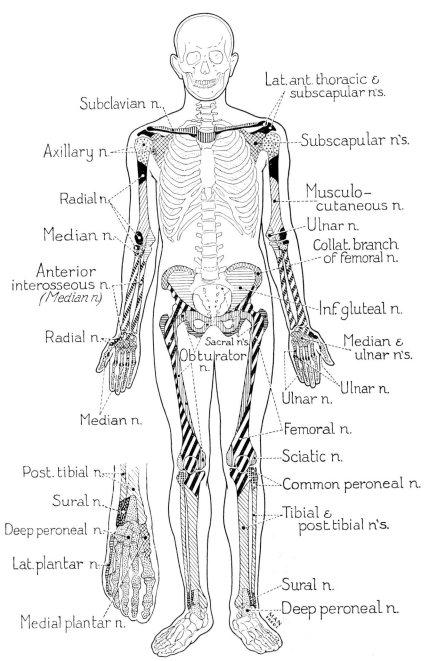

FIGURE 35. *The Peripheral Nerve Supply of the Skeleton from the Anterior Aspect.* The various peripheral nerve fields are indicated by different types of shading. (Modified after Dejerine, 1914.)

which have penetrated from the attached muscles. For example, the nerve to the quadratus femoris muscle sends twigs to the part of the bony pelvis to which this muscle is attached. Some parts of the skeleton, especially in the regions of joints, receive branches directly from nerve trunks: for instance, the anterior interosseous nerve (from the median) terminates as an articular branch which supplies the wrist joint and carpus. The phalanges receive their nerve supply from independent nerve filaments: for example, the periosteum and joints of the little finger are innervated by terminal branches of the ulnar. The tissues of the finger joints receive their innervation by way of tendons attached to the fingers, the nerves concerned being the median and ulnar. The same principle of innervation applies to the toe joints.

The diagrams of the peripheral nerve innervation of the skeleton used in this text are substantially those of Dejerine (1914) but modified in the light of the description given in *Cunningham's Textbook of Anatomy* (1951). These diagrams differ in many respects from those by Foerster (1929). For innervation of finger and toe joints, see also Lehmann (1916).

Disorders of Bones and Joints
Following Peripheral Nerve Lesions

Rarefaction of bone, or *osteoporosis*, is frequently encountered in peripheral nerve palsies. The condition develops more rapidly and tends to be more severe in partial interruption associated with pain, indicating that immobilization is an important etiological factor. Osteoporosis may also occur in the absence of motor paralysis and sensory deficit in association with Sudeck's atrophy of bone.

The most frequent site of osteoporosis is in the phalanges, where it centers about the joints and the tips of the distal phalanges. Median nerve palsies are most apt to be accompanied by this change, especially when causalgia exists. In such instances the bones of the thumb and index and third fingers have been observed to be most seriously affected. Articular lesions may also be confined to the region of distribution of an interrupted nerve, the axillary, for instance, in which striking atrophy of the lateral part of the neck and head of the humerus with new bone formation has been reported in association with shoulder joint arthropathy (Creutz, 1932; see also Dejerine and Schwartz, 1915). Arthropathy following peripheral nerve interruption is occasionally as severe as in the Charcot joints of tabes dorsalis.

Fibrosis of *joint and periarticular tissues* with consequent ankylosis is also a feature of peripheral nerve palsies. The condition tends to develop more readily in the presence of pain. Since the joint changes are frequently selective, they are not regarded as due solely to immobilization. Thus, in interruption of the radial nerve in the midhumeral region the elbow joint is most prone to suffer; in tibial nerve palsies the interphalangeal joints of the foot are the ones predominantly affected, and in palsies of the common peroneal nerve the ankle. Probably the most severe ankylosis occurs in painful lesions of the median nerve, the sites involved being the interphalangeal and metacarpophalangeal joints and occasionally the wrist joint. In such cases there is sometimes a partial ankylosis of the metacarpophalangeal joints of the thumb, allowing only abduction and adduction of the digit (Pollock, 1944). In ulnar nerve palsies the ankylosis, which is usually limited to the fourth and fifth fingers, is variable in degree and occasionally so advanced as to necessitate amputation of the little finger.

Examination of the Peripheral Nervous System

T HIS SECTION deals first with examination of the peripheral nervous system in the acutely injured battle casualty, with emphasis on a few simple tests by means of which peripheral nerve injuries may be quickly recognized. This phase of the subject concluded, the text moves on to the examination of motor function after the acute phase of the injury has passed. The anatomy of movement is presented in detail since a knowledge of it is the crux of accurate diagnosis of peripheral nerve injuries.

CHAPTER 5

Manifestations of
Peripheral Nerve Injuries

THE MANIFESTATIONS of peripheral nerve lesions vary considerably depending upon the time that has elapsed since injury. For this reason acute and chronic injuries are discussed separately in the pages that follow. Early and repeated examinations are of the utmost importance in establishing the presence of paralyses since delay in treatment often prejudices the subsequent usefulness of the part affected.

It should be emphasized at the outset that no method is as yet available for determining whether loss of function of a nerve is due to anatomical or to physiological interruption; i.e., whether a nerve is severed or is intact but rendered functionless by compression or other factor. Without surgical intervention the only means of differential diagnosis is the subsequent course: if improvement sets in, the interruption must have been physiological. Total interruption may be recognized by the following changes in the field of distribution of the nerve: (1) complete paralysis of all muscles distal to the site of interruption, (2) rapid and pronounced atrophy of the paralyzed muscles, and (3) sensory deficit. In addition there is a complete reaction of degeneration and an absence of sensation when pressure is applied to the distal portion of the involved nerve.

The extent to which an examination of the peripheral nervous system is carried out depends on the condition of the patient. If he is seriously wounded, all efforts should be directed toward saving life and treating the injury. When this is accomplished the significant data related to the trauma should be recorded at the examiner's earliest opportunity: the time of the injury, the nature of the trauma (missile, stab wound, etc.), as well as associated injuries, such as fractures and contusions. Of importance also are the position of the patient when the wound was inflicted, the exact site of entrance and exit of the missile, the type of pain experienced at the time of injury (i.e., stabbing, lancinating, or like an electrical shock; sudden or delayed), and whether subsequently there was numbness, total loss of feeling, or local or radiating pains. The appearance of the wounded region should be described, with special attention to induration, discoloration, and the degree of hemorrhage. There should be a record of the color and temperature of the affected and unaffected limb and of the presence or absence of arterial pulsations and of sweating. The history of the case should include information as to whether or not a tourniquet was applied and, if it was, for how long. Finally, it is of utmost importance that a record be made of any operative procedures, such as débridement, the ligation of vessels, the repair of tendons, and the removal of foreign bodies.

When, in the judgment of the medical officer, the examination of the peripheral nerve function is practicable, an estimate of nerve damage can be made quickly by applying a few selected tests. The most valuable information is yielded by muscle tests in which specific movements are carried out against resistance, special efforts being made by the examiner to observe and palpate muscles and tendons to make doubly sure that the muscles tested are contracting. A number of the tests outlined below may be performed even when the limbs are encased in plaster of paris. Sensory examination is of importance, and therefore should be made routinely. The use of a pin in testing sensibility is desirable, but pinching of a fold of skin or of the tip of certain digits usually is adequate. The patient may be aware of the presence of cutaneous anesthesia and able to describe its limits with considerable precision.

Errors in diagnosis may be avoided if certain factors are not overlooked. Pain associated with fracture may greatly curtail movement; damage to vessels may render a limb useless by reason of ischemia, and severed tendons and lacerated muscles may give clinical manifestations suggestive of peripheral nerve palsies. A patient's failure to cooperate will often invalidate the results of the examination.

In performing the examination it is desirable to start at the periphery of the injured limb, then to proceed proximally.

Detection of Recently Acquired Palsies of the Upper Extremity

Ulnar Nerve

One of the simplest tests for disclosing an ulnar nerve palsy is to have the patient attempt to adduct his little finger (Fig. 36). Inability to perform this movement indicates complete interruption of the nerve above the wrist. Adduction of the little finger may in some instances be performed by the extension digiti quinti. The ability to spread the fingers apart and to bring them together serves as another index of the functional integrity of the ulnar nerve. The strength of approximation of the fingers may be tested by interposing them with those of the examiner (Fig. 37). If the ulnar nerve is interrupted the fingers are unable to retain grasp on the examiner's fingers.

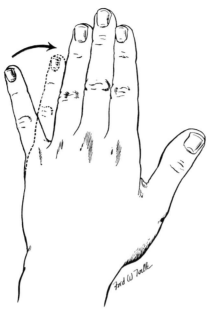

FIGURE 36.   *Failure of Adduction of the Little Finger in Ulnar Palsy.* In complete
interruption of the ulnar nerve the patient is unable to adduct the
little finger, i.e., to bring it to the position indicated by the broken
lines.

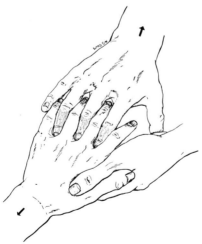

FIGURE 37.   *Failure of Adduction of the Fingers in Ulnar Palsy.* The examiner has
interposed his fingers with those of the patient. In ulnar palsy the
interlocking movement is impossible because of paralysis of the interossei.

Since the tip of the fifth finger is supplied exclusively by the ulnar nerve, it is totally anesthetic when the nerve is interrupted. The lack of sensation when the tip of the little finger is tightly squeezed may be regarded as unequivocal evidence of complete interruption of the ulnar nerve. When the ulnar nerve is divided above the elbow, firm pressure exerted on the nerve in the region where it passes near the medial epicondyle of the humerus no longer gives rise to the tingling in the fingers which this maneuver customarily provokes.

Median Nerve

When confronted by a patient wounded in the arm, the examiner can readily determine whether the median nerve has been damaged by requesting the patient to flex the distal phalanx of the index finger (Fig.

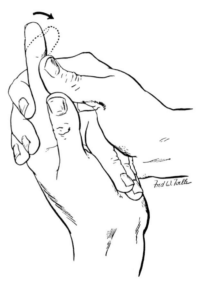

FIGURE 38.   *A Test for Median Nerve Palsy.* This is to illustrate that in complete interruption of the median nerve above the elbow or of its flexor digitorum branch below the elbow, the patient cannot flex the distal phalanx of the index finger (in the manner indicated by the broken lines).

38). Inability to perform this movement is irrefutable evidence of interruption of the median nerve above the level of innervation of the flexor digitorum profundus. Paralysis of hand and finger flexors also is evident. The functional status of the flexor carpi radialis may be determined by palpating its tendon (at the wrist) when plantar flexion of the hand is attempted. If information on the integrity of the nerve proximal to the wrist is desired, the power of the opponens pollicis, which is innervated usually by the median, may be tested. Normally this muscle carries out flexion of the first metacarpal, and, together with the abductor pollicis brevis and the superficial head of the flexor pollicis brevis, rotates the thumb inward so that the palmar surface of its distal phalanx comes in contact, in turn, with the palmar surfaces of the other digits.

Interruption of the median nerve can be confirmed by the sensory examination. Since the tip of the index finger is supplied exclusively by

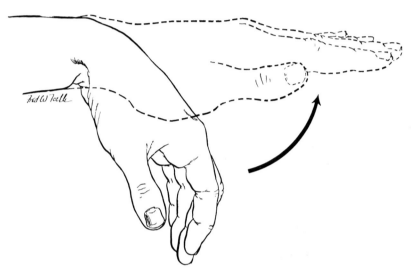

FIGURE 39.   *Wrist-drop in Radial Nerve Palsy.* In complete interruption of the radial nerve the patient is unable to dorsiflex the hand at the wrist, as illustrated by the broken lines.

the median nerve, firm pressure applied to it fails to elicit pain or other feeling.

Combined Ulnar and Median Palsy

The disabilities in combined ulnar and median palsy are the sum of those just described. Loss in power of adduction of the little finger and inability to flex the distal phalanx of the index finger provide adequate evidence of damage to the ulnar and the median above the level of the wrist and mid-forearm respectively.

Radial Nerve

Inability to dorsiflex the hand at the wrist or the fingers at the metacarpophalangeal joints indicates damage to the posterior cord of the brachial plexus or to the radial nerve above the level of the elbow (Fig. 39). An effort should be made to determine the level of the injury. If the lesion is at a level higher than the mid-humeral region, the brachi-oradialis muscle fails to contract when flexion at the elbow is tested against resistance; if the damage is at the axillary or a higher level, the heads of the triceps do not contract when extension at the elbow is attempted.

When the proximal part of the forearm is wounded, in which case wrist-drop may be incomplete, it is desirable to test separately those muscles with accessible tendons. Thus, in the event that function is

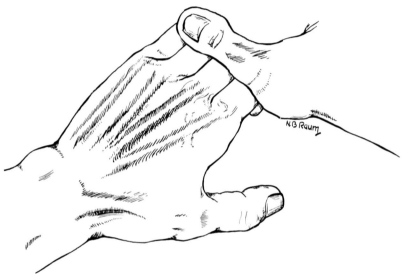

FIGURE 40.   *The Stretch of the Tendons on the Back of the Hand When the Proximal Phalanges Are Extended Against Resistance.* Extension at the metacarpal joints is impossible in radial nerve palsy. If the palsy involves a part of the extensor digitorum, only the tendons of the unaffected portion become taut when the test is performed.

preserved, the tendons of the extensor digitorum and those of the extensors of the thumb will stand out prominently when extension at the metacarpophalangeal joints is resisted by the examiner (the interphalangeal joints being simultaneously flexed in order to eliminate action of the small muscles of the hand) (Fig. 40). The degree of tenseness of the tendons of the extensor carpi ulnaris (Fig. 67), the extensor carpi radialis longus (Fig. 68), the extensor pollicis longus (Fig. 83) and of the abductor pollicis longus (Fig. 77) when appropriate actions are undertaken, also will give information as to the site of radial nerve damage.

As regards sensory changes in radial nerve palsy, a zone of total analgesia often is found on the dorsum of the hand in the region of the first and second metacarpals (Figs. 231, 235). In some instances the sensory loss is somewhat less extensive than that indicated in these figures.

Combined Radial and Median or Ulnar Palsy

In the presence of radial nerve palsy the question may arise as to whether the median or the ulnar nerve is also affected. Normal median

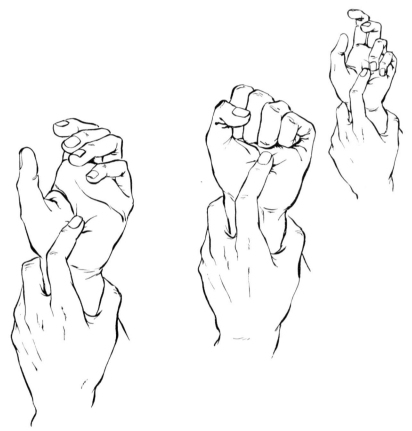

FIGURE 41.   *The Testing of Full Finger Flexion (Median and Ulnar Nerves) in the Presence of Radial Nerve Palsy.* Because of wrist drop, which prevents the making of a tight fist, the hand is first brought into dorsiflexion (*to left*). Success in making a tight fist (*middle*) indicates that the median and ulnar nerves are intact. The attitude of benediction (*to right*) indicates median nerve palsy.

nerve function can be determined by the patient's ability to make a fist, but this is difficult in the radial nerve palsy because the hand is incapable of the dorsiflexion on which the making of a fist is dependent. Hence in testing median nerve function in the presence of radial nerve palsy it is necessary for the examiner to dorsiflex the patient's hand and then ask him to make a fist (Fig. 41). This can be done by grasping the patient's wrist with the examiner's index finger resting under the palm of the patient's hand and then raising the patient's hand so that it is brought into a position of dorsiflexion.

In the presence of radial nerve palsy the function of the ulnar nerve can be tested by grasping the wrist in the same manner and with aid of the forefinger bringing the hand to the mid-position, parallel to the forearm, and then asking the patient alternately to separate his fingers and bring them together again.

Other Nerves

The examination of the upper limb may be concluded by palpating muscle bellies when certain movements of the forearm and shoulder are tested. Lack of contraction of the biceps brachii indicates interruption of the musculocutaneous nerve; of the deltoid, the axillary nerve; of the supraspinatus and infraspinatus, the suprascapular nerve; of the pectoralis major, the anterior thoracic nerves; and so on. The technics of performing these tests are described in Chapter 6.

Detection of Recently Acquired Palsies of the Lower Extremity

Tibial and Posterior Tibial Nerves

Inability to plantarflex the toes indicates interruption of the tibial nerve (Fig. 42) or of the posterior tibial nerve in its uppermost part:

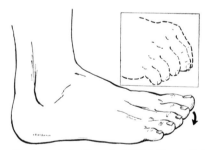

FIGURE 42.   *Plantar Flexion of the Toes in Tibial Nerve Palsy.* In paralysis occasioned by interruption of the tibial nerve, plantar flexion of the toes (a position indicated by broken lines) cannot be performed.

i.e., at a point proximal to the level of innervation of the flexor digitorum longus (Fig. 250). Plantar flexion at the ankle also is lost when the tibial nerve is interrupted (Fig. 43).

In interruption of either the tibial or the posterior tibial nerve the sensory examination reveals anesthesia and analgesia of the sole of the foot and of the plantar surface of the toes.

Common Peroneal Nerve and Its Branches

Foot-drop is a well known sign of interruption of the common peroneal nerve or of the uppermost part of the deep peroneal nerve. When the foot is moved passively into full dorsiflexion the patient is unable to maintain the position (Fig. 44). This also applies to the toes

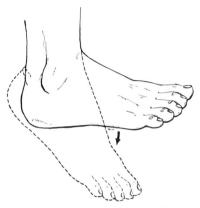

FIGURE 43.   *Plantar Flexion of the Foot in Tibial Nerve Palsy.* In tibial nerve palsy the foot is incapable of plantar flexion, a position indicated by the broken lines.

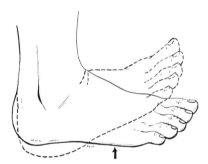

FIGURE 44.   *Dorsiflexion of the Foot in Common Peroneal Nerve Palsy.* In palsy of the common peroneal or of the uppermost part of the deep peroneal nerve, the foot is unable to dorsiflex at the ankle (in the manner indicated by the broken lines).

(Fig. 45). Interruption of the more distal part of the deep peroneal nerve leads only to sensory loss in a small area of skin on the dorsum of the foot between the first and second metacarpals (Fig. 254, p. 295).

Damage to the superficial peroneal is revealed by sensory loss over the central part of the dorsum of the foot. When the uppermost part of this nerve is involved, ability to evert the foot is lost, and the peronei cannot be felt to contract when the movement is attempted.

Other Nerves

If opportunity permits and if indicated, the power of other movements may be tested. Lack of contraction of the hamstring muscles indicates interruption of the corresponding part of the sciatic; of the

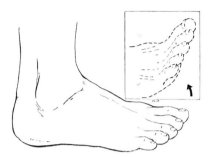

FIGURE 45.   *Dorsiflexion of the Toes in Common Peroneal Nerve Palsy.* In palsy of the common peroneal nerve or of the uppermost part of the deep peroneal nerve, elevation of the toes (in the manner indicated by the broken lines) is impossible.

gluteus maximus, the inferior gluteal nerve; of the adductors of the thigh, the obturator; and of the quadriceps, the femoral. The methods of performing these tests are described in Chapter 6.

An Analysis of the Movements Tested in a Neurological Examination

ACCURATE KNOWLEDGE of the muscles employed in executing various movements is a prerequisite to localization of peripheral nerve lesions. Certain combinations of motor deficit can point only to peripheral nerve injury, others only to plexus injury, still others only to root injury.

In examining a patient with suspected peripheral nerve injury, the attempt should be made to test separately the function of each accessible muscle in the field concerned. Illustrations in the following pages deal with these tests in some detail. When a given movement is dependent on one muscle and that muscle fails to contract there is an obvious paralysis, but when several muscles participate in a movement and only one muscle is affected, then the disability is manifested by weakness of the movement. The illustrations are intended to serve as the basis for the diagnosis of such disabilities.

In performing tests of motor function it is essential that certain conditions be met. Since some movements are restricted when the limbs are stiffened by cold, it is important that the patient be warm before the examination is begun. Distraction may influence the results of the examination adversely; therefore, if possible, the patient and the examiner should be alone. If fatigue and inability to concentrate set in, the examination should be halted, and resumed when the patient is rested.

In order to gain the cooperation of the patient it is important that he understand the purpose of the examination and the part he is to play in the tests. There are two ways of determining the status of motor function: (1) the patient carries out the prescribed movements against the examiner's resistance; (2) the examiner does most of the work while the patient resists. For instance, in testing flexion of the forearm at the elbow (Fig. 63), the patient may be told to flex his forearm still more while the examiner resists his efforts, or the patient may be asked to keep his arm flexed and not allow the examiner to move it. Both methods should be employed, but the latter is preferable because the patient understands more readily what is required of him, and the examiner is better able to gauge the power of the movement.

The *influence of gravity* should always be taken into consideration in testing movements. Gravity may induce a movement of which the patient is not actively capable or, on the other hand, it may prove an obstacle to contraction of an enfeebled muscle. In order to evaluate the true range of a weakened movement it is necessary, therefore, that motor power be tested with the limb in a neutral position. To illustrate: Gravity may induce (1) pronation when, with the forearm flexed and in a position midway between pronation and supination, the elbow is moved away from the body through an angle of 90 degrees, and (2) extension at the elbow when, with forearm flexed, the arm is abducted and then externally rotated. To the contrary, certain movements nullified by gravity may be accomplished when the limb is placed in a neutral position. Thus, extension at the knee, ill-performed when the patient is standing with the thigh flexed, may be carried out to advantage when the patient lies on his side with his lower limb supported by the examiner; also abduction of the arm may be much impeded when the patient is standing but may be performed with facility when the patient is recumbent. A weakened movement may prove effective when certain other maneuvers are carried out: thus, although in common peroneal nerve palsy an active dorsiflexion of the foot is impossible, the foot may be capable of maintaining dorsiflexion after having been placed in that position by the examiner. Furthermore, when in radial nerve palsy the hand cannot actively dorsiflex from the resting position, it may do so after the examiner lifts the hand to a position horizontal with the forearm.

In *testing the power of movements*, the examiner will find it highly advantageous to identify the participating muscles. Those accessible, together with their tendons, should be palpated and observed routinely, for only in this manner can the functional status of the muscles be determined. The strength of movement of the affected side should always be compared with that of the active side. In recording the results of examination, regular use should be made of a grading scale of 0 to 3+, as follows:

     0......no contraction
     1+......perceptible contraction
     2+......active movement against gravity, but not against resistance
     3+......active movement against gravity and resistance.

Such a record is particularly useful in estimating the degree of improvement in muscle strength during the course of successive examinations. In this respect, dynometer readings are preferable when there is sufficient muscle power for objective measurement (Lewey, Kuhn and Juditski, 1947; Newman, 1949).

Certain *deformities*, occurring both at rest and during movement, may give valuable information concerning the denervation of muscles.

Deformities present when the limb is at rest are not readily seen in the acute phase of injury. The classical "simian hand" of combined median-ulnar nerve paralysis, the "benediction hand" of median nerve paralysis and the ulnar "griffe" represent deformities that develop from the unopposed action of antagonists when prime movers are paralyzed. Deformity occurring during muscle contraction may be illustrated by the common ulnar deviation of the hand when, in median nerve paralysis, an effort is made to flex the hand and by the scapular protrusion typical of trapezius and serratus anterior muscle paralyses.

In addition to the factors already discussed, the examiner should be aware of the voluntary motor movements that have been described as *trick or supplementary or deceptive movements*. These are movements that seem to be adequately performed even though those muscles responsible for their execution are denervated. Such substitutive movements are never as powerful or as functionally useful as the normal muscle movement. When prime movers are paralyzed, trick movements may be initiated in the following ways:

1. By anomalous nerve supply to muscles and less commonly by anomalous muscle insertion. The opponens pollicis, for instance, may be wholly or partially supplied by the ulnar nerve rather than by the median. Anomalous muscle-tendon insertions of the long extensors of the fingers may be present and thus obliterate the classical ulnar "griffe," there may be a variation in the insertion of the IIId lumbrical muscle, and so on.

2. By sudden release of strongly contracting antagonist muscles. This allows rebound of the paralyzed prime movers—of the dorsiflexors of the toes, for instance, after release of the plantar flexors.

3. By supplementary action of a muscle so placed that it may reproduce the action of a prime mover. As an example may be cited the well known observation that when the flexors of the hand are paralyzed, the hand can still be flexed by the abductor pollicis longus.

4. By the passive tendon action of paralyzed prime movers when the antagonists are forcibly contracted. Thus, in paralysis of the flexor digitorum profundus, some degree of trick flexion can be produced by extension at the wrist.

5. By the action of an accessory tendinous insertion of an intact muscle into the tendon of a denervated muscle. An illustration is afforded by radial nerve paralysis in which the terminal phalanx of the thumb may be extended by the abductor pollicis brevis. (Pollock, 1919; Jones, 1921; Highet, 1943 a and b; Sunderland, 1944 b and c.)

In the description of movements in the text that follows, the muscles, nerves and spinal segments listed in **boldface type** have the controlling influence on the performance of the movements.

Upper Extremity

MOVEMENTS AT THE SHOULDER JOINT

As has been shown by Inman, Saunders and Abbott (1944), all shoulder movements are participated in by all adjacent muscles and joints, with the muscles acting in concert to provide a "scapulohumeral rhythm" of movement (see also Woodhall, 1952). In the performance of this rhythmic movement, in which thoracal muscles also participate, a given muscle may act as a fixator during the first phase of a movement and as a "motor" in the remainder. For instance, while the arm is being abducted to 90 degrees the superior third of the trapezius has a fixator (supportive) function, but on abduction above that level it becomes a scapular rotator. In the following pages an effort is made to distinguish "motors" and fixators of movements, for this is an important key to the understanding of shoulder movements.

Abduction of the Arm from the Resting Position at the Side of the Body (Figs. 46, 47)

The patient attempts to abduct the arm while the examiner resists the movement. This maneuver is well suited to test the functions of the

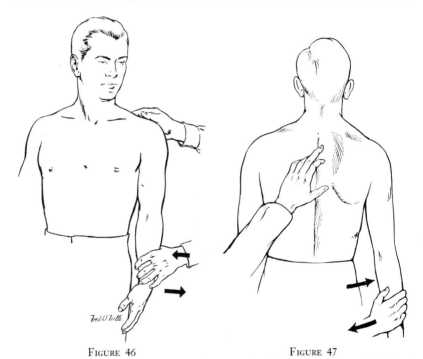

FIGURE 46   FIGURE 47

FIGURES 46, 47.   *Abduction of the Arm from the Resting Position at the Side of the Body.* In this movement two muscles may be tested to advantage: the *supraspinatus* (supplied by the suprascapular nerve), which assists in abducting the arm (Fig. 46) and the lower two thirds of the trapezius (the lower one half or two thirds of the trapezius is supplied by cervical nerves, the remainder by the accessory nerve), which aid in fixing the scapula (Fig. 47).

supraspinatus and *trapezius* muscles. Contraction of the supraspinatus, which is innervated by the suprascapular from spinal segments C4 and

C5, can be readily detected by palpation (Fig. 46). During this movement the lower two thirds of the trapezius also visibly contract in order to provide scapular fixation (Fig. 47).

Abduction of the Arm Toward the Horizontal (Fig. 48)

The patient abducts his arm so that the angle between the arm and the side of the body is approximately 60 degrees. He then attempts to

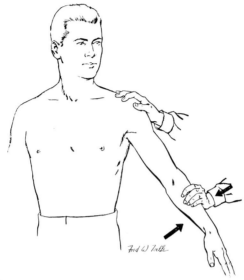

FIGURE 48.   *Abduction of the Arm Toward the Horizontal.* This movement tests the power of the deltoid muscle, which is supplied by the axillary nerve. The influence of gravity is avoided if the patient is recumbent.

hold the arm in this position against the examiner's resistance. The contraction of the deltoid muscle can be both seen and felt. This muscle is supplied by the axillary nerve from spinal segments C5 and C6. The supraspinatus and other shoulder muscles also participate.

Abduction of the Arm to the Horizontal (Fig. 49)

The patient abducts his arm to an angle of 90 degrees, and attempts to hold it there against resistance. Although the deltoid, assisted by the supraspinatus, is the muscle chiefly concerned, the movement usually cannot be performed without the aid of the lateral (external) rotators of the humerus (infraspinatus and teres minor) which, with the subscapularis, also function as depressors of the humerus.

Pure abduction of the arm to 45 degrees in the presence of deltoid and supraspinatus paralysis may be performed by scapular rotation initiated by the trapezius muscle. In paralysis of the trapezius muscle, an inefficient pure abduction may be performed by the deltoid and supraspinatus muscles to the point at which, in normal scapulohumeral rhythm, the action of the lower four digitations of the serratus anterior checks further progress. If at this point the extremity is externally rotated, abduction proceeds and is completed. Some patients with trapezius muscle paralysis are unable to abduct the arm above 45 degrees.

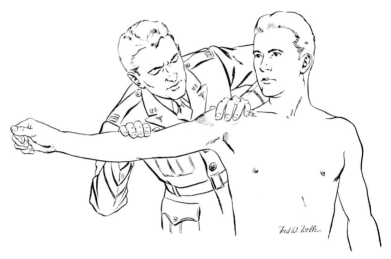

FIGURE 49.   *Abduction of the Arm to the Horizontal.* Although this movement tests the deltoid and supraspinatus muscles (axillary and supra-scapular nerves respectively) it is contingent on fixators of the scapula (supplied by suprascapular and subscapular nerves).

Other participants in this movement are discussed in the next paragraph.

MUSCLES TESTED IN ABDUCTION OF ARM TO HORIZONTAL PLANE
Deltoid
Supraspinatus
Lateral (external) rotators of scapula (infraspinatus, teres minor)

PERIPHERAL NERVES TESTED
Axillary N.
Suprascapular N.

SPINAL SEGMENTS TESTED
C5, C6

Elevation of the Arm Over the Head (Fig. 50)

Elevation of the arm at the shoulder may be achieved in two ways: through abduction or through forward flexion. An essential difference between the two, so far as muscle action is concerned, is that elevation of the arm in flexion requires participation of the pectoralis major while elevation in abduction does not. The lateral (external) rotators of the scapula have a role in elevating the arm to the horizontal; however, they do not come into full play until elevation is above that level.

Furthermore, in flexion the lower four digitations of the serratus anterior muscle participate more forcibly in scapular rotation than they do in the movement of pure abduction. The serratus anterior muscles, with the aid of the levator scapulae and rhomboids, fix the scapula to

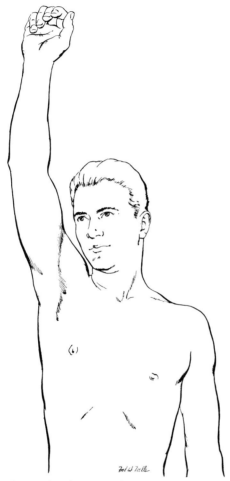

FIGURE 50.   *Elevation of the Arm over the Head.* This movement, because of its complexity, is not adapted for examination of individual nerve palsies but should be performed in order to observe scapulohumeral rhythm: any break in the rhythm suggests disability in muscles or joints.

the chest wall as the upper extremity remains in the dependent position. The serratus anterior and trapezius muscles alternate their supportive and rotatory function as the arm is raised in full abduction. In testing this and other shoulder movements it is important to observe scapulohumeral rhythm. This rhythm, which is dependent not only on the shoulder joint proper but also on the clavicular and scapulothoracic joints, should be smooth: any break in it immediately suggests disability in muscles or joints.

MUSCLES TESTED
Deltoid
Supraspinatus
Lateral rotators of humerus
Trapezius
Serratus anterior

PERIPHERAL NERVES TESTED
Axillary (circumflex) N.
Suprascapular N.
Accessory N.
Long thoracic N.

SPINAL SEGMENTS TESTED
C5, C6, C7

Elevation (Shrugging) of the Shoulders (Figs. 51, 52)

The patient shrugs his shoulders against resistance. In performing the test the examiner should stand first in front of the patient (Fig. 51) to

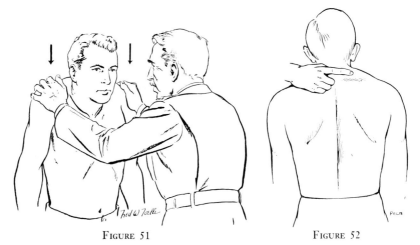

FIGURE 51   FIGURE 52

FIGURES 51, 52.   *Elevation (Shrugging) of the Shoulders.* This movement tests the upper part of the trapezius, which is supplied by the accessory nerve. Although the power of gross movement can be assessed when the examiner is in front of the patient (Fig. 51) it is necessary to examine from behind (Fig. 52) in order adequately to palpate the trapezius.

feel the levator scapulae contract. This muscle, innervated from segments C3, C4 and C5, is situated along the anterior border of the trapezius. The test should be repeated with the examiner behind the patient (Fig. 52) in order to detect contraction of the upper part of the trapezius, which is mainly responsible for this movement. The upper one third or one half of the trapezius is supplied by the accessory nerve.

Bracing the Shoulders (Figs. 53, 54)

The trapezius is the chief muscle concerned in keeping the shoulders braced. When the shoulders are moved back (adducted), the contraction of the lower two thirds of the trapezius can be noted along the vertebral border of the scapula. When the examiner resists this movement by bringing the patient's shoulder forward, the bulge of the trapezius in this region can be seen and felt (Fig. 53).

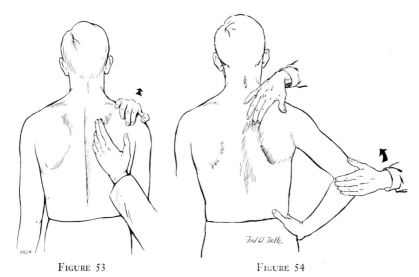

FIGURE 53   FIGURE 54

FIGURES 53, 54.   *Bracing the Shoulders.* The movement is well suited to demonstrate contraction of the middle part of the *trapezius* (Fig. 53), innervated by the accessory, and contraction of the *rhomboids* (Fig. 54), supplied by the dorsal scapular nerve.

Bracing the shoulders also brings the *rhomboids* into play. These muscles, supplied by the dorsal scapular nerve from spinal segments C4 and C5, serve to adduct the shoulders. Their contraction can best be brought about by having the patient place his hand on his hip and then bring his shoulder backward, while the examiner, by pushing the elbow forward, resists the movement (Fig. 54). During this maneuver the contraction of the rhomboid muscles can be readily felt and frequently seen.

The *rhomboid muscles* also have an important function with respect to scapular position during the act of lowering the arm from the vertical. During elevation, the serratus anterior draws the scapula outward and upward, in a rotational movement; with descent of the arm the rhomboids assist greatly in guiding the scapula back to its original position, and in so doing also counteract the tendency of the still contracting deltoid to draw the scapula away from the thoracic cage. The contraction of the rhomboid muscles during this movement can be both seen and felt.

The Pushing Test (Fig. 55)

The patient pushes firmly against a wall or other object. Normally the scapulae retain their position close to the thoracic cage. The main-

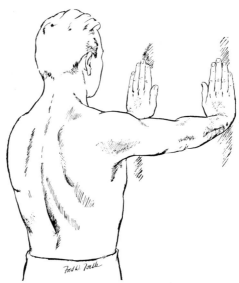

FIGURE 55.   *The Pushing Test.* Thrusting the arms forward and pushing on a stationary object tests the function of the serratus anterior which keeps the scapulae close to the thoracic cage. The serratus anterior is supplied by the long thoracic nerve.

tenance of the shoulder blade close to the thoracic wall for movements of pushing is chiefly a function of the serratus anterior, which is supplied by the long thoracic nerve from spinal segments C5, C6 and C7.

Medial (Internal) Rotation of the Arm at the Shoulder (Fig. 56)

The forearm is flexed to a right angle to provide a lever arm with which to test the strength of the movement. The patient attempts medial rotation of the arm at the shoulder, while the examiner tries to rotate the arm in the reverse direction. In testing medial rotation, the observer must always guard against the effects of gravity, which, when the patient is upright, constantly act to induce this movement. If the movement is weakened, it is necessary to palpate accessible muscles in order to determine which are affected.

MUSCLES TESTED

Subscapularis
Teres major

Anterior fibers of deltoid
Latissimus dorsi
Pectoralis major
    (The latter two especially
    when movement is resisted)

PERIPHERAL NERVES TESTED

Subscapular N's.
Axillary N.
Thoracodorsal N.
Lateral & medial anterior thoracic N's.

SPINAL SEGMENTS TESTED

C5, C6, C7

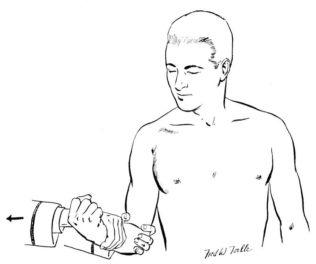

FIGURE 56.   *Medial (Internal) Rotation of the Arm at the Shoulder.* This movement depends chiefly on the subscapular and the teres major muscles. Weakness of this movement constitutes evidence of interruption of the subscapular and thoracodorsal nerves.

Lateral (External) Rotation of the Arm at the Shoulder (Figs. 57, 58)

The forearm is brought into the same position as in the previous test. The patient resists the examiner's attempt to rotate the arm inward (Fig. 57). The test should also be performed with the examiner behind the patient so that he may be able to see and feel the infraspinatus muscle contract (Fig. 58).

MUSCLES TESTED

Infraspinatus   Teres minor
                                              Posterior fibers of deltoid

PERIPHERAL NERVES TESTED

Suprascapular N.   Axillary N.

SPINAL SEGMENTS TESTED

C4, C5, C6   **C5, C6**

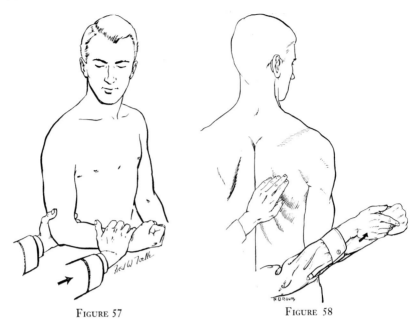

FIGURE 57   FIGURE 58

FIGURES 57, 58.   *Lateral (External) Rotation of the Arm at the Shoulder.* This
movement is dependent chiefly on the infraspinatus muscle,
which is supplied by the suprascapular nerve. The strength of
the movement may be gauged by the procedure illustrated in
Figure 57 and contraction of the infraspinatus muscle as shown
in Figure 58.

Adduction of the Arm Against the Body (Figs. 59, 60)

The arm is first abducted and flexed at the elbow and then the patient
is asked to retain the position while the examiner attempts to abduct
the arm further, at the same time palpating the contracting pectoralis major (Fig. 59). By testing the power of abduction in the manner shown in Figure 60 the strength of the movement may be gauged,
and the hand employed for palpating the latissimus dorsi.

MUSCLES TESTED
Pectoralis major (sternocostal portion)
Teres major
Latissimus dorsi

PERIPHERAL NERVES TESTED
Lateral & medial anterior thoracic N's.
Subscapular N. (lateral)
Thoracodorsal N.

SPINAL SEGMENTS TESTED
C5, C6, C7, C8, T1

Adduction of the Horizontally Abducted Arm (Fig. 61)

This movement is designed to test the functions of the teres major, the latissimus dorsi and the sternocostal and clavicular parts of the pectoralis major. Contraction of the first two muscles can best be produced when the patient attempts to adduct his horizontally abducted arm against the examiner's resistance. Contraction of the two parts of

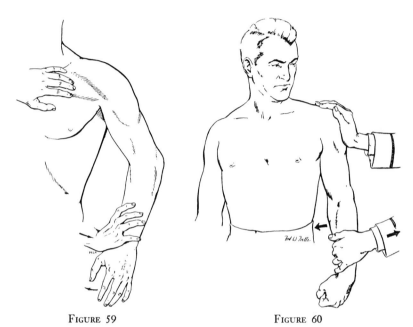

FIGURE 59   FIGURE 60

FIGURES 59, 60.   *Adduction of the Arm Against the Body*. This movement depends on the action of the pectoralis major, the teres major and the latissimus dorsi. In Figure 59 the contracting pectoralis major is being palpated. The strength of adduction may be assessed as illustrated in Figure 60 but this mode of testing is unsatisfactory since muscles participating in the movement are not being palpated.

the pectoralis major is shown to advantage when, from the starting point indicated in the illustration the patient attempts to bring his elbow forward against resistance. During these movements the contraction of the participating muscles should be verified by palpation.

The teres major is supplied by the lower subscapular nerve (from segments C5 and C6), the latissimus dorsi by the thoracodorsal nerve (from C6, **C7** and C8), the sternocostal part of the pectoralis major predominantly by the medial anterior thoracic nerve (from C5, C6, **C7, C8** and **T1**) and the clavicular portion by the lateral anterior thoracic nerve (from **C5, C6, C7,** C8 and T1).

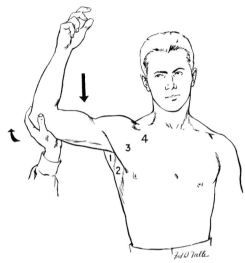

FIGURE 61.   *Adduction of the Horizontally Abducted Arm.* This movement tests in particular (1) the teres major muscle (lateral subscapular n.), (2) the latissimus dorsi (thoracodorsal n.) and (3) the sternocostal and (4) the clavicular parts of the pectoralis major (medial and lateral anterior thoracic nerves respectively). The contraction of the two parts of the pectoralis major is shown to best advantage when the patient brings his elbow forward against the examiner's resistance (indicated by the lateral arrow).

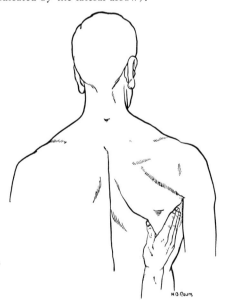

FIGURE 62.   *Test for Function of the Latissimus Dorsi.* The examiner firmly grasps the latissimus dorsi in the region of the inferior angle of the scapula. Normally the muscle can be felt to contract when the patient coughs. The latissimus dorsi is supplied by the thoracodorsal nerve.

Another means of testing latissimus dorsi function is to grasp between thumb and index finger the tissues on either side of the inferior angle of the scapula (where a slip of the latissimus takes origin) and then, by means of a pincers movement, to bring the tissues together under the scapula (Fig. 62). When the patient coughs the examiner can feel the latissimus dorsi contract.

MOVEMENTS AT THE ELBOW

Flexion of the Forearm at the Elbow (Fig. 63)

The patient flexes the forearm at the elbow and resists the examiner's attempt to straighten the arm. During the movement the biceps can be

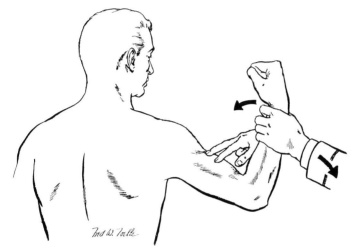

FIGURE 63.   *Flexion of the Forearm at the Elbow.* The movement, when tested with the forearm fully supinated, is dependent almost entirely on the biceps and brachialis muscles, which are supplied by the musculocutaneous nerve.

seen and felt to contract. Full supination of the forearm during the test minimizes participation of the brachioradialis muscle.

MUSCLES TESTED
Brachialis
Biceps brachii
Brachioradialis
Pronator teres

PERIPHERAL NERVES TESTED
Musculocutaneous N.
Radial N.
Median N.

SPINAL SEGMENTS TESTED
C5, C6

Test for Brachioradialis Function

The forearm is placed in a position midway between pronation and supination and the patient is requested to bend the arm at the elbow. When resistance to the movement is offered, the belly of the brachioradialis muscle (**C5**, **C6**) stands out prominently (Fig. 64). Even when biceps and brachialis are completely paralyzed, the brachioradialis still is capable of flexing at the elbow, providing the forearm is sufficiently

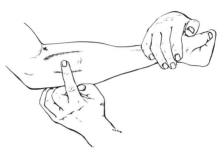

FIGURE 64.   *Test for Brachioradialis Function.* The brachioradialis muscle is tested to best advantage when the forearm, in a position midway between pronation and supination, is flexed against resistance. The muscle is supplied by the radial nerve.

pronated (*a supplementary action*). Contraction of this muscle can also be demonstrated during the act of steadying a glass while raising it to the lips.

Extension of the Forearm at the Elbow (Fig. 65)

With the arm somewhat abducted (to eliminate the effect of gravity) and the forearm slightly flexed, the patient attempts to extend the forearm at the elbow while the examiner resists. During the movement the contraction of the three heads of the triceps can be seen and felt. In Figure 65 the long head of the triceps (1) is being palpated.

MUSCLES TESTED
Triceps brachii
Anconeus

PERIPHERAL NERVE TESTED
Radial N.

SPINAL SEGMENTS TESTED
C7, C8, T1

MOVEMENTS AT THE RADIAL-ULNAR JOINTS

Supination of the Forearm (Fig. 66)

The forearm is flexed to a right angle and the elbow is kept in contact with the body. With the forearm in slight pronation the patient

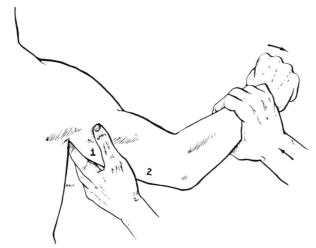

FIGURE 65.   *Extension of the Forearm at the Elbow.* This movement is dependent on the triceps muscle, supplied by the radial nerve. The contracting long head of the triceps (1) is being palpated. By palpating at a lower level (2) all the parts of the muscle may be felt to contract.

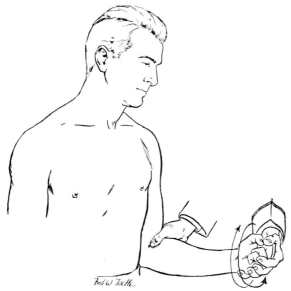

FIGURE 66.   *Supination and Pronation of the Forearm.* The arrows indicate the direction of the attempted rotation of the hand when supination and pronation of the forearm, respectively, are attempted against the examiner's resistance. Supination depends on the biceps and the supinator muscles, which are innervated by the musculocutaneous and radial nerves, respectively; pronation is performed mainly by the pronator teres and pronator quadratus, both of which are supplied by the median.

attempts to supinate while the examiner tries to pronate the hand. The accessible participating muscles should be palpated during the maneuver. Supination can also be carried out by these muscles, including the biceps brachii, when the arm is extended (Woods, 1919).

MUSCLES TESTED
Biceps brachii
Supinator
Brachioradialis

PERIPHERAL NERVES TESTED
Musculocutaneous N.
Radial N.

SPINAL SEGMENTS TESTED
C5, C6

Pronation of the Forearm (Fig. 66)

The forearm is bent to a right angle, the arm is externally rotated at the shoulder, and the elbow is kept continually in contact with the trunk. The patient attempts to pronate while the examiner tries to turn the forearm in the reverse direction. This movement depends chiefly on the pronator teres muscle, which is innervated from spinal segments C6 and **C7**.

When testing for pronation the greatest care should be exercised to rule out the effect of gravity. If the test is carried out as illustrated in Figure 66, gravity does not influence the movement. The role of gravity may be illustrated as follows: Flex and supinate forearm, keeping the elbow to the side. The palm is up. Maintain the spatial position of the hand. Now allow the elbow to drift away from the side and be carried outward and forward. The hand will fall into pronation without conscious effort. In this movement the shoulder is abducted and internally rotated to maintain the fixed spatial position of the hand in front of the body.

MUSCLES TESTED
Pronator teres
Pronator quadratus
Flexor carpi radialis
Palmaris longus
(the last two when
resistance is offered)

PERIPHERAL NERVE TESTED
Median N.

SPINAL SEGMENTS TESTED
C6, C7, C8

MOVEMENTS AT THE WRIST

Dorsal Flexion ("Extension") of the Hand at the Wrist

In testing the power of dorsal flexion of the hand, the various participating muscles should be palpated separately. The contraction of the

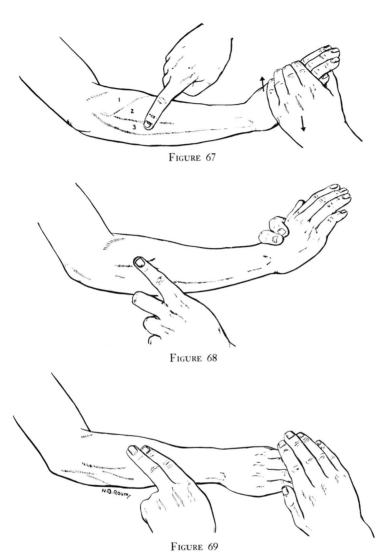

FIGURE 67

FIGURE 68

FIGURE 69

FIGURES 67, 68, 69.   *Dorsal Flexion of the Hand at the Wrist.* The movement is dependent on the extensors of the hand and fingers. In the first sketch (Fig. 67) the sites of the extensor carpi radialis longus (*1*), the extensor digitorum (*2*) and the extensor carpi ulnaris (*3*) are indicated. In Figure 67 the extensor carpi ulnaris is being palpated; in Figure 68 the extensor carpi radialis longus, and in Figure 69 the extensor digitorum. All these muscles are supplied by the radial nerve.

In performing these tests it is easier *to observe* the muscles and *to feel* the tendons than to feel both the muscle bellies and the tendons.

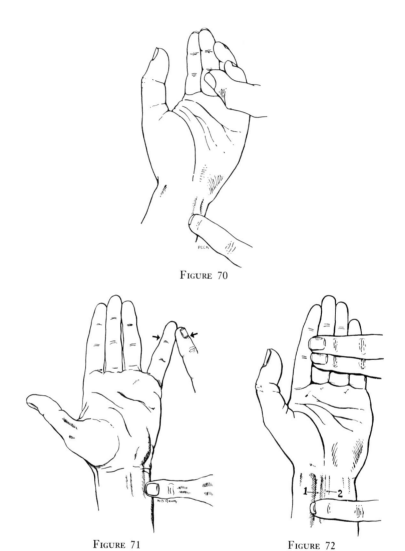

FIGURE 70

FIGURE 71   FIGURE 72

FIGURES 70, 71, 72.   *Palmar Flexion of the Hand at the Wrist.* The muscles
chiefly responsible for this movement are the flexor carpi
radialis longus, innervated by the median, and the flexor carpi
ulnaris, innervated by the ulnar. In Figures 70 and 71 the
tendon of the flexor carpi ulnaris is being palpated. The contraction illustrated in Figure 71 is due to fixation by the flexor
carpi ulnaris of the point of origin of the abductor digiti
quinti. In Figure 72 the tendon of the flexor carpi radialis
longus (*1*) comes into particular prominence and the tendon
of the palmaris longus (*2*) to a lesser degree.

extensor carpi ulnaris (C7 and C8), the extensor carpi radialis longus (C6 and C7) and the extensor digitorum (C7 and C8) can be felt to contract when the tests are performed in the manner indicated in Figures 67, 68 and 69 respectively.

MUSCLES TESTED
Extensor carpi radialis longus
Extensor carpi radialis brevis
Extensor carpi ulnaris
Extensors of the digits

PERIPHERAL NERVE TESTED
Radial N.

SPINAL SEGMENTS TESTED
C6, **C7**, C8

Palmar Flexion of the Hand at the Wrist

The flexor carpi ulnaris and flexor carpi radialis are the muscles chiefly concerned in this movement. Simple tests for eliciting contraction of the flexor carpi ulnaris (**C7** and C8) are carried out as follows: the examiner presses on the palmar surface of the outstretched little finger (Fig. 70) and resists abduction of the little finger (Fig. 71). In both tests a tightening of the tendon of the muscle can be seen and felt. The function of the flexor carpi radialis (**C7** and C8) may be tested by plantar-flexing the hand against resistance. When this is done the tendon of the muscle stands out prominently (Fig. 72) and the belly of the muscle can be felt to contract.

MUSCLES TESTED
Flexor carpi radialis
Flexor carpi ulnaris
Abductor pollicis longus
Flexors of fingers
   (sublimis & profundus)
Palmaris longus
   (the last two especially
   against strong resistance)

PERIPHERAL NERVES TESTED
Median N.
Ulnar N.
Radial N.

SPINAL SEGMENTS TESTED
C6, **C7**, C8

MOVEMENTS OF THE THUMB AND FINGERS

Adduction of the Thumb

The thumb may be adducted in two ways: in the plane of the palm (ulnar adduction) and in a plane at right angles to that of the palm (palmar adduction). In order to illustrate graphically the various motions of the thumb, the patient's hand, with ulnar border down, should be placed at right angles to a flat surface, as shown, for example, in Figures 75 and 82. When the thumb is at rest, its dorsal and palmar surfaces are parallel to the surface of the table. If, from this position, the thumb is fully extended, it lies almost parallel to the other fingers, or in a position of radial abduction. Starting from this position, ulnar adduction

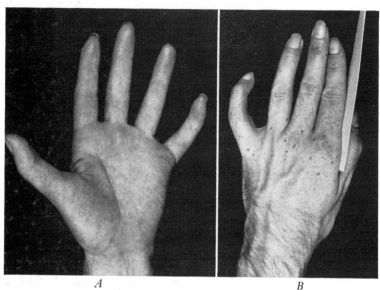

A   *B*

FIGURE 73.   *Median-Innervated Thumb and Interosseous Muscles in a Case of Complete Ulnar Palsy. A* Illustrates the lack of atrophy of muscles of the ball of the thumb and the ability to spread the fingers, indicating that muscles ordinarily supplied by the ulnar nerve are innervated by the median. Intact adductor function of the thumb due to action of the first dorsal interosseous muscle is illustrated in *B.* (H.H.)

consists of a downward movement which brings the ulnar surface of the thumb against the radial border of the palm (Fig. 75). The movement may be continued still further by sliding the thumb over the palmar surface of the head of the second metacarpal.

In ulnar adduction of the thumb a number of muscles, chiefly the adductor pollicis, come into play. The power of this movement should be tested by having the patient resist the examiner's attempt to withdraw a piece of paper grasped between the thumb and the radial border of the hand (Fig. 75).

MUSCLES TESTED

Adductor pollicis   Extensor pollicis longus
                                                Opponens pollicis
                                                Flexor pollicis longus
                                                Flexor pollicis brevis

PERIPHERAL NERVES TESTED

Ulnar N.   Radial N.
                               Median N.

SPINAL SEGMENTS TESTED

C8, T1   C7, **C8, T1**

The muscles concerned in ulnar adduction of the thumb may occasionally be supplied solely by the median nerve. An example of such *anomalous innervation* is illustrated in Figure 73.

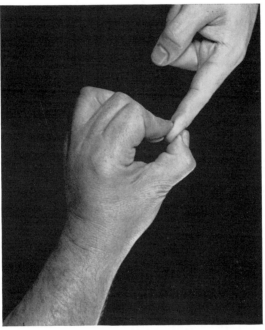

FIGURE 74.   *Irreparable Ulnar Nerve Paralysis Following Laceration of Middle Third of Left Forearm by a Door Handle of a Car.* The photograph was taken eight months after the injury. The following supplementary muscle movements are coordinated to insure the important function of "pinch": (a) stabilization of the metacarpophalangeal articulation of the thumb and flexion of its distal phalanx by the flexor pollicis longus; (b) flexion of the proximal phalanx and extension of the distal phalanx of the index finger by median-innervated musculature to stabilize the proximal interphalangeal and metacarpophalangeal articulations of this digit; and (c) the use of the long finger (i.e., the third) to stabilize the index finger. (DUH, D-13367.)

In *palmar adduction of the thumb* (Fig. 76), in which the power of the movement is tested by attempting to withdraw a piece of paper from between the thumb and palm, the muscles tested and their sources of innervation are as follows:

MUSCLES TESTED

1st interossei   Extensor pollicis longus
(dorsal & palmar)

PERIPHERAL NERVES TESTED

Ulnar N.   Radial N.

SPINAL SEGMENTS TESTED

C8, **T1**

In lesions completely interrupting the ulnar nerve, adduction of the thumb from the position either of palmar or of radial abduction can be performed by the *supplementary action* of the extensor pollicis longus

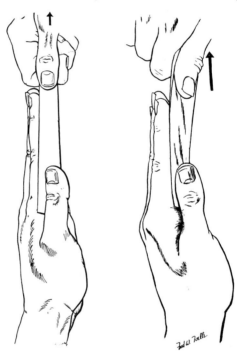

FIGURE 75   FIGURE 76

FIGURES 75, 76.   *Adduction of the Thumb.* In ulnar adduction of the thumb (Fig. 75), the adductor pollicis is the chief muscle tested. In palmar adduction (Fig. 76) the interossei come into play. Both movements are dependent principally on the ulnar nerve.

and flexor pollicis longus muscles with simultaneous flexion of the distal phalanx of the thumb (Fig. 225; p. 259). The *supplementary movements* concerned in pinch function of the thumb and index finger are more complicated (Fig. 74).

Abduction of the Thumb

The position of the hand during performance of abduction of the thumb should be the same as that described under adduction. This movement may be performed in two ways: by moving the thumb upward in the same plane as that of the palm (radial abduction) and by moving it outward in a plane at right angles to the plane of the palm, inside the radial margin of the hand and index finger (palmar abduction). Both movements should be carried out against resistance and the tendons of the responsible muscles palpated.

In *radial abduction of the thumb* (Fig. 77) the participants are the following:

MUSCLES TESTED

Abductor pollicis longus
Extensor pollicis brevis
Extensor pollicus longus
Abductor pollicis brevis

PERIPHERAL NERVES TESTED

Radial N.
Median N.

SPINAL SEGMENTS TESTED

C7, C8

FIGURE 77   FIGURE 78

FIGURES 77, 78.   *Abduction of the Thumb.* Radial abduction of the thumb (Fig. 77) depends on the abductor pollicis longus, the extensor pollicis longus and the extensor pollicis brevis (innervated by the radial) and on the abductor pollicis brevis (innervated by the median). Palmar abduction (Fig. 78) is due chiefly to the action of the abductor pollicis brevis (supplied by the median nerve) and the flexor pollicis brevis (supplied by both median and ulnar, or by the ulnar alone).

In *palmar abduction of the thumb* (Fig. 78) the muscles and sources of innervation concerned are as follows:

MUSCLES TESTED

Abductor pollicis brevis
Flexor pollicis brevis (both heads)
Abductor pollicis longus
Opponens pollicis

PERIPHERAL NERVES TESTED

Median N.
Ulnar N.
Radial N.

SPINAL SEGMENTS TESTED

C8, T1

True palmar abduction of the thumb is usually lost in the presence of paralysis of the thenar muscles. *Supplementary* palmar abduction may, however, be performed (Fig. 79)

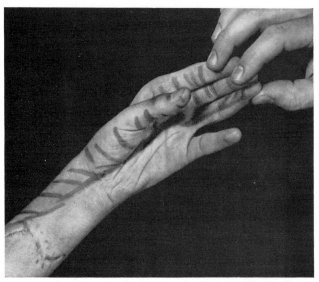

FIGURE 79. *Supplementary Palmar Abduction of the Thumb in Median Nerve Paralysis.* The median nerve in its course through lower half of the forearm was lacerated in an automobile accident two months prior to surgical exploration. The palmar abduction illustrated here was accomplished by stabilization of the thumb by the palmaris longus and by the combined action of the abductor pollicis longus and ulnar-innervated opponens pollicis. Adequate abduction may also be carried out through anomalous or double innervation of the abductor pollicis brevis or the superficial head of the flexor pollicis brevis. Variability in size of the ulnar-innervated head of the flexor pollicis brevis may influence the strength of supplementary palmar abduction. (DUH, D-38700.)

Extension of the Thumb

The patient's hand, with ulnar edge down, is placed at a right angle to a flat surface, and the thumb assumes the position of palmar abduction. Taking this as the starting position, the thumb is moved into moderate extension (Fig. 81). This motion tests chiefly the function of the extensor pollicis longus (which extends primarily at the interphalangeal joint and secondarily at the metacarpophalangeal) and the function of the extensor pollicis brevis (which extends at the metacarpophalangeal and carpometacarpophalangeal joints). With further extension the extensor pollicis longus comes into greater play. Its tendency to tilt the metacarpus toward the ulnar side is partly counteracted by the abductor pollicis longus and the abductor pollicis brevis. In this movement the tendon of the extensor pollicis longus and those of the extensor pol-

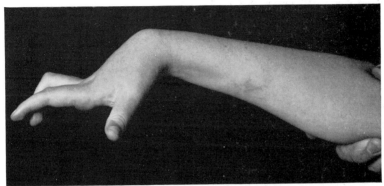

FIGURE 80.   *Supplementary Full Extension of the Distal Phalanx of the Thumb in a Missile Wound of the Radial Nerve and Upper Arm.* The photograph was taken twenty-four hours after the injury. (DUH, C-59555.)

licis brevis and abductor pollicis longus come into full prominence, forming the dorsal and volar boundaries of the *anatomical snuffbox* of the hand (Fig. 82).

Extension of the distal phalanx of the thumb may conveniently be tested by resisting the examiner's attempt to flex at the interphalangeal joint (Fig. 83), and extension of the proximal phalanx by resisting the examiner's attempt to flex at the metacarpophalangeal joint (Fig. 84) (in each instance palpating the contracting muscle); but since both of these movements are dependent on other muscles as well, it is desirable to test the two phalanges in the manner illustrated in Figures 85 and 86.

Extension of Distal Phalanx	*Extension of Proximal Phalanx*
MUSCLES TESTED	
Extensor pollicis longus	**Extensor pollicis brevis** Extensor pollicis longus
PERIPHERAL NERVE TESTED	
Radial N.	
SPINAL SEGMENTS TESTED	
C7, C8	**C7, C8**

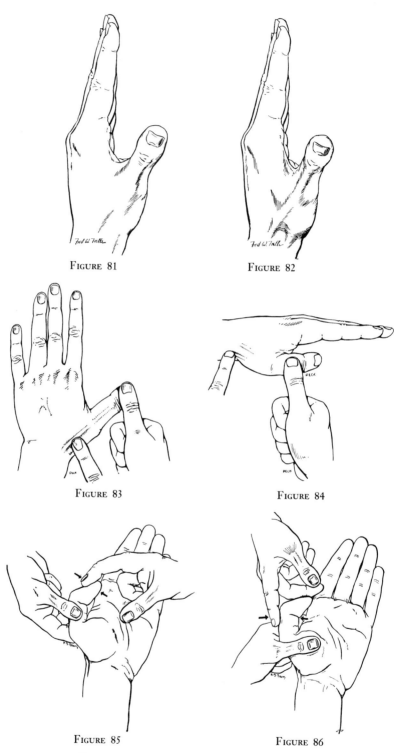

FIGURE 81

FIGURE 82

FIGURE 83

FIGURE 84

FIGURE 85

FIGURE 86

FIGURES 81–86.   See opposite page for legend.

In a large proportion of patients with complete radial nerve division the ability to extend the distal phalanx of the thumb is preserved. This *supplementary*, or *trick*, movement is subserved by the action of a slip of the abductor pollicis brevis which passes round the radial aspect of the thumb and inserts into the tendons of the extensor pollicis longus. The trick movement is, therefore, usually associated with palmar abduction of the thumb and may be inhibited by firm palmar adduction of the thumb during testing. Flexion at the wrist may also extend the distal phalanx of the thumb through tendon action of the paralyzed extensor musculature (Fig. 80).

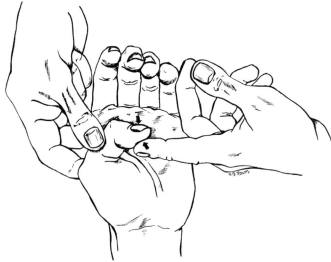

FIGURE 87.   *Flexion of the Distal Phalanx of the Thumb.* This movement tests the function of the flexor pollicis longus, which is supplied by the median nerve.

Flexion of the Thumb

In testing flexion of the distal phalanx of the thumb, the examiner immobilizes the proximal phalanx and then attempts to extend the flexed distal phalanx (Fig. 87). This maneuver tests the action of the flexor pollicis longus. It is of importance that the test be carried out with the

FIGURES 81–86.   *Extension of the Thumb.* In moderate extension of the thumb (Fig. 81) the extensor pollicis longus and extensor pollicis brevis come chiefly into play; in full extension (Fig. 82) the abductors of the thumb take part. The remaining illustrations indicate methods of testing extension of the thumb against resistance. The tests shown in Figures 83 and 84 have the advantage of permitting palpation of the tightened tendon of the extensor pollicis longus and of the extensor pollicis brevis respectively; those illustrated in Figures 85 and 86 are equally as satisfactory since the extensor pollicis longus and the extensor pollicis brevis are the only muscles tested.

thumb in a position of palmar adduction to preclude the action of other muscles.

In testing flexion at the metacarpophalangeal joint of the thumb, the finger is placed in a position of palmar adduction, the metacarpal is immobilized, and then the movement is attempted against resistance. This action depends chiefly on the flexor pollicis longus and flexor pollicis brevis.

Flexion of Distal Phalanx	*Flexion of Proximal Phalanx*
MUSCLES TESTED	
Flexor pollicis longus	**Flexor pollicis longus** **Flexor pollicis brevis** Abductor pollicis brevis Adductor pollicis
PERIPHERAL NERVES TESTED	
Median N.	**Median N.** Ulnar N.
SPINAL SEGMENTS TESTED	
C7, C8, **T1**	C7, C8, **T1**

Loss of active flexion of the distal phalanx of the thumb has been considered irrefutable evidence of complete division of the median

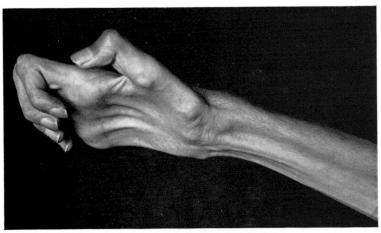

Figure 88.   *Supplementary Flexion of Terminal Phalanx of the Thumb in Combined Median and Ulnar Nerve Injury Due to Low Brachial Plexus Injury.* The photograph was made three years after injury. (DUH, C-93624.)

nerve. In Figure 88, the wrist is hyperextended and the thumb radially abducted, thus placing tension upon the tendons of the paralyzed long flexor, with the result that the distal phalanx is flexed. This *trick movement* is readily unmasked by testing with the thumb in firm palmar adduction.

Opposition of the Thumb and Little Finger

The power of opposition of the thumb and the little finger should be tested separately. In opposition, the thumb advances across the palm in a wide arc, rotating en route through about 60 degrees, so that at

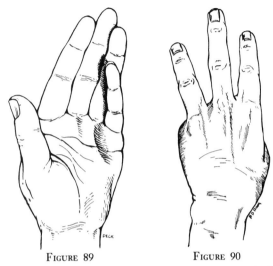

FIGURE 89   FIGURE 90

FIGURES 89, 90.   *Attitude of the Hand When Opposition of the Little Finger Is Performed.* There is cupping of the hand (Fig. 89) and rounding of the dorsal metacarpal arch (Fig. 90).

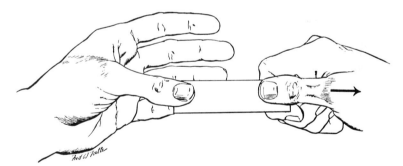

FIGURE 91.   *Opposition of the Thumb and Little Finger.* In this combined movement the thumb is drawn over the palm chiefly by its opponens muscle, which is supplied by the median nerve. Opposition of the little finger, a movement for which the ulnar nerve is necessary, depends on palmar elevation of the fifth metacarpal as well as on the action of the opponens muscle.

the end of the movement the palmar surface of the thumb comes in contact with the palmar surface of the base of the little finger.

In opposition of the extended little finger, its tip, describing a short arc, moves toward the thumb: this movement is dependent not only on the ability of the little finger to move toward the radial side of the hand but also on palmar elevation of the head of the 5th metacarpal. When opposition is full there is cupping of the palm (Fig. 89) and rounding of the dorsal metacarpal arch (Fig. 90).

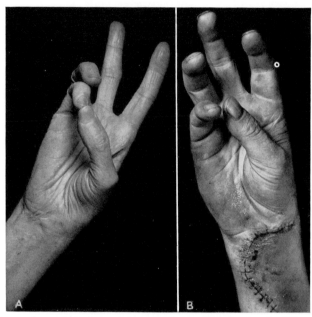

FIGURE 92.   *Anomalous Innervation of Thenar Muscles by the Ulnar Nerve in Complete Median Nerve Division.* In *A* there was a complete interruption of the median nerve at the wrist due to laceration by a window pane six months previously. Note loss of opponens pollicis muscle mass. There was moderate rigidity of the metacarpophalangeal articulation of the thumb. Opposition was carried out through stabilization of the joint by the flexor pollicis longus and through the anomalous ulnar innervation of the abductor pollicis brevis and flexor pollicis brevis. (DUH, C-92197.) In *B*, the median nerve was lacerated in the region of the wrist. Note the lack of atrophy of the opponens pollicis and abductor pollicis brevis muscles and normal opposition of thumb. (DUH, C-96146.)

Opposition of the thumb and little finger may be tested in one maneuver (Fig. 91). Under normal conditions, opposition of the thumb and little finger is such that when both are extended their tips meet, the two digits forming a vertical arch over the palm. The strength of the combined movement may be gauged by the patient's ability to retain his grasp on a paper which the examiner attempts to pull away.

Opposition of Thumb	*Opposition of Little Finger*
CHIEF MUSCLES TESTED	
Opponens pollicis	**Opponens digiti quinti**
Flexor pollicis brevis	Flexor digiti quinti
(deep head)	
Abductor pollicis brevis	

PERIPHERAL NERVES TESTED

Median N.   **Ulnar N.**
Ulnar N.

SPINAL SEGMENTS TESTED
C8, **T1**   C8, **T1**

Since the thenar contribution to opposition of the thumb is controlled exclusively by those intrinsic thumb muscles supplied by the median nerve, any *supplementary movement* of opposition must be due to anomalous ulnar innervation or to double innervation of the abductor pollicis, opponens, and/or flexor pollicis brevis (Fig. 92).

Adduction of the Fingers (Excluding Thumb) (Fig. 93)

This movement consists of bringing the fingers tightly together. The degree of functional integrity may be determined by having the patient attempt to retain between adjacent fingers a piece of paper which the

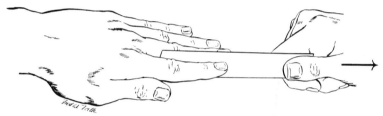

FIGURE 93.   *Adduction of the Fingers (Excluding Thumb)*. The fingers are adducted by the palmar interossei, which receive their nerve supply from the ulnar. In this figure the power of the first palmar interosseous muscle is being tested.

examiner tries to dislodge. By performing the test with the palmar aspect of the hand up, the muscles can sometimes be felt to contract. Adduction of the fingers may also be tested in the manner illustrated in Figure 37 (p. 59).

MUSCLES TESTED
Palmar interossei

PERIPHERAL NERVE TESTED
Ulnar N.

SPINAL SEGMENTS TESTED
C8, **T1**

Abduction of the Fingers (Excluding Thumb) (Fig. 94)

With the fingers fully extended and spread apart, the patient endeavors to resist the examiner's attempt to bring them together. The examiner usually can see and feel the bellies of the respective interosseous muscles contract. In Figure 94 the strength of the 1st dorsal interosseous muscle is being tested.

MUSCLES TESTED
Dorsal interossei
Lumbricals
Abductor digiti quinti

PERIPHERAL NERVE TESTED
Ulnar N.

SPINAL SEGMENTS TESTED
C8, **T1**

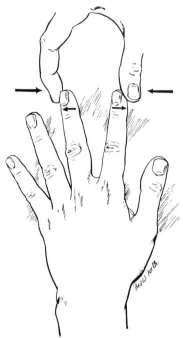

FIGURE 94.   *Abduction of the Fingers (Excluding Thumb).* In this movement the
dorsal interossei, supplied by the ulnar, are the chief muscles tested.
The power of the movement is assessed in the manner indicated.

Extension of the Fingers (Excluding Thumb)

Extension at the metacarpophalangeal and interphalangeal joints
should be tested separately. In testing the power of extension at the
proximal interphalangeal joint of the index finger, the metacarpophalangeal joint is extended and the proximal interphalangeal joint is partly
flexed. The patient then attempts extension at the proximal interphalangeal joint against the resistance offered by the examiner (Fig. 95).
This maneuver tests the function of the 1st lumbrical and dorsal and
palmar interosseous muscles. Full extension at all interphalangeal joints
is carried out by the lumbricals and dorsal and palmar interossei with
the aid of the extensor digitorum. The interossei and 4th and 3d lum-

bricals are innervated by the ulnar (from C8 and **T1**) and the 2d and 1st lumbricals by the median (from C7 and C8). The action of the extensor digitorum on the interphalangeal joints is most pronounced when the fingers are in flexion at the metacarpophalangeal joints and is nil when the fingers are in hyperextension.

Extension of the fingers at the metacarpophalangeal joints is brought about by the extensor digitorum, aided by the extensors of the index

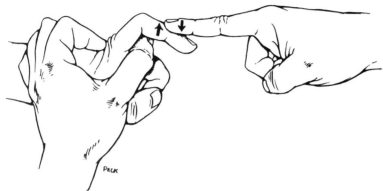

FIGURE 95.   *Extension of the Middle Phalanx of the Index Finger.* This movement tests the function of the 1st lumbrical (median nerve) and the palmar and dorsal interossei (ulnar nerve). In the presence of hyperextension at the metacarpophalangeal joint, as shown here, the extensor digitorum is powerless to act.

and little fingers, all innervated by the radial from spinal segments **C7** and C8.

THE MOVEMENTS PERFORMED IN MAKING A FIST

The significance of the failure to make a fist is readily comprehended when the component movements are analyzed. Each of the following movements should be tested against resistance and the contraction of the participating muscles verified by palpation.

Flexion of the Distal Phalanges (Fig. 96)

This movement is accomplished by the flexor digitorum profundus. The portions of the muscle going to the second and third fingers are supplied by the median nerve, those reaching the fourth and fifth by the ulnar (both from spinal segments C7, C8 and **T1**).

Flexion of the Middle Phalanges (Fig. 97)

This motion is performed by the flexor digitorum sublimis, which is innervated solely by the median nerve (from spinal segments C7, **C8** and **T1**). For this test of the function of the sublimis to be valid, the distal phalanges must be completely flaccid; otherwise the flexor digitorum profundus may aid in flexing the middle phalanges.

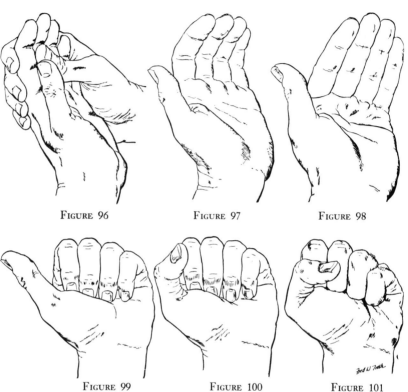

FIGURE 96   FIGURE 97   FIGURE 98

FIGURE 99   FIGURE 100   FIGURE 101

FIGURES 96–101.   *Various Movements Performed in Making a Fist.* Flexion of the distal phalanges (Fig. 96) is carried out by the flexor digitorum profundus, flexion of the middle phalanges (Fig. 97) by the flexor digitorum sublimis. Flexion at the metacarpophalangeal joints and simultaneous extension at the interphalangeals (Fig. 98) is due to combined action of the lumbricals and interossei (*palmar* and *dorsal* interossei in extension of the interphalangeal joints, and *palmar* in flexion at the metacarpophalangeal joints), aided by the extensor digitorum. Flexion at all the joints (Fig. 99) requires combined profundus and sublimis action. Bringing the distal phalanx of the thumb over the fingers preparatory to making a fist (Fig. 100) is due to combined action of the flexor pollicis longus, the flexor pollicis brevis and the abductor pollicis brevis. In tightening the fist (Fig. 101) the thumb opposes and further flexes, the sublimis and profundus go into full action, and the extensors of the hand (at the wrist) contract to fix the wrist.

Simultaneous Extension of Phalanges (Fig. 98)

Opinions vary as to the muscles responsible for this movement. Most authors (e.g., in Cunningham, 1951; Highet, 1942b) have stated that the lumbricals and both interossei act as flexors of the fingers at the metacarpophalangeal joints and that, through their attachment to the extensor tendons and continuation to the base of the distal phalanges, they act as extensors of the fingers at the interphalangeal joints, a combined movement which is impossible when these muscles are paralyzed. Kendall and Kendall (1949) have contended that in this combined action (1) flexion at the metacarpophalangeal joints is brought about by the lumbricals aided by the *palmar* interossei, and (2) extension at the finger joints is carried out by the lumbricals and *both* interossei. Thus, the interossei differ in their action, the *dorsal* aiding in the extension at

FIGURE 102.   *Test for Function of the Lumbrical Muscles.* The holding of a newspaper or a book in the position illustrated is dependent on normal functioning of the lumbricals. The dorsal and palmar interossei and the extensor digitorum aid in this form of grasp movement. (Redrawn from Kendall and Kendall, 1949.)

the phalangeal joints and the *palmar* having this function plus that of assisting in flexion at the metacarpophalangeal joints. The lumbricals are important in both aspects of this combined movement, as is also the extensor digitorum (Fig. 102). The interossei and the 4th and 3d lumbricals are innervated by the ulnar, the 2d and 1st lumbricals by the median (all from spinal segments C7, C8 and T1), the extensor digitorum by the radial.

Flexion of the Fingers at All Joints, with Extension of the Thumb (Fig. 99)

In this phase of making a fist the fingers are being folded into the palm. The flexion of the fingers is due to combined profundus and sublimis action, with the profundus serving at all the joints and the sublimis only at the proximal interphalangeal and metacarpophalangeal joints. The extensor carpi ulnaris and the radial extensors of the hand at the wrist aid in flexion of the fingers by synergically extending at the wrist. The thumb owes its extension chiefly to contraction of the extensor pollicis longus and brevis.

Flexion of the Fingers at All Joints, with Flexion of the Thumb (Fig. 100)

Flexion of the thumb prior to bringing it across the palm is essentially a median nerve function. The thumb is flexed at the phalangeal joint by the flexor pollicis longus muscle, and at the metacarpophalangeal joint

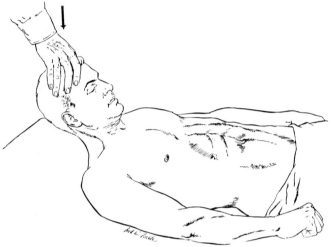

FIGURE 103.   *Abdominal Tenseness.* This maneuver brings the abdominal muscles into contraction, fixing the umbilicus. In paralysis of parts of the abdominal musculature, the shift of the umbilicus during the performance of this test is in the direction away from the part paralyzed. In paralysis of the upper abdominal musculature, for instance, the direction of the shift of the umbilicus during the performance of this test is downward.

by the flexor pollicis longus and brevis as well as by the abductor pollicis brevis.

Tightening the Fist (Fig. 101)

The power of a fist depends on (1) the ability of the thumb to brace the flexed fingers and (2) the degree of fixation at the wrist by synergists. In the tightly made fist the flexed thumb has moved into a position of opposition; the movement as a whole is, therefore, the result of combined median and ulnar nerve action. Virtually all the long muscles of the forearm, especially the extensors, participate in fixation at the wrist.

Abdomen

The abdominal muscles may be tensed by having the patient flex the head against resistance (Fig. 103). When using this test in the examination for paralysis, particular attention should be paid to migration of the umbilicus. When only a portion of the abdominal muscles are involved, the umbilicus moves in a direction opposite to the affected part. Paralysis of the upper half of the rectus abdominis results in downward movement of the umbilicus when the abdominal wall is tensed; paralysis of the right upper oblique causes the umbilicus to move downward and to the left; and so on.

MUSCLES TESTED

Rectus abdominis
External oblique
Internal oblique

PERIPHERAL NERVES TESTED
Lower thoracic N's.

SPINAL SEGMENTS TESTED
T6 to L1

Lower Extremity

The complexity of movement being less in the lower than in the upper extremity, there are fewer deceptive movements and, therefore, less chance for error to occur in the assessment of muscle function. Tests should be done in such a way that gravity does not in itself induce a movement. It is important also to guard against leverage as a source of error: when, for instance, the patient is lying on his back with the heel pressed firmly on the bed a shift of other parts of the body may produce movements at the ankle or elsewhere of which the patient is not actively capable.

MOVEMENTS AT THE HIP JOINT

Flexion at the Hip (Figs. 104, 105)

Two methods of testing flexion at the hips are illustrated. The extended leg may be brought off the bed and maintained in that position against resistance (Fig. 104), or the leg may be brought to a position in which the angle between the trunk and the thigh is a little less than 90 degrees, the lower leg being flexed at the knee and supported on the examiner's arm—the patient then attempting further flexion at the hip against resistance (Fig. 105). The latter test is preferable since fewer supporting muscles come into play. This movement is dependent chiefly on the iliopsoas muscle. The iliac muscle is supplied by the femoral nerve (L2, L3 and L4), the psoas by branches of anterior primary rami of segments L2 and L3, and in some instances by those of L1 and L4 as well.

MUSCLES TESTED

Iliopsoas	Gluteus medius & minimus
Rectus femoris	(anterior fibers only)
Sartorius	Tensor fasciae latae
Pectineus	Adductors longus & brevis

PERIPHERAL NERVES TESTED

Femoral N.	Superior gluteal N.
	Obturator N.

SPINAL SEGMENTS TESTED

L1, **L2**, L3, L4

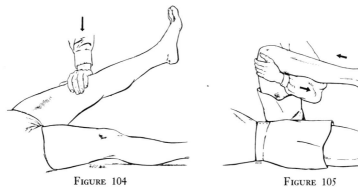

FIGURE 104   FIGURE 105

FIGURES 104, 105.   *Flexion at the Hip.* This movement tests the function of the iliopsoas muscle, which is supplied by the femoral nerve (L2, L3 and L4) and by branches of anterior primary rami of spinal segments L2 and L3 (L1 and L4 also in some instances). The test illustrated in Figure 105 is the more satisfactory since muscles aiding the iliopsoas do not come as much into play.

Test for Function of the Sartorius Muscle (Fig. 106)

The sartorius muscle, by reason of its attachments to the anterior superior iliac spine above, and medial surface of the shaft of the upper tibia below, is a flexor at both the hip and the knee as well as a lateral rotator of the thigh. In all these actions, its role is, however, relatively minor. The adducting action of the sartorius is negligible.

The sartorius is supplied by the femoral nerve from spinal segments **L2**, L3 and L4. Its functional status can be ascertained by having the patient lie on his back with the knee moderately flexed and with the thigh both flexed and laterally rotated at the hip; the patient then tries to flex at the knee against resistance offered at the ankle by the examiner. During this maneuver the contracted sartorius can be readily seen and felt.

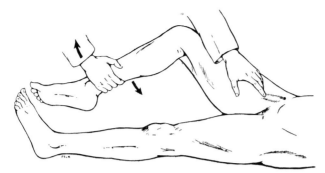

FIGURE 106.   *Test for Function of the Sartorius Muscle.* With the leg in the position indicated and the lower leg flexed against resistance the proximal part of the sartorius can be readily seen and felt.

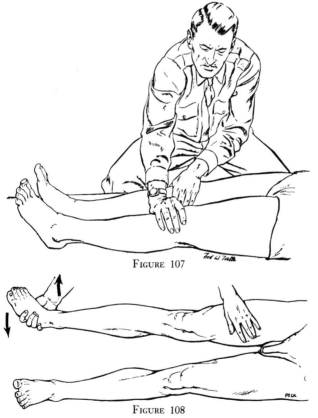

FIGURE 107

FIGURE 108

FIGURES 107, 108,   *Adduction of the Thigh.* In performing adduction of the thighs in the manner shown in Figure 107 an estimate of power of the two legs can be made. Each leg should then be tested separately and the contraction of the adductors verified by palpation, as is indicated in Figure 108. The adductor muscles are supplied by the obturator nerve.

Adduction of the Thigh (Figs. 107, 108)

The examiner may determine the power of adduction of both legs by testing in the manner shown in Figure 107. It is necessary also to test adduction of each leg separately, confirming the contraction of the adductors by means of palpation (Fig. 108). The most powerful of the group is the adductor magnus, which is innervated both by the obturator (from segments L3 and L4) and the sciatic (from L4 and L5).

MUSCLES TESTED

Adductor magnus	Gluteus maximus (lower fibers)
Adductor brevis	Quadratus femoris
Adductor longus	

PERIPHERAL NERVES TESTED

Obturator N.	Inferior gluteal N.
Sciatic N.	N. to quadratus femoris

SPINAL SEGMENTS TESTED
L2, L3, L4

Abduction of the Thigh (Fig. 109)

The recumbent patient attempts to abduct his extended leg against resistance. The muscles employed and their innervation are much the

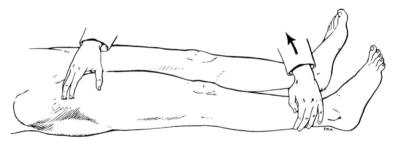

FIGURE 109.   *Abduction of the Thigh.* In this movement the contracting gluteus medius is being palpated. This muscle is supplied by the superior gluteal nerve.

same as those concerned in medial rotation of the thigh (see next heading). The most powerful abductor of the thigh is the gluteus medius (**L4,** L5 and S1).

Medial (Internal) Rotation of the Leg at the Hip (Fig. 110)

This test may conveniently be carried out by having the patient lie prone, with the lower leg flexed at the knee. The patient endeavors to turn the lower leg laterally, thus attempting medial rotation at the hip, while the examiner, using the lower leg as a lever arm, tries to pull the leg medially. During this maneuver the gluteus medius can be felt to contract. Other tests for gluteus medius functions are described on page 306.

MUSCLES TESTED
Gluteus medius
Tensor fasciae latae
Gluteus minimus

PERIPHERAL NERVE TESTED
Superior gluteal N.

SPINAL SEGMENTS TESTED
L4, L5

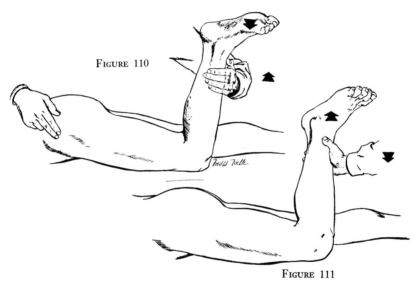

FIGURE 110

FIGURE 111

FIGURE 110.   *Medial (Internal) Rotation of the Leg at Hip.* This movement depends on the action of the gluteus medius, supplied by the superior gluteal nerve.

FIGURE 111.   *Lateral (External) Rotation of the Leg at Hip.* Combined action of a number of muscles, especially the gluteus maximus, is essential for this movement.

Lateral (External) Rotation of the Leg at the Hip (Fig. 111)

The patient assumes the same position as for the test just described. He then attempts to turn his lower leg medially (to produce lateral rotation at the hip) whereas the examiner tries to pull it laterally. The gluteus maximus is the muscle mainly responsible for this movement, but the short rotators at the hip (obturator internus and gemelli, obturator externus and quadratus femoris), especially the obturator internus and the gemelli, are also of importance. The test is of value only in detecting paralysis of the gluteus maximus.

MUSCLES TESTED

Gluteus maximus
  (its lower fibers)
Obturator internus
  & gemelli

Quadratus femoris
Obturator externus
Adductor magnus
Adductor brevis
Piriformis

PERIPHERAL NERVES TESTED

Inferior gluteal N.
N. to obturator internus

N. to quadratus femoris
Obturator N.
Twigs from rami S1 & S2

SPINAL SEGMENTS TESTED
L4, L5, S1, S2

Extension at the Hip (Fig. 112)

The patient lies prone, lifts his leg, flexed at the knee, off the bed; he then attempts to hold the position while the examiner tries to move the

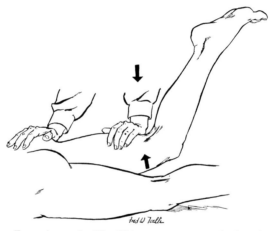

FIGURE 112.   *Extension at the Hip.* This movement tests the function of the gluteus maximus muscle, which is supplied by the inferior gluteal nerve.

leg back to the bed. During this maneuver the contracted belly of the gluteus maximus (L5, **S1** and **S2**) can be readily seen and felt.

MUSCLES TESTED

Gluteus maximus
Gluteus medius
  (posterior fibers)

Biceps femoris (long head)
Semitendinosus
Semimembranosus

PERIPHERAL NERVES TESTED

Inferior gluteal N.
Superior gluteal N.

Sciatic N.

SPINAL SEGMENTS TESTED
L5, S1, S2

MOVEMENT AT THE KNEE

Extension at the Knee (Figs. 113, 114)

The power of extension at the knee may be assessed in the manner illustrated in Figure 113; the patient attempts to keep the leg extended

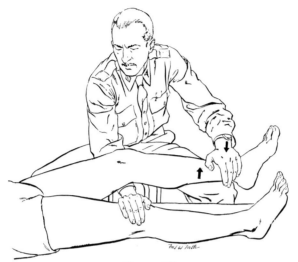

FIGURE 113

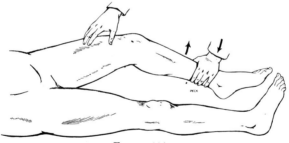

FIGURE 114

FIGURES 113, 114.   *Extension at the Knee.* This movement tests the function of quadriceps muscle, supplied by the femoral nerve. The test illustrated in Figure 113 may be used to assess the power of the movement, and that in Figure 114 to verify contraction of the quadriceps by palpation.

at the knee while the examiner, with right arm used as a fulcrum, tests the patient's ability to maintain that position. As shown in Figure 114, it is important also to palpate the contracting quadriceps. (See page 68 for another test.)

MUSCLE TESTED
Quadriceps femoris

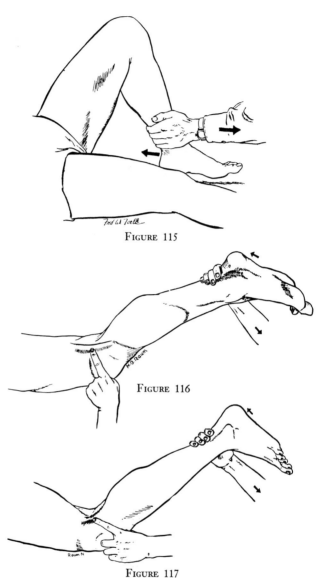

FIGURE 115

FIGURE 116

FIGURE 117

FIGURES 115–117.   *Flexion at the Knee.* Performance of the test as illustrated in Figure 115 has certain disadvantages (see text). The power of flexion at the knee is best determined in the manner shown in Figures 116 and 117. The tendons of the semitendinosus and semimembranosus are being palpated in Figure 116 and that of the biceps femoris in Figure 117. The muscles responsible for flexion at the knee are supplied by the nerve to the hamstrings.

PERIPHERAL NERVE TESTED
Femoral N.

SPINAL SEGMENTS TESTED
L2, **L3**, L4

Flexion at the Knee (Figs. 115–117)

In performing flexion at the knee as indicated in Figure 115, care should be taken that the foot is clear of the bed. The disadvantage of this test is that simultaneous flexion at the hip may lead to the false conclusion that power of flexion exists at the knee. Moreover, when the test is performed in this way the examiner has difficulty in seeing and feeling the hamstring muscles contract.

The desired method of testing flexion at the knee is illustrated in Figures 116 and 117. The patient lies prone with the lower leg flexed at the knee. He attempts to keep the leg in that postion while the examiner, by pulling the foot toward the bed, tests the patient's ability to maintain flexion. This maneuver tests the functions of the hamstring muscles: the tendons of the semitendinosus and semimembranosus (situated medially) (Fig. 116) and biceps femoris (situated laterally) (Fig. 117) can be seen and felt to contract.

MUSCLES TESTED
Biceps femoris
Semitendinosus
Semimembranosus

PERIPHERAL NERVE TESTED
Sciatic N.

SPINAL SEGMENTS TESTED
L5, **S1**, **S2**

MOVEMENTS AT THE ANKLE

Dorsal Flexion of the Foot (Figs. 118–120)

When the patient dorsiflexes his foot against resistance, the tibialis anterior and the extensor digitorum longus come into full prominence (Fig. 118). The contracted belly of the tibialis anterior (**L4**, L5) may be palpated in the manner shown in Figure 119; also the degree of tightening of its tendon should be observed. The power of the extensor digitorum longus (L5 and S1) may be tested by attempting to depress the patient's dorsiflexed toes, at the same time palpating the tendons as illustrated in Figure 120.

MUSCLES TESTED

Tibialis anterior   Peroneus tertius
Extensor digitorum **longus**
Extensor hallucis **longus**

PERIPHERAL NERVES TESTED

Deep peroneal N.   Deep peroneal N.

SPINAL SEGMENTS TESTED
L4, L5, S1

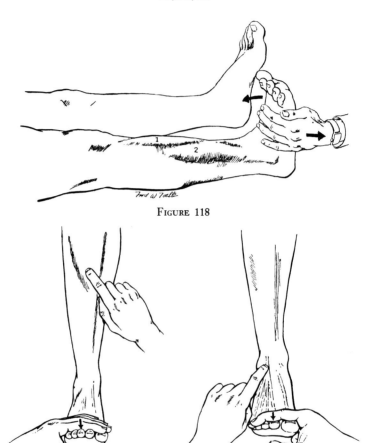

FIGURE 118

FIGURE 119   FIGURE 120

FIGURES 118–120.   *Dorsal Flexion of the Foot.* In Figure 118 the muscles brought
into prominence are the tibialis anterior (*1*) and the extensor
digitorum longus (*2*). In Figure 119 the power of the tibialis
anterior is being tested, and in Figure 120 that of the extensor
digitorum longus. Both are supplied by the deep peroneal
nerve.

Plantar Flexion of the Foot (Figs. 121, 122)

The patient attempts to maintain plantar flexion while the examiner
offers resistance and palpates the contracting gastrocnemius (S1 and

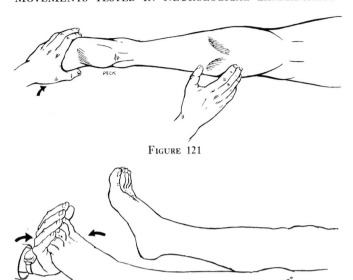

FIGURE 121

FIGURE 122

FIGURES 121, 122.   *Plantar Flexion of the Foot.* In Figure 121 the gastrocnemius is being palpated while the patient plantarflexes the foot against resistance. Performance of the test as shown in Figure 122 is unsatisfactory because the gastrocnemius cannot be seen or adequately palpated. This muscle and others of the back of the lower leg on which this movement depends, are supplied by the tibial nerve.

S2) (Fig. 121). Performance of the test as shown in Figure 122 is inadequate because the position makes palpation of the gastrocnemius difficult.

MUSCLES TESTED

Gastrocnemius	Peroneus longus
Soleus	Peroneus brevis
Tibialis posterior	
Flexor digitorum longus	
Flexor hallucis longus	

PERIPHERAL NERVES TESTED

Tibial N.	Superficial peroneal N.
Posterior tibial N.	

SPINAL SEGMENTS TESTED
L5, S1, S2, S3

MOVEMENTS AT THE INTERTARSAL JOINTS

Inversion of the Foot (Fig. 123)

The patient has turned his foot inward (inversion) and is resisting the attempt of the examiner to turn the foot outward (eversion). During this maneuver the tendons of the posterior and anterior tibial muscles stand out prominently. In Figure 123 the index finger is palpating the tendon of the tibialis posterior, which is just behind the medial malleolus.

MUSCLES TESTED

Tibialis posterior   **Tibialis anterior**
Flexor digitorum longus   Extensor hallucis longus
Flexor hallucis longus
Gastrocnemius
Soleus

PERIPHERAL NERVES TESTED

Posterior tibial N.   **Deep peroneal N.**
Tibial N.

SPINAL SEGMENTS TESTED
L4, L5, S1, S2

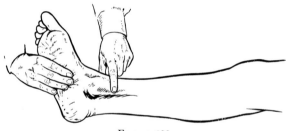

FIGURE 123

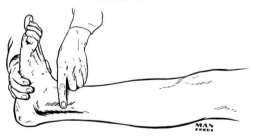

FIGURE 124

FIGURES 123, 124.   *Inversion and Eversion of the Foot.* Inversion of the foot (Fig. 123) depends on the power of the tibialis posterior (supplied by the posterior tibial nerve) and the tibialis anterior (supplied by the deep peroneal). In this figure the tendon of the tibialis posterior is being felt. Eversion of the foot (Fig. 124) is dependent chiefly on the peronei, innervated by the superficial peroneal nerve. In this figure the tendons of these two muscles are being palpated.

Eversion of the Foot (Fig. 124)

The foot is moved into a position of eversion. The patient tries to hold the position while the examiner attempts to invert. During this maneuver the tendons of the peroneus longus and brevis, which are situated a little above and behind the external malleolus, can usually be felt to tighten.

MUSCLES TESTED

Peroneus longus	Extensor digitorum longus
Peroneus brevis	Peroneus tertius

PERIPHERAL NERVES TESTED

Superficial peroneal N.	Deep peroneal N.

SPINAL SEGMENTS TESTED

L5, S1, S2

MOVEMENTS OF THE TOES

Dorsal Flexion (Extension) of the Toes

This movement is carried out chiefly by the following muscles: (1) the *extensor hallucis longus* (L5, **S1** and **S2**), which extends the great

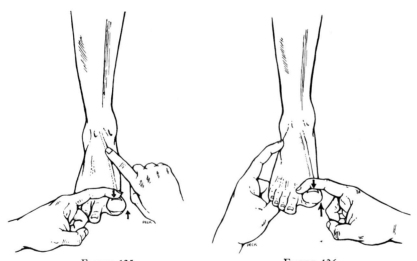

FIGURE 125   FIGURE 126

FIGURES 125, 126.   *Dorsal Flexion of the Great Toe.* In Figure 125 the tendon of the extensor hallucis longus is being palpated, and in Figure 126 the belly of the extensor digitorum brevis. Both muscles are supplied by the deep peroneal nerve.

toe, (2) the *extensor digitorum longus* (L5 and S1), which extends all the other toes, and (3) the *extensor digitorum brevis* (S1 and S2), which extends all toes except the little one.

In Figures 125 and 126 the technic of testing extension of the great toe is illustrated. The patient dorsiflexes the digit and attempts to hold it in that position against the examiner's resistance. In Figure 125 the tendon of the extensor hallucis longus is being palpated, and in Figure 126 the belly of the extensor digitorum brevis.

Dorsal Flexion of Great Toe	*Dorsal Flexion of the Other Toes*
MUSCLES TESTED	
Extensor hallucis longus	Extensor digitorum longus
Extensor digitorum brevis	Extensor digitorum brevis
PERIPHERAL NERVE TESTED	
Deep peroneal N.	
SPINAL SEGMENTS TESTED	
L5, S1, S2	L5, S1

Plantar Flexion of the Toes (Fig. 127)

Plantar flexion of the toes is brought about mainly by two muscles: the *flexor digitorum longus* (L5 and S1) and the *flexor digitorum brevis*

FIGURE 127.   *Plantar Flexion of the Great and Second Toes.* Plantar flexion of the great toe is due to action of the flexor hallucis longus and flexor hallucis brevis; that of the second toe, to action of the flexor digitorum longus and flexor digitorum brevis. These muscles are supplied by the posterior tibial nerve.

(S1 and S2). Each flexes all toes except the great one. The former acts chiefly at the distal interphalangeal joints, the latter at the metatarsophalangeal and proximal interphalangeal joints. In addition, these toes are flexed at the metatarsophalangeal joints (and extended at the interphalangeals) by the lumbricals and interossei.

The great toe is flexed at the metatarsophalangeal joint by the flexor hallucis brevis and longus and at the interphalangeal joint by the flexor hallucis longus.

The mode of testing plantar flexion of the great and second toes is illustrated in Figure 127. The patient flexes the digits and attempts to maintain the position against resistance.

Plantar Flexion of Great Toe	*Plantar Flexion of the Other Toes*
MUSCLES TESTED	
Flexor hallucis brevis	Flexor digitorum longus
Flexor hallucis longus	Flexor digitorum brevis
Abductor hallucis	Flexor digiti quinti brevis
Adductor hallucis	Abductor digiti quinti

PERIPHERAL NERVES TESTED

Posterior tibial N.
(and its branches, the medial
and lateral plantar N's.)

SPINAL SEGMENTS TESTED

S1, S2

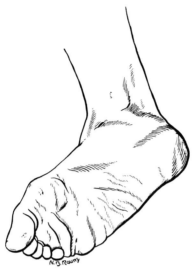

FIGURE 128.   *Cupping of the Sole of the Foot.* The cupping is due to action of the small muscles of the foot.

Cupping of the Sole of the Foot (Fig. 128)

The movement of cupping is performed by the small muscles of the foot, which are supplied by the medial and lateral plantar nerves (Fig. 250; p. 290).

Classification, Causes and Symptomatology of Peripheral Nerve Injuries

THIS SECTION is introduced by a presentation of the different degrees of nerve injury in terms of pathological changes, then moves on to a discussion of the causes and general symptomatology of nerve injuries, and concludes with a series of special tests of value in diagnosis and prognosis. Thus the section serves as a necessary preliminary to the presentation of individual nerve injuries in Section IV.

CHAPTER 7

The Various Degrees of
Peripheral Nerve Injury and
Their Clinical Significance

SUNDERLAND (1952a) has provided a simple classification of peripheral nerve injuries which takes into consideration five different degrees of injury. Each degree of pathological change incurred is correlated with the clinical outcome. The classification does not deal with nerve injuries due to traction or to widespread ischemia (as in Volkmann's contracture), but rather with those in which a relatively small segment of a nerve is implicated.

Sunderland's classification, which we have slightly modified and supplemented, is as follows:

First Degree Injury

By first degree injury is meant the loss of conductivity of axis cylinders at the site of the injury without any grossly apparent break in continuity of the structures comprising the nerve trunk. This degree of injury may be induced by instantaneous violence (e.g., missile wound or fracture) or by sudden or prolonged compression (e.g., by a crutch), and is to be ascribed to ischemia, petechial hemorrhages in or near the nerve sheath and/or mechanical deformation of the axis cylinders.

In an experimental study (on cats) of the effects of a blow on a nerve or of compression by means of a clip or a tourniquet, Denny-Brown and Brenner (1944a, b, c) observed that when the inflicting force is mild to moderate a first degree injury to the nerve is incurred, but that when severe the nerve injury is of second degree. Thus, following light percussion the sheath of Schwann is ruptured longitudinally and the damaged myelin escapes into the endoneurial spaces, but the axis cylinders remain intact. The nerve trunk rapidly swells because of the development of edema and the accumulation of macrophages intent on removing the destroyed myelin. The "pseudo-neuroma" thus formed may persist for weeks. Under such conditions sensibility is retained but there is a transient total block of impulses in motor fibers.

Functional alterations following mild compression for a relatively short period of time give rise to transient paralysis unassociated with a gross defect in sensibility, the functional dissociation being ascribed to differences in axoplasmic properties rather than to differences in fiber size. The "intermittent" demyelination which occurs in the nerve sheath was regarded as due entirely to ischemia.

Under first degree injury should also be included those cases in which a nerve trunk is exposed to the energy wave of a high velocity missile. A clinical example is illustrated in Figure 135. The sciatic nerve from such a case was studied pathologically by Spielmeyer (1915). At operation the nerve, found near the missile tract, was neither thickened nor thinned, but it felt softer than the adjoining proximal and distal seg-

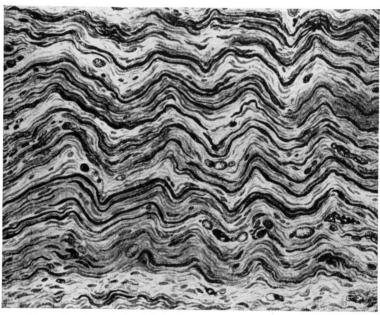

FIGURE 129.   *Section of the Sciatic Nerve in First Degree Injury.* This section was stained to bring out myelin sheaths. A fair number of myelin sheaths have disappeared or have degenerated, as indicated by their greyness in this photograph. The ringlets are evidence of wallerian degeneration. The time interval from injury to operation is not known. (From Spielmeyer, 1915.)

ments. The epineurium was pale grey-red. On microscopic examination approximately one third of the myelin sheaths had disappeared. This was a diffuse disappearance, not focal (Fig. 129). Many axis cylinders in the region of demyelination were intact; however, about 25 to 30 per cent of the nerve fibers were destroyed. In the region near the nerve trunk there were residual small hemorrhages. For similar observations by others, see Wexberg (1919).

Puckett and his associates (1946) have shown by means of micro-second roentgenograms in cats that just after a high velocity bullet has passed near a nerve trunk a large cavity is formed momentarily in the tissue and that as the cavity expands, the nerve is rapidly blown aside. As a result of being thus compressed and stretched, the nerve displayed numerous lesions, consisting of "(1) large breaks within the nerve, in which the continuity of a large bundle of fibers was broken; (2) a separation of the individual fibers; (3) an extreme 'kinking' of the fibers, as though they had undergone excessive stretching and (4) a series of multiple microscopic injuries scattered along the nerve trunk for a considerable distance." As Livingston, Davis and Livingston (1945) have shown clinically, some high velocity injuries fall in the category of first degree injury, others in the second and even the third.

First degree injury in man is characterized by a loss of motor function, loss of muscle tone, and a reduction in proprioceptive sensibility (postural and appreciation of vibration). In many instances, touch and pain sensibility are spared, but if affected they recover more rapidly than do motor and proprioceptive functions. Touch usually suffers to a greater degree than pain, and occasionally there may be anesthesia in the absence of analgesia for several weeks (Seddon, 1943). If at the time of the initial examination some functional restoration has occurred, the only sensory manifestations may be numbness or paresthesias and a proprioceptive defect. The most resistant components of the nerve are the sympathetic fibers; if affected, they are the first to recover. Electrical excitability is usually retained in the nerve trunk below the level of the injury and in the paralyzed muscles as well. Seddon (1943) has cited some cases in which the response to faradism was slightly weaker than normal, an observation which led him to conclude that a certain number of muscle fibers had degenerated as a consequence of degeneration of a few nerve fibers. When recovery of function is rapid, muscle wasting does not occur, but should recovery be delayed the wasting will be maximal in the involved muscles. The coexistence of normal, paretic and paralyzed muscles in a given limb in cases of this kind may be explained on the basis of individual variation of susceptibility of the motor fibers themselves and by the varying degree of protection the fibers are afforded by their position within the nerve trunk.

Recovery of function of the paralyzed muscles may set in within a few minutes, or the onset may be delayed for a period of several weeks, seldom, however, more than four weeks. Motor function recovers simultaneously in all the affected muscles, with the progress of the recovery being more rapid in some muscle groups than in others; there is none of the orderly distally-advancing functional restoration characteristic of the regenerating completely divided nerve. As to sensibility, pain sensibility recovers first, then touch, and finally, after considerable delay, proprioceptive sensibility. Paresthesias, appearing during the first few days, are usually evanescent. Functional restoration, considered over-all, is usually complete in three or four months after the injury. Exceptions are cases of concussion, in which function is fully restored in a few days or in two or three weeks.

Second Degree Injury

In second degree injury the axons are severed, with wallerian degeneration ensuing, but the pattern of the neural structures is not altered and endoneurial tubules retain their integrity. The regenerating axons advance distally in the endoneurial tubules they originally occupied, not in foreign tubules, and thus each is directed back to the end-organ to which it was originally connected. Since the fiber pattern after re-innervation is the same as that prior to the injury, function is usually fully restored.

Clinically there is complete loss of motor, sensory and sympathetic functions in the *autonomous* region of distribution of the injured nerve. The axonal degeneration is complete by about the nineteenth hour following injury, after which time the nerve fails to react to electrical stimulation and the muscles undergo atrophy and display the typical reaction of degeneration.

The duration of the latent period elapsing between the occurrence of the injury and the onset of recovery varies greatly because it depends on a number of factors, each of which is subject to individual variation.

Among these factors, which apply also to the more severe degrees of injury about to be discussed, is that of chromatolysis of nerve cells of the anterior horns and posterior root ganglia resulting from nerve injury. In animal experiment it has been observed that the period of latency corresponds to the degree of chromatolysis, which is by far the most striking in posterior root ganglia and thus explains the customary lag in sensory re-innervation as compared to motor. Chromatolysis is more intense following avulsion of a nerve than after simple section or ligation and more intense the closer the site of interruption is to the spinal cord (Marinesco, 1901). Also a certain number of chromatolytic nerve cells perish (Fleming, 1897; Ranson, 1909; Collier and Buzzard, 1903; see also Kelly, 1951).

Another factor is that of retrograde degeneration, the intensity of which varies inversely as the distance of the site of damage from the parent cell (Sunderland, 1952b).

Because of these and other factors, the latent period is considerably longer than after first degree injury. The onset of functional restoration commences in the region of the injury and proceeds in serial order from proximal to distal, the proximally-innervated muscles and cutaneous areas recovering before those supplied at more distal levels. Hoffmann-Tinel's sign is a reliable guide to recovery.

Third Degree Injury

By third degree is meant an injury of such severity as to disorganize the internal structure of the funiculi, the essential change being a loss in continuity of the endoneurial tubules. There is also axonal destruction and consequent wallerian degeneration. Epineurium and perineurium are often intact. Some injuries of this degree may be complicated by intrafunicular hemorrhage, edema and ischemia. Both the endoneurial injury and the complications favor the development of intrafunicular fibrosis, which serves as a serious obstacle to the regenerating nerve fibers. The endoneurial fibrosis may lead to fusiform swelling (neuroma-in-continuity) of the involved funiculus, which may or may not be visible externally. Third degree nerve injury is illustrated in Figure 130, and a cross section of a nerve showing normal funicular arrangement in Figure 131.

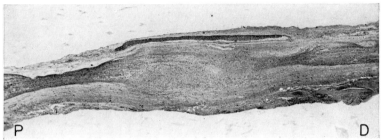

FIGURE 130.   *Third Degree Nerve Injury.* Rifle bullet wound of right forearm, with comminuted fracture of radius and paralysis of the median nerve. The small fascicle in the upper part of the nerve passes through the region of injury without interruption. The larger fascicle expands to form a fairly symmetrical neuroma. (WR-184; from Lyons and Woodhall, 1949.)

The onset of regeneration (and recovery) is delayed longer than in second degree injury largely because the regenerating axons meet greater endoneurial obstruction and many that are capable of growing through it are deflected from their course and enter foreign tubules, the ultimate result being faulty re-innervation. Retrograde degeneration is another important factor.

The degree of re-innervation achieved depends on the nature of the funiculus or funiculi damaged. In the discussion of the funicular pattern of peripheral nerves on page 45, it was pointed out that an incoming nerve branch ascends the nerve trunk for a distance as a discrete funiculus and that at a certain point the funiculus anastomoses with other funiculi, until at proximal levels any one funiculus contains fibers from many sources, though in various combinations and proportions. The more proximal the level the more heterogeneous are the fibers in any given funiculus, excepting those funiculi formed at proximal levels by the entrance of nerve branches into the nerve trunk. Funiculi of both types are present at all levels.

Damage inflicted on a funiculus which contains fibers from one source is much less serious functionally than injury of a funiculus containing fibers from many sources inasmuch as the resulting paralysis is sharply localized and the sensory deficit discrete. Since all routes in such a funiculus lead to the same or a related tissue, those regenerating axis cylinders which are diverted into foreign tubules can vitiate the pattern of re-innervation in only a restricted region.

On the other hand, injury inflicted on a funiculus which is composed of fibers from several different and functionally unrelated sources has

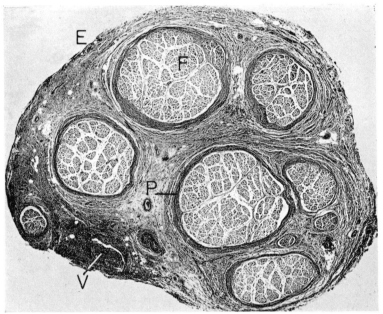

FIGURE 131.   *The Proximal Segment of a Completely Divided Nerve with Preservation of the Nerve Pattern.* Perforating shell fragment wound of right arm with paralysis of radial nerve on April 18, 1945. End-to-end suture was performed on Sept. 22, 1945. The photograph shows fibrotic epineurium (*E*) and six large edematous fascicles (*F*) and several smaller ones surrounded by thickened perineurium (*P*). The interfascicular tissue is also fibrotic and thickened. The fascicles are composed of clusters of regenerating axons in the previously vacuolated tubules. A thrombosed vein is visible in the epineurium (*V*). (VA-128A.)

serious consequence because a considerable number of the regenerating axons grow through foreign tubules to reach endings of a different category than previously. The new fiber pattern may have suffered so much distortion in comparison with the old that functional recovery is minimal.

Because of the factor of increasing intermixture of fibers at successively more proximal levels, a funicular lesion at a proximal level will have a more serious effect on distally-innervated than on proximally-innervated structures. Involvement of a single proximal funiculus is characterized by widely distributed paresis and/or sensory impairment, whereas involvement of all funiculi is manifested by complete loss of motor, sensory and sympathetic functions distal to the level implicated.

Third degree injuries followed by poor functional restoration are difficult to cope with when examination of the nerve trunk at operation fails to reveal swelling or epineurial damage, as is sometimes the case.

Under such circumstances the intrinsic blood vessels of the nerve may have been affected more severely than usual. Intimal proliferation of peri-neurial and endoneurial vessels of the distal stump of an injured nerve is the rule and not infrequently, especially in traction injuries, there is vascular thrombosis followed by recanalization (Highet and Holmes, 1943; Lyons and Woodhall, their Plate V, 1949; Woodhall and Davis, 1950). Anatomical aspects of peripheral nerve vascularization as they are concerned in periph-eral nerve injuries have been discussed in detail by Sunderland (1945).

As to the course of recovery, there is usually the same serial order of re-innervation as in second degree injury, though some irregularity in its sequence occurs as the result of retardation of the growth of re-generating axons through the fibrotic obstruction. Moreover, recovery of function is slower than in second degree injury, and paresis and/or sensory deficit usually persist. Hoffmann-Tinel's sign is regarded as an unreliable guide to the quality of recovery.

Fourth Degree Injury

This degree of injury is characterized by disruption of all the funic-uli of a nerve trunk, or of most of them; consequently there is more or less complete loss of motor, sensory and sympathetic functions in the field served by the nerve. The disorganization of the funiculi is such that their demarcation from perineurium and epineurium may no longer be visible. Continuity of the nerve trunk is retained, but the injured segment is converted into a slender cord of tissue composed of a tangled mass of connective tissue, proliferating Schwann cells, and regenerating axons. A neuroma may form. The severance of the axons results in con-spicuous wallerian degeneration. Fourth degree injury is illustrated in Figure 132.

Regeneration is more defective than in third degree injury. This is due to the more pronounced retrograde effects, the greater tendency of regenerating axons to advance down foreign tubules, and the greater disorganization of the nerve trunk whereby the regenerating axons tend to grow into interfunicular connective tissue from which they are in-capable of extricating themselves.

In partial involvement of the funiculi, the nature of the peripheral disturbance depends, as in third degree injury, on the fiber constitu-tion of the funiculi damaged. When all funiculi are affected, the spontaneous return of function is too slight to serve a useful purpose. In this type of injury the damaged segment should be excised, and repair instituted.

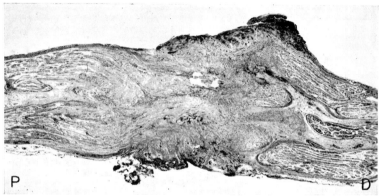

FIGURE 132.   *Fourth Degree Nerve Injury.* S/Sgt. sustained a perforating shell fragment wound of left arm, upper third, on April 26, 1945, with immediate median nerve paralysis. No spontaneous improvement occurred. Resection of neuroma-in-continuity and end-to-end suture were performed on July 21, 1945. The specimen shows the proximal nerve segment (*P*) with small proximal neuroma fused to the distal nerve sgment (*D*) by mass of scar tissue involving all components of the nerve structure and thus completely interrupting the nerve. (VA-67C.)

Fifth Degree Injury

By fifth degree injury is meant severance of the nerve trunk with consequent total loss of motor, sensory and sympathetic functions in the nerve's autonomous field of supply. The nerve ends may be separated or they may be joined by a slender strand of connective tissue which after sufficient lapse of time becomes transformed into a fibroblastic and endoneurial cell framework into which degenerating axons have grown. In due time a neuroma usually develops on the proximal stump ("proximal neuroma") but may form on the distal stump as well ("distal glioma"). Wallerian degeneration in the distal part of the nerve is the inevitable result of such injuries. Fifth degree injury is illustrated in Figure 133.

Recovery of function in untreated fifth degree injuries is negligible, and for several reasons. Retrograde neuronal effects are severe, and owing to the high incidence of axonal degeneration the number of surviving axons is significantly reduced. Moreover, most of the regenerating axons fail to reach the distal stump even when the two ends are relatively close together, and those which do attain this stump encounter difficulty in getting much further: this is due mainly to the shrinkage of the cross-sectional area of the distal stump (Sunderland and Bradley,

1950) and the dissimilarity in the funicular pattern of the two ragged nerve ends (Sunderland, 1945). Also there is a marked tendency for the axons to enter foreign tubules in the distal stump.

The suturing of the nerve ends at the optimal time provides the regenerating axons with a route by which they may reach the periphery, but frequently the recovery of function is submaximal or highly de-

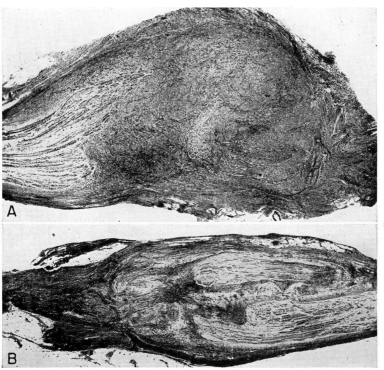

FIGURE 133.   *Fifth Degree Nerve Injury.* Mortar shell fragment wound of ulnar nerve with complete disruption of nerve segment. End-to-end suture was performed eight months after injury. In *A*, the proximal nerve segment is characterized by fascicles fanning out to form a typical swollen, neuromatous bulb, surrounded by fragments of scar tissue (proximal neuroma). *B* Illustrates the distal glioma of the same specimen. The distal fascicles are embedded in firm scar tissue and the tip of the glioma is covered by adhesions. (HGH-195; from Lyons and Woodhall, 1949.)

fective because of the degeneration of axons in the region of the injury, which reduces their number, and because of distortion of the fiber pattern brought about by the downward passage of the regenerating axons in the wrong tubules. The downward growth of sensory axons in the distal stump can be detected by the Hoffmann-Tinel test, but the test gives no indication of the nature of the injury or of the quality of the end result.

Partial and Mixed Injuries

Within any given funiculus-in-continuity the component axons may suffer variously, from first degree to complete disorganization (Fig. 134). Such partial or mixed injuries result in the complete loss of motor, sensory and sympathetic function in the autonomous field of supply of the nerve affected. The injury of the nerve trunk being uneven, the de-

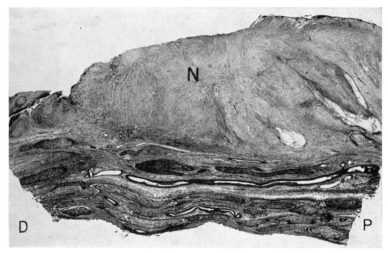

FIGURE 134.   *Partial Fourth Degree Nerve Injury.* The patient incurred a shell fragment wound of the left posterior thigh on April 21, 1945, with partial sciatic nerve division. Resection of the neuroma-in-continuity and end-to-end anastomosis were done on July 30, 1945. The specimen is that of a neuroma-in-continuity in which about four fifths of the nerve segment has been transformed into a lateral neuroma (N), with one fifth of the fibers remaining intact. The epineurium adjacent to the normal fibers is not disrupted. (VA-12C.)

gree of recovery in the fields of the various branches of the nerve will depend on the relative extent of each type of injury and the nature of the injury sustained by the individual fibers. Partial and mixed injuries are thus explicable in terms of the five degrees of injury outlined.

It is apparent from the foregoing that a knowledge of the neuropathology of peripheral nerve injuries is essential to the diagnosis of injury. A fuller knowledge of this subject may be obtained from the companion piece of this text, namely the volume by Lyons and Woodhall, entitled *Atlas of Peripheral Nerve Injuries* (W. B. Saunders Co., 1949).

CHAPTER 8

Causes and Manifestations of Peripheral Nerve Injuries

Indirect Nerve Wounds from Low and High Velocity Projectiles, and Distinction Between Complete and Incomplete Interruption of Nerves

Concussion

As a high velocity projectile passes through a limb or any other part of the body, the tremendous energy released exerts a destructive effect on tissues for a considerable distance along the projectile's path. This is due to oscillating positive and negative pressures engendered by the release of energy and to the violent radial thrust of the tissue particles lying in the projectile's path, a thrust of sufficient force to cause momentary cavity formation in the wake of the projectile and a compression and stretching of the tissues. Destructive effects of high velocity missiles vary as the first power of the mass and as the cube of the velocity. Thus, a fourfold increase in mass would raise the projectile's destructive effects in tissue 4 times, and a fourfold increase in velocity, 64 times. Numerous other factors contribute to the tissue damage, such as the degree of density of the tissue, the "tumble" of a bullet, the angle of incidence, and the lacerating effect of shell fragments (Black, Burns and Zuckerman, 1941; Callender, 1943; Puckett et al., 1946).

As a consequence of the passage of low or high velocity projectiles through tissues, the nerve trunks within range of the energy wave suffer to varying degrees depending upon the amount of released energy to which they are exposed. Should the degree of damage incurred by the nerve be relatively mild (first degree injury of Sunderland's classification; p. 123) then *concussion* can be said to have occurred. Paralysis and numbness of the part develop immediately and usually involve all parts distal to the site of the wound. The paralysis and numbness begin to regress in a few hours and usually disappear within two or three days. Sensibility is much less affected, although, as a rule, there is a loss of proprioceptive sensibility. The corresponding deep reflexes are absent. Electrical irritability is usually normal. An example of early return of function after concussion is shown in Figure 135. The functional loss is considered to be due to mechanical deformation (brusque local stretching due to pressure exerted on one side of the nerve) of axis

133

cylinders and to myelin damage of the order described by Spielmeyer and by Denny-Brown and Brenner (pp. 123, 124).

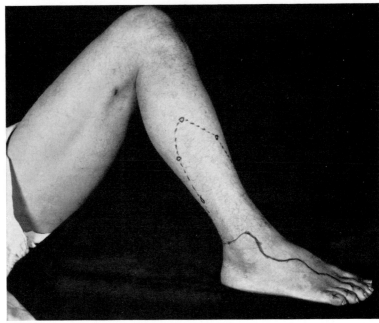

FIGURE 135.   *The Sensory Changes in First Degree Nerve Injury.* Accidental .45 cal. automatic pistol wound of lower third of right thigh, studied three and one half months after injury. The wound of exit is visible. Rapid resolution of motor and sensory paralysis occurred, leaving residual weakness of the posterior tibial, flexor hallucis longus and brevis and flexor digitorum longus muscles. Burning pain developed one week after injury. Residual hypalgesia, hypesthesia and diminished response to heat and cold are indicated by the continuous line. There was loss of sense of position in fifth, fourth and third toes. Over-response (dysesthesia or hyperalgesia) to pain is outlined by the dotted line. (Case D-52706; DUH.)

The Problem of Delayed Recovery of Function in Nerves-in-Continuity and in Partially and Completely Severed Nerves

In the majority of cases the destructive effects of the passage of high velocity projectiles in the vicinity of a nerve are such that functional return is delayed for weeks or months. During the first few weeks the side effects of wounding usually resolve so that the degree of nerve injury can be determined. *Complete severance of a nerve* is characterized by total paralysis and loss of tone of all the muscles it supplies, a sharply defined cutaneous area of loss of all qualities of sensibility in the nerve field in question, and a loss of deep sensibility (appreciation of pressure) in the region of the affected muscles. Toward the end of the first week the chronaxia begins to rise and the paralyzed muscles begin to fibrillate. At about the end of the second week the complete reaction of degeneration (R.D.) of the affected muscles sets in, and at the end of a month muscle atrophy becomes noticeable. Hoffmann-Tinel's sign continues to be absent. No improvement in motor function occurs, and the same is true in regard to sensibility except for shrinkage of the autonomous zone. Time is also required for resolution before an *incomplete severance of a nerve* can be established. Relatively early manifestations of such lesions are paresis instead of paralysis, partial sensory loss in the cutaneous area of supply, a difference in degree of motor and sensory deficit, and a retention of deep sensibility (appreciation of pressure). Dissociated paralysis also tends to occur, i.e., loss of motor power in only some muscles supplied by the nerve in question. Loss of cutaneous sensibility in part of the field of a nerve is another characteristic of a partially interrupted nerve. Irritative symptoms such as pain tend to occur early. After a three to four week period the R.D. may be partial though nerve irritability is retained, and about this time Hoffmann-Tinel's sign becomes positive and hyperpathia may be noted. As time passes, gradual improvement of motor function and sensibility occurs. The various clinical aspects of completely and incompletely severed nerves are discussed in subsequent pages of this chapter.

When total functional loss persists for two or three months or longer it is difficult if not impossible to determine whether the nerve in question is anatomically intact but damaged by an energy wave, whether the nerve has been completely severed, or whether it has been partially severed and the remainder of the segment damaged through the release of energy. End-organs are denervated under all three conditions, and therefore the sensory and motor deficits in these three conditions do not differ. In exploring a nerve which, after three months' observation, one has every reason to believe is completely severed, one commonly finds that it is grossly normal, though encased by scarred connective tissue. Such was reported by Spielmeyer (1915) in 14 of 90 cases subjected to exploratory operation three months or longer after injury, during which time paralysis had remained complete and R.D. total. Grossly normal nerves in the presence of persistent paralysis have been observed in 10 of 148 cases by Wexberg (1935). In 234 such cases described by Strotzka (1942), the nerves most frequently concerned were the median, ulnar, radial, and sciatic, in that order. In Livingston, Davis and Livingston's (1945) operative experience with 53 cases of high velocity projectile injuries involving one or more of the three major nerves to the hand, mainly at proximal levels, there were 26 in which the nerve in question was found intact and grossly non-neuromatous.

Where, during operation, a nerve is found grossly intact its response to faradic stimulation will give an indication as to whether or not motor fibers have degenerated. A negative response does not, however, necessarily mean that functional recovery will not occur.

Such a case was reported by Livingston, Davis and Livingston (1945). The patient had had an ulnar palsy following a missile wound in the upper third of his forearm. Exploration five months after injury failed to disclose the level of maximal injury, and there was no response of the flexor carpi ulnaris or any of the hand muscles to faradic stimulation. Ulnar palsy was still complete eleven months after injury when the nerve was again explored. Stimulation at this time induced a contraction of the flexor carpi ulnaris muscle. Four months later the nerve was well on the road to a satisfactory recovery of function.

Information concerning the integrity of a nerve may also be obtained by means of the sweating test. Anhidrosis is a sign of loss of nerve function, though it provides no information as to the type or degree of a nerve lesion. Sweating occurring in the presence of total paralysis and anesthesia, as has been occasionally observed, may be taken as dependable evidence of complete or partial integrity of a nerve and a sign of impending restoration in motor and sensory functions.

In short, clinical evaluation of the nature and degree of a nerve injury in cases of delayed recovery of function is difficult, and often the answer can be obtained only on exploration of the wound. The decision as to whether to operate and when hinges on the exact point of the injury, its distance from the first innervated muscle, time after injury, and the results of various electrodiagnostic studies, such as percutaneous stimulation and electromyography. The surgical aspects of peripheral nerve injuries, all exceedingly complex, are not dealt with in this volume.

Muscle Atrophy and Motor Irritative Phenomena

Immediately after severance of a nerve the muscles it supplies lose all power of voluntary contraction and become atonic, or flaccid. During the first week after interruption, the nerve undergoes degeneration, but little if any histological alteration occurs in the muscle. Between the second and third week the paralyzed muscles rather abruptly undergo fibrillation and fasciculation, irritative phenomena which persist until advanced atrophy has occurred. At about the same time, the affected muscles begin to undergo a reduction in size. Sunderland and Ray (1950) found in opossums that after nerve section there was a rapid initial loss in muscle weight, i.e., 30 per cent in twenty-nine days. After sixty days, when the weight loss amounted to 50 to 60 per cent, the process slowed down and at about 120 days became stabilized. Even after 485 days the general form of each muscle was fully retained. Atrophy of individual muscle fibers also occurred rapidly in early stages so that at about sixty days the average fiber cross-sectional area was reduced by 70 per cent. In the next sixty days the atrophy had advanced only another 10 per cent. From that time onward the muscles had undergone 80 to 90 per cent atrophy. There was no significant decrease in the number of muscle fibers. Despite denervation, the muscle fibers continued to be striated for well over a year, although the striations were sometimes less prominent than normally. Motor end-plates and neuromuscular spindles also retained their characteristic morphological appearance. The connective tissue content of the muscle increased relatively and absolutely in the form of a thickening of the perimysium and endomysium.

Much the same changes have been observed by Bowden and Gutmann (1944) in human denervated muscle. Their material consisted of 140 biopsies from 86 cases in which muscles had been denervated from forty-two days to thirty years. Up to three months after denervation the pattern of innervation persisted and the individual Schwann tubules could be followed to their end-plates. Thereafter the essential changes consisted of progressive but unequal shrinkage of the muscle fibers, progressive depletion of the sarcoplasm of the end-plates, and progressive distortion of the pattern of innervation and vascularization. It seemed that vascular permeability (as reflected in perivascular infiltrates of lymphocytes) initiated progressive thickening of vessel walls and that the increasing connective tissue formation emanating from such vessels was the factor responsible for reducing and distorting the anastomotic network of capillaries in the involved muscles. Cross-striations persisted for many months, although they showed reduction of stainability rather soon after denervation. Only from three years onward were disruptive changes in muscle observed. Up to that time, despite considerable shrinkage, few, if any, muscle fibers had undergone complete disintegration.

Tonic contracture and convulsive movements occurring immediately after nerve injury and lasting for a few seconds or minutes are other examples of motor irritation. Flexor muscles are most concerned.

One marine found that he could not get up from his prone posture until he had loosened, with his normal hand, the tight grasp of the fingers of his wounded arm on the grass and weeds in which he lay; another man found that the fingers of his wounded extremity were so tightly clasped on the hand grip of his machine gun that he continued to fire the gun involuntarily until the jarring of the recoil bounced his hand off the gun; and a corpsman was certain that his hand had been shot off until he caught sight of it, behind his forearm, sharply flexed at the wrist, jerking in a prolonged series of convulsive movements. (Livingston, Davis and Livingston, 1945.)

Persistent clonic and athetoid movements after nerve injuries have also been reported (Krambach, 1920a, Götze, 1942, Becker, 1940).

Where motor irritative phenomena persist after muscle function and sensibility have been regained, a shell fragment or other foreign body should be sought.

Alterations of Cutaneous Sensibility

The Factor of Overlap

As a nerve approaches the skin it divides into a number of bundles, and upon entering the skin the bundles form a nerve plexus. Fibers

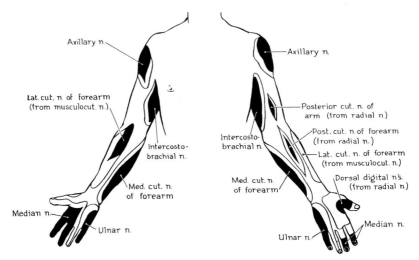

FIGURE 136.   *Sensory Deficit Following Interruption of Individual Nerve Trunks of the Upper Limb.* The black areas represent the autonomous zones and the surrounding lines indicate the approximate border of tactile anesthesia and thermoanesthesia. The cutaneous area between the autonomous zone and the encircling border of retained pain sensibility is referred to as the "intermediate zone." The autonomous zones depicted here by Foerster (1929) represent the smallest he encountered in the hundreds of cases studied by him from this standpoint.

given off by the plexus undergo repeated dichotomous branching, with each fiber terminating in multiple endings. Interlocked between these are the endings of adjacent branches. Any one end-organ receives two or more fibers, which reach it from different directions.

All cutaneous nerves overstep their gross anatomical boundaries (i.e., those established by gross dissection) to assist in the innervation of adjacent fields (Trotter, 1926; see also Walshe, 1942). Because of the *overlap* and because of the anastomotic branches which each nerve receives from others, the region of sensory loss following section of a nerve is smaller than the cutaneous area supplied by that nerve. The area of complete sensory loss signifies the part of the anatomical field supplied exclusively by the nerve which has been interrupted. This is called the *autonomous zone* (the dark areas in Figs. 136 and 137). The size of the autonomous zone is subject to variation not only in accordance with the nerve implicated, but also from individual to individual. This is explicable on the basis of differing degrees of overlap and of anastomosis between nerves. Among the autonomous zones subject to wide variation is that of the radial nerve: in some cases of radial nerve palsy no autonomous zone is detected, while in others it is represented only on the radial half of the dorsum of the hand and thumb (Figs. 230, 231, 235).

Where a nerve is left intact and all those adjoining it are sectioned, the sensory area of the intact nerve is larger than its gross anatomical field: this area is referred to as the *maximal zone* (Fig. 138). The difference in size between the autonomous and maximal zones is due, as stated, to nerve overlap and to the contributions received from neighboring nerves through anastomoses. A study of Figure 138, which depicts the maximal zone of the ulnar nerve, will reveal that fibers conveying pain sensibility extend over into the fields supplied by the median and radial nerves, and that those conveying tactile and thermal sensibility are much less widespread. Pain fibers of the maximal fields of the median and radial nerves extend also on to the anatomical field of the ulnar nerve, and the tactile and thermal fibers to a much less extent, and thus after total interruption of the ulnar nerve it is understandable that the zone of total anesthesia, including analgesia (the autonomous zone) should be smaller than the areas of tactile anesthesia and thermoanesthesia. In between the border of the autonomous zone and that of tactile and thermal deficit, the appreciation of pain is intact: this is called the *intermediate zone* (in legend of Fig. 136).

Decrease in Size of the Autonomous Zone

Within a few days after complete interruption of a nerve, at a time when recovery of nerve function through regeneration is impossible, the autonomous zone begins to shrink, and as it does so the intermediate zone enlarges correspondingly (Pollock, 1919, 1921, 1929). The increment in the intermediate zone is apparently due to a resumption of function of adjacent normal nerve fibers already present in this zone, especially those conveying tactile sensibility (Guttmann, 1940; Highet, 1942). The reduction in the size of the autonomous zone advances less rapidly after missile wounds than after simple section, the reason being, according to Foerster (1937), that concussion of adjacent nerve trunks delays functional recovery of the respective nerve terminals. That the enlargement of the intermediate zone might be due to actual ingrowth of fibers from adjacent normal nerves is suggested by experiment (Speidel, 1935; Weddell, Guttmann and Gutman, 1941).

It is highly important to recognize that the autonomous zone of total anesthesia may continue to shrink during the first few weeks through processes other than regeneration of the damaged nerve trunk. Whether the recovery of function is due to return of sensation to the area of

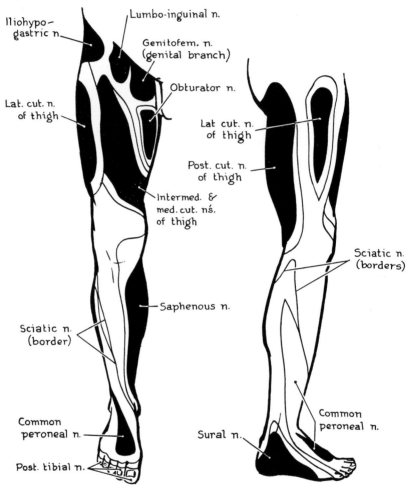

FIGURE 137.   *Sensory Deficit Following Interruption of Individual Nerve Trunks of the Lower Limb.* The pattern has the same significance as in Figure 136. (From Foerster, 1929.)

overlap or to regeneration of the damaged nerve trunk may be determined by *procaine block* of the affected nerve or of the neighboring nerves. According to Highet (1942), blockage of neighboring nerves is preferable because one can then be certain that the block is complete. After these nerves have been blocked, the sensory examination and the sweating test are again performed. If, for instance, the median nerve is completely severed, there will be no sweating or sensation in the median area after block of the ulnar and radial nerves. Nerve block may be regarded as complete when there is full vasodilatation, anhidrosis, anes-

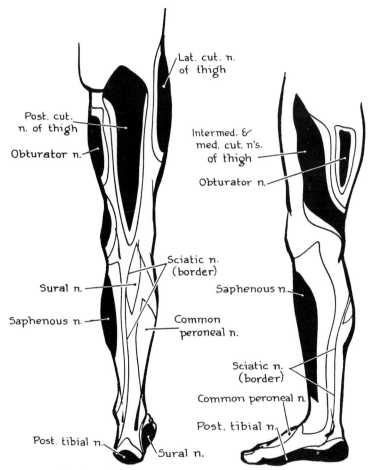

FIGURE 137.   Continued.

thesia and analgesia in the autonomous zone of the nerve, and when paralysis of the muscles concerned is complete and prolonged.

Alterations of Deep Sensibility

Immediately after severance of a nerve trunk the denervated muscles are found to be insensitive to deep pressure, an alteration which persists until the muscles are re-innervated. The problem of disturbed joint sensibility, i.e., loss of appreciation of position or passive movements, revolves on the innervation of joint tissues (Figs. 34 and 35). Nerve branches reach these tissues via the insertional areas of adjacent tendons.

In injuries of nerve trunks there is seldom any clinically significant disturbance of deep sensibility as long as the other nerves which supply the joints are intact. Severance of the *median nerve* abolishes joint sensibility only in the region of the middle phalanges of the index and middle fingers because the joints of the thumb and ring fingers are innervated also by the radial. By the same token, in *ulnar nerve* palsy

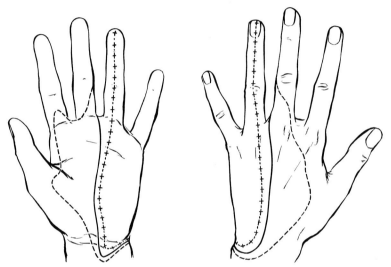

FIGURE 138.   *The Maximal, or Total, Area of Supply by the Ulnar Nerve.* In this instance a missile completely divided the median, radial and musculocutaneous nerves and the medial cutaneous nerve of the forearm. The *broken line* indicates the boundary of pain perception, the *solid line* that of touch perception, and the *cross and dot line* that of temperature perception. (From Foerster, 1929.)

joint sensibility is lost only in the little finger. In interruption of the *radial nerve* no alterations of joint sensibility occur, the reason being that the joints concerned are also supplied by the median nerve. When the *sciatic* is severed, sensibility of foot and toe joints is entirely lost. Interruption of either the *common peroneal* or the *tibial nerve* fails to interfere with sensibility of foot or toe joints, although Lehmann (1916) has asserted that in tibial nerve lesions such sensibility is lost.

Median or ulnar nerve injury in the more distal part of the hand does not interfere with joint sensibility since under such conditions the branches of the respective nerves reaching the joint tissues via the long flexors remain intact.

In *total plexus injuries* the alterations in deep and superficial sensibility run parallel. However, in *partial plexus injuries* joint sensibility usually suffers to a greater degree, a dissociation which becomes more pronounced as functional restoration sets in (Foerster, 1918). The high susceptibility of the proprioceptor fibers to injury is generally ascribed to their relatively large size.

Hyperesthesia of deep tissues is evident in some cases of peripheral nerve injury, even when the overlying skin is totally anesthetic. Thus, in median nerve palsy marked tenderness may be induced by compressing the palm of the hand, or in sciatic nerve palsy by exerting pressure on the calf or foot.

Nerve trunk and plexus injuries are also characterized by loss of appreciation of vibration. The area of pallanesthesia usually corresponds rather closely to the area of sensory loss, as has been reported by numerous older observers (Redlich, 1916; Krambach, 1920b). The best results are obtained with a tuning fork of 64 frequencies.

Spread of Sensory and Motor Deficit after Nerve Injury

A recent review of the spread of sensory and motor deficit after nerve injury, by Kelly (1952), sums up what is known of the subject. Briefly, damage inflicted on a nerve is in some instances followed by a spread of sensory and/or motor deficit beyond the field of the injured nerve. For instance, sensory loss due to brachial plexus injury may spread to the field of the cervical plexus, or ulnar palsy due to a missile wound of the palm of the hand may be complicated by paralysis of the medial part of the flexor digitorum profundus. The most common site of sensory spread seems to be from the field of the ulnar nerve to that of the medial cutaneous nerve of the forearm. Extensive spread in either motor or sensory realm is frequently misdiagnosed as hysterical.

The spread to the field of a primarily uninjured nerve occurs a few days after the injury. Recovery usually ensues within one month, but may take longer. The sensory change in the affected field may consist of numbness and tingling or hyperalgesia or sensory deficit; seldom is sensibility completely abolished.

In offering an explanation of the pathogenesis of the phenomenon of spread, Kelly cited evidence (1) that chromatolysis occurs both in sensory ganglia and in anterior horns after nerve injury and that especially in sensory ganglia a fairly large number of nerve cell bodies disappear (see also Sunderland, 1952b, on this point), and (2) that non-myelinated axis cylinders of sensory fibers (as many as 61 per cent) undergo branching as they course through spinal roots, nerve trunks and peripheral nerves—much more branching, in fact, than do myelinated sensory axons or motor fibers. On the basis of these observations, he concluded that chromatolysis of the parent cell bodies of the branching axons is responsible for the spread. The predominance of sensory spread over motor was ascribed to the greater degree of branching in sensory fibers.

One wonders whether unrecognized real injury may not have coexisted in these cases, for neither of us has observed the phenomenon of spread of sensory and motor deficit.

Alterations of Reflex Activity

The status of the reflexes, both deep and superficial, is not as important in the diagnosis of peripheral nerve injuries as motor function and sensory deficit, the reason being that reflex arcs are not dependent on the integrity of a single nerve. When occurring, the reflex deficit is apparent at the time of the injury and it usually persists for some time after other functions have been restored.

In injuries of the radial nerve the triceps reflex is lost; those of the musculocutaneous, the biceps reflex; those of the femoral nerve, the patellar reflex; and in those of the sciatic or tibial nerve, the tendo Achilles reflex—and so with others. Sometimes instead of being lost they are paradoxical; for instance, in radial nerve palsy a contraction of the biceps and brachialis muscles occurs when the triceps tendon is tapped, or in median or ulnar nerve palsy there may be a contraction of the biceps and brachialis muscles (instead of the finger flexors) when the flexor tendons of the lower forearm are tapped.

Since reflexes may no longer be elicitable after partial interruption of certain nerves they cannot be taken as an index of the severity of a lesion. Furthermore, some components of a muscle group may be unresponsive when interruption is partial. Thus, the triceps reflex may be elicited if the long head of the triceps muscle is spared and the tendo Achilles reflex may be active when the only muscle capable of contracting is the soleus. Moreover, the brachioradial reflex may be preserved when part of its efferent arc is broken; for instance, although the biceps and brachialis muscles are paralyzed by musculocutaneous nerve injury, the brachioradialis muscle may still contract.

Cutaneous reflex activity parallels the degree of sensory loss. Muscles are unresponsive when an anesthetic field is stimulated. Cutaneous reflexes usually recover before tendon reflexes. For instance, in sciatic or tibial nerve injuries the plantar reflex frequently becomes elicitable at a time when the loss of the tendo Achilles reflex persists. In the presence of hyperesthesia the cutaneous reflexes may be exaggerated.

In tibial nerve injuries the plantar reflex may be extensor (i.e., the great toe and often the other toes undergo dorsiflexion—the so-called "peripheral Babinski reflex") when proprioceptive and cutaneous sensibility has been restored in the absence of significant return of motor function of the muscles of the sole of the foot or of the flexor muscles of the toes. Moreover, a para-doxical tendo Achilles reflex may occasionally be noted. This consists of contraction of the tibialis anterior and extensor digitorum muscles on percussion of the Achilles tendon (Foerster, 1918).

Disturbances in Vasomotor Activity, Sweating, and Pilomotor Reaction

Interruption of autonomic fibers in a peripheral nerve gives rise, in the cutaneous area supplied, to the triad consisting of loss of vasomotor control, lack of spontaneous sweating, and abolition of the pilomotor, or "gooseflesh," response. The autonomous area which any one nerve supplies with autonomic fibers is relatively small because of the con-siderable overlapping of autonomic fibers from adjacent areas. More-over, there is great variation in autonomic overlap from individual to individual. As a consequence autonomic fields are somewhat less constant than sensory fields.

Vasomotor Disturbances

In complete division of a peripheral nerve the denervated region of the skin has a pink or rosy appearance because of vasodilatation brought about by interruption of sympathetic fibers to the part. As a rule the vasodilatation and accompanying elevation of skin temperature last about two weeks, after which the skin of the anesthetic area usually be-comes cold and exhibits vasoconstriction.

Prolonged vasomotor disturbances are most apt to occur in partial nerve injuries, especially when causalgia exists. The most common manifestation consists of mottling of the skin, i.e., combined pallor and cyanosis. The skin under such conditions has a lowered temperature.

Edema, ascribed to decrease in the flow of lymph coincident to im-mobilization of the part and to vasomotor disturbances, usually over-reaches the field of disturbed sensibility. Procaine-induced vasodilata-tion as a diagnostic sign is discussed on pages 141 and 189.

Alterations of Sweating

When a peripheral nerve is completely interrupted, sweating no longer occurs in its field of distribution. Anhidrosis constitutes an ex-cellent objective sign of the extent of an injury because it is not influ-enced by the mood of the patient or by the vagaries of interpretation on the part of the examiner. In numerous clinics a sweating test is performed routinely; on the area of anhidrosis is superimposed the boundaries of the area of sensory loss (indicated by lines, dots and other identifying marks, depending on the number of modalities test-ed), after which a photograph of the part is made as a permanent record.

The close correspondence of areas of anhidrosis and the cutaneous distribution of nerves will be noted in Figure 139. Ordinarily the area of anhidrosis is slightly larger than that of sensory deficit.

Increased tendency to sweat is frequently noted in partial nerve palsies, especially when irritative phenomena such as early tonic contracture exist or after regeneration has commenced. The sweating may occur either spontaneously or under the duress of emotion, and not infrequently extends beyond the anatomical confines of the nerve con-

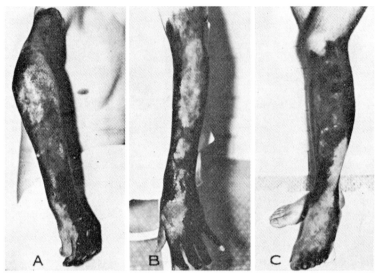

FIGURE 139.   *Three Cases of Peripheral Nerve Palsy Showing Areas of Anhidrosis.* Sodium chinizarin 2–6 disulfonate was employed in the test for sweating. The darkened portions of the limbs indicate the region of sweating, the lighter portions the zones of anhidrosis. In *A* there is anhidrosis in the region of the wound as well as over the cutaneous distribution of the ulnar nerve. In *B* the area of anhidrosis is in the field of the radial nerve. In *C* the field of the superficial peroneal nerve is affected. (W.R.) (Courtesy of Rose and Everts.)

cerned. Following nerve resection, Klar (1943) observed normal or slightly increased sweating when all other signs pointed to complete division of a nerve (total anesthesia, complete R.D.) and in such cases spontaneous recovery in function subsequently occurred. From such observations the importance of the sweating test in detecting early nerve regeneration is evident.

Trophic Disorders

Trophic disorders occur fairly frequently in palsies involving the hands and feet, especially when irritative phenomena such as pain exist or when the part is subjected to continued trauma or to the application of excessive heat or cold, of which the patient is unaware because of the sensory loss. At first the delicate indentations of the skin become more shallow, and before long the skin grows inelastic and smooth. In time the skin tends to become transparent and shiny, i.e., atrophic (Fig. 140). Cutaneous pigmentation and a keratotic eczema-like change may develop, with their border sometimes corresponding so closely to that of the sensory loss that diagnosis as to the nerve injured may be made at a glance (Fig. 141). These changes are of localizing value only

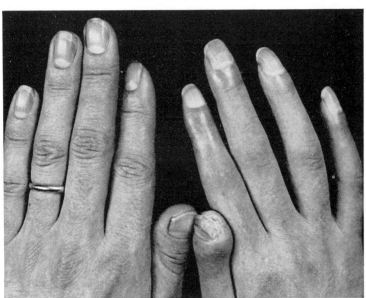

FIGURE 140.   *Trophic Changes in a Case of Combined Radial, Median and Ulnar Nerve Palsy.* The fingers taper and have a "glossy" appearance. The nails are ridged, their beds pale. On the thumb, which is decidedly clubbed, a healed ulcer is visible. (W.R.)

in the chronic stages of an injury, for in early stages they may be widespread, overstepping the cutaneous boundary of the interrupted nerve.

In the region of sensory loss the skin lacks its normal resistance to noxious influences. When subjected to pressure, trauma, or to excessive cold or heat, which ordinarily would do little harm, the skin breaks down and may ulcerate. Healing is retarded unless regeneration of the affected nerve occurs. Such trophic ulcers seldom heal spontaneously. Sites of predilection are the fingers (in median and ulnar nerve palsies) and the toes, the sole and the heel (in tibial and sciatic nerve injuries).

Fibrosis of the subcutaneous tissue may also occur but is uncommon unless interruption is partial. Skin thus affected tends to be fissured and thrown into heavy folds. Local shriveling of subcutaneous tissue is a feature in a few cases of peripheral nerve injury, particularly median and ulnar. Fingers are most subject to these changes: they may, in fact, taper to a remarkable degree, and their tips may be severely atrophic and be marked off from the rest of the finger by an indentation (Fig. 142). The condition is also characterized by a loss of the furrow

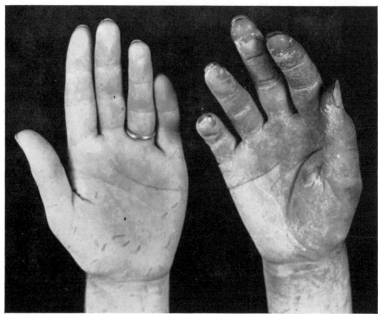

FIGURE 141.   *Pigmented, Hyperkeratotic Cutaneous Lesion Complicating Partial Median Nerve Injury.* The lesion corresponds rather closely to the region of distribution of the median nerve. On April 20, 1945, the soldier received a penetrating bullet wound of the right arm just beneath the level of the axilla. Combined complete ulnar and median nerve paralysis occurred immediately. There was no osseous or major vascular injury. Burning pain set in at once in the palm of the involved hand and became extreme. No functional recovery having occurred by May 8, neurolysis of both nerves was done, as a consequence of which the causalgia lessened about 25 per cent.

The photograph was taken June 28, 1945. By that time it was evident that the patient had had a partial median nerve injury. Causalgia persisted in the field of distribution of both the median and the ulnar nerve, chiefly the former. On July 5, 1945, preganglionic sympathectomy was performed. Neurosurgical evaluation in November disclosed complete relief of the causalgia with only paresthetic residues in the median nerve area. (P.J.H.)

which normally separates finger tip and nail, the furrow having been eliminated through the continued adherence of the soft tissue to the nail as the latter grows (Fig. 142). As a consequence of the distal projection of the soft tissues of the finger, hemorrhage often occurs when the fingernails are clipped. Clubbing of finger tips also has been noted (Fig. 143).

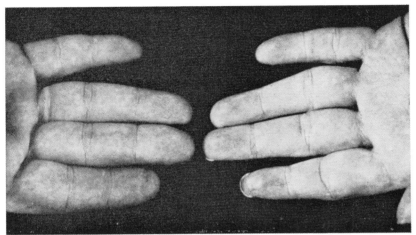

FIGURE 142.   *Trophic Changes of the Fingers in a Case of Partial Ulnar and Median Nerve Palsy, Left (to the reader's right).* Owing to "atrophy" of subcutaneous tissues, the fingers of the left hand, especially the index, show considerable tapering. The skin of the index finger has become glossy. Notice the slight cutaneous indentation running across the index finger just proximal to the finger tip, due to the distal projection of the subungual tissue through its adherence to the growing nail. The patient had sustained a gunshot wound of the upper arm four months previously. (W.R.)

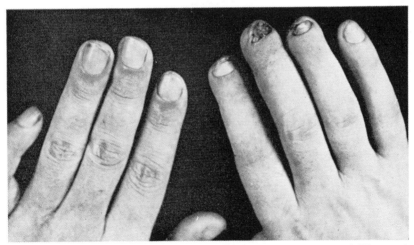

FIGURE 143.   *Trophic Changes in Fingernails in a Case of Combined Ulnar and Median Palsy, Right.* Injury of ulnar and median nerves occurred eight months previously when a missile penetrated the wrist. The nails of three of the fingers are irregular and their growth stunted. Clubbing of finger tips is conspicuous. (W.R.)

Fingernails undergo characteristic changes, especially in the region of most striking sensory deficit. They may acquire transverse broad white stripes and become thickened, ridged, brittle, and curved (like claws) (Figs. 140, 143, 221). The nail changes become progressively worse during the first four or five months after injury and then either

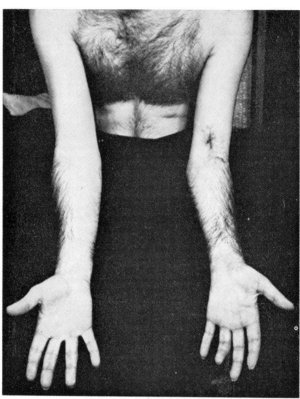

FIGURE 144.   *A Case in Which Severe Pain (Non-causalgic) Began in the Left Hand and Arm Three Days after Median Nerve Injury, with Gradual, Spontaneous Resolution.* In the forearm and hand there are diffuse atrophy and a change in color which is only suggested in this photograph; note also the hypertrichosis of the left forearm. (W.R.)

persist or, with re-innervation, regress, sometimes fully. The changes in the toenails are less conspicuous, probably because of longstanding atrophic changes brought about by the wearing of shoes. In measuring nail growth after denervation, Sunderland and Ray (1952) found retardation of growth in the denervated digits in some cases but not in others. When, however, arterial ligation was superimposed on denervation, nail growth was consistently and markedly retarded. The retardation could not be ascribed solely to the vascular injury because

(1) it outlasted the period of circulatory embarrassment, (2) the non-denervated digits of the involved hand remained unaffected, and (3) complete nerve recovery resulted in an equality of growth in the involved and corresponding normal digits.

Hair in the region of sensory deficit may fall out or may occasionally exhibit increased growth (Fig. 144). Hypertrichosis has most frequently been noted on the forearm in radial nerve and median nerve injuries, and occasionally in injuries of the brachial plexus.

Pain

Causalgia

Burning pain over the region of distribution of a nerve occurring in connection with penetrating missile wounds of large mixed nerves was first referred to by Weir Mitchell (1872) as causalgia (*kausos*, heat; *algos*, pain). Weir Mitchell and his associates (1864, 1872) observed that the burning pain varies in intensity "from the most trivial burning to a state of torture." Putting weight upon this variance, some authors (e.g., Echlin, Owens and Wells, 1949) have divided the disorder into "major causalgia" and "minor causalgia," depending on the severity of the pain, although when Homans (1940) coined the term "minor causalgia" he intended it to include only painful osteoporosis, Sudeck's atrophy, etc., due to trauma, thrombosis and other factors, in which hyperesthesia was the major complaint. Most current authors have avoided use of the term "minor causalgia" and have reserved the term "causalgia" only for those cases in which the burning pain is severe. White, Heroy and Goodman (1948) have applied the term "causalgia" only to those cases of nerve injury characterized by the triad of hyperpathia (burning pain and hyperesthesia), trophic changes, and autonomic phenomena (vasomotor and sudomotor overactivity).

In virtually all published series of cases of peripheral nerve injury the incidence of causalgia was between 2 to 5 per cent, but in Echlin, Owens and Wells' (1949) 310 cases of peripheral nerve injury, the incidence ("major" at some time during the course of disorder) was 19.6 per cent.

In full-blown "major causalgia" the more distant parts of the affected limb are the seat of constant intense and diffuse burning pain. The pain seems to predominate deep in the tissues. Because of a lowered threshold of the entire body for sensory stimuli, the pain in the affected part may be aggravated—often in an explosive manner—by exposure of the body to warmth or cold or by contact, motion, or moving air. Conditions or events which excite emotional reactions aggravate the pain. This superimposed pain spreads beyond the anatomical confines of the injured nerve—possibly through the intermediation of branching fibers in the spinal roots and nerve trunks (Sunderland and Kelly, 1948) —and may persist for a considerable time after it has developed.

Causalgia, whether "major" or "minor," is most common in the hand and foot, in the field of distribution of the median and tibial nerves respectively. Shumacker (1948) listed the following order of incidence among 230 cases collected from the literature (in per cent): sciatic, 34.3; median, 25; brachial plexus, 13; median and ulnar, 8; median, ulnar and radial, 6; other upper limb nerves, 5.7; other lower limb nerves (tibial nerve predominating), 8.

The pain develops at varying intervals within the first week after the injury or sometimes longer, and frequently appears at the moment of the injury—in 36.7 per cent of 98 cases reported by Rasmussen and Freedman (1946) and as high as 58.7 per cent in the 75 cases of Ulmer and Mayfield's (1946) series. The intensity of the pain bears no relation to the degree of injury of the nerve, which, according to objective examination, is usually mild and is seldom attended by fracture, widespread soft tissue injury, or injury of major blood vessels. Causalgia may also occur following total interruption of a nerve, as has been noted by Nathan (1947) in 4 of the 22 cases of causalgia. The actual incidence is doubtless higher when one considers that in battle casualties partial interruption of peripheral nerves is twice as common as complete interruption (Nathan, 1947; see also Shumacker, 1948).

Because of the pain, the patient treats the affected part with the utmost indulgence, not permitting it the least movement. Some patients carry a cool or warm moist compress for immediate use when the pain becomes aggravated; others keep the part wrapped in soft cloth, and still others pour cold water into the shoe so that the shoe can be tolerated in walking. Desquamating skin is too sensitive for them to wash, and the fingernails too painful to cut. The anxious facial expression as well as the tense, protective bodily attitude tell the physician at once the nature of the condition from which the patient is suffering (Fig. 145). Not infrequently such patients become "emotional derelicts."

In the presence of causalgia in the region of distribution of the median nerve, the hand may display either vasodilatation or vasoconstriction or no apparent alteration in blood flow. (A lack of such changes in one third of his patients was reported by Shumacker, 1948.) It seems that vasodilatation predominates in early stages. Where vasodilatation exists, the hand is pinker and warmer than that of the normal hand and it tends to be dry. The pinkness indicates increased rapidity of blood flow, and nail-bed microscopy under such conditions reveals dilatation of capillary loops, precapillaries and postcapillary veins. In the presence of vasoconstriction the part is colder than its mate and it is mottled or cyanotic and is usually moist. According to Philippides (1942b), in such cases there may be reflex sweating in the other hand and even of more distant regions. When the median nerve is sufficiently damaged to cause anhidrosis in the region of its supply, the adjacent skin innervated by the ulnar may be moist. Glossiness of the skin, of fairly common occurrence and tending to develop after prolonged vasodilatation, has been ascribed to accelerated proliferation of deeper epithelium together with rapid desquamation of the superficial layer; Weir Mitchell and his associates (1864) described glossy skin as "shining as though it had been skillfully varnished." The small muscles of the hand often undergo atrophy even though paralysis is mild and there may be thinness and tapering of the fingers. Fingernails are often shiny and may grow faster. They also tend to suffer trophic changes. There may or may not be osteoporosis. Owing to pain induced by movement, the hand or foot is kept immobile, with the result that the joints become exceedingly stiff. According to Mayfield (1951), the hair on the back of the hand and forearm tends to become long and coarse in the presence of vasodilatation and to fall out when there is vasoconstriction. The trophic changes are similar in all respects to those in comparable nerve injuries without causalgia. Hyperkeratotic cutaneous lesions may develop in the region of distribution of the involved nerve (Fig. 141).

With the passage of time the pain may slowly become worse, but as a rule it gradually abates.

Numerous views as to the *pathogenesis of causalgia* are extant. The evidence indicates that the pain is the cardinal feature of causalgia and that the vascular and nutritional disturbances, including the osteoporosis, are secondary manifestations. It has long been known that nerve impulses may be deflected in a cut or crushed region of the nerve. In 1944, Granit, Leksell and Skoglund demonstrated that when an anterior root is electrically stimulated the nerve impulses may be transmitted to the sensory fibers in a crushed region of the nerve and can be picked up in the posterior root of the same segment. In this way the traumatized region of the nerve may serve as an "artificial synapse" through which down-coming impulses are shunted to the sensory fibers, and thus are returned to the spinal cord where they give rise to the sensation of pain. On the basis of clinical observations, Doupe, Cullen and Chance (1944) agreed with this view and suggested that the sensory fibers are stimulated by efferent sympathetic impulses. The injection of procaine distal to the site of injury usually afforded relief from the pain, suggesting that the predominant site of interaction is in the more distal part of the extremity, where, according to Doupe and his associates, the pain is induced by a metabolic disturbance brought about by edema, ischemia or some other factor determined by the injury to the limb. In those instances in which pain was not thus relieved, the site of interaction was considered to be in the region of the injury. Their view, that the

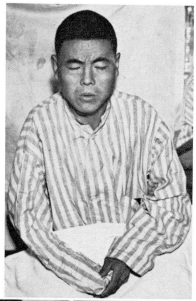

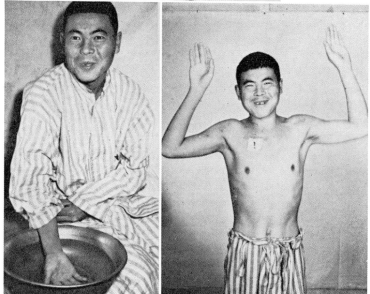

FIGURE 145.   *A Case of Causalgia Following Gunshot Wound Involving the Upper Part of the Median Nerve.* The pains were alleviated by drawing the sleeve over the hand. Immersion in cold water was even more helpful. The pains disappeared after removal of sympathetic ganglia (displayed on the patient's chest). The differences in facial expression are revealing. Following ganglionectomy an aneurysm of the brachial artery was removed. (20th G.H.)

sympathetic fibers are implicated, is consistent with the well recognized fact that causalgia may be cured by sympathectomy (Fig. 145). The observation that a major artery is frequently adherent to the injured nerve makes one wonder whether periarterial sympathetic fibers may not also be implicated. Homans (1940) stressed reflex arterial spasm in the pathogenesis of causalgia. Mayfield (1951) has suggested that whereas in causalgia there is burning hyperesthesia due to involvement of superficial sensory organs, in Sudeck's atrophy and painful osteoporosis the shunting of impulses in the region of injury of small nerves which supply tendons and ligaments is expressed as an aching, throbbing sensation rather than as burning pain.

Certain other views have been set forth, and they may be supplementary to those just expressed.

Livingston (1944) elaborated the thesis that the altered nerve impulse activity originating in the damaged part of the nerve creates an abnormal state of activity in the internuncial neuron centers of the grey matter of the spinal cord and that grey matter activity, in turn, gives rise to efferent discharges responsible for the muscle spasm and the vasomotor and other phenomena. Despite supportive evidence such as the fact that causalgia may occur following amputation, this view rests still in the realm of theory. Gerard (1951) has also contended that in the search for the mechanism responsible for causalgia one must look to the spinal cord for some kind of maintained disturbance.

Directing his attention to cutaneous hyperalgesia in causalgia, Lewis (1936) reached the conclusion that burning pain is brought about by the secretion of a pain substance (H substance) at the terminals of fibers belonging to the posterior root system. Since these fibers appeared to be neither somatic, sensory nor sympathetic he called them "nocifensor nerves." There has been no real confirmatory evidence that nocifensor fibers exist. Jung (1941) expressed the opinion that causalgia is dependent on central and peripheral reflex mechanisms, both brought into activity through irritative phenomena at the level of the lesion. The symptoms, he thought, were partly due to the production of H substance in the peripheral tissues through the intermediation of antidromic impulses of somatic sensory fibers coursing through the injured region of the nerve and that secondary spinal and sympathetic overactivity occurs. Later (1951) he accepted the concept of the "artificial synapse." Nathan (1947) has completely repudiated Lewis's hypothesis of the genesis of causalgia.

Accepting the theory of the liberation of H substance in peripheral tissues, but feeling that the substance was elaborated through activation of cholinergic efferent vasodilator fibers traversing posterior roots, de Takats (1943) reasoned that the resulting vasodilatation is the essential basis for a number of disorders, including Weir Mitchell's causalgia, Sudeck's atrophy and Leriche's post-traumatic painful osteoporosis (in both of which the pain is of an aching, throbbing quality and is apt to occur in the region of small joints), the chronic traumatic edema of Klassen, the peripheral trophoneurosis of Zur Verth, and the *état physiopathique* of Vulpian. He subdivided the vascular aspects of the causalgic state into three stages: during the *first*, the limb is warm, flushed and dry, the subcutaneous and periarticular spaces edematous, and blood flow and oscillometric curves indicate increased circulation to the part; during the *second*, the warmth and flushing are less conspicuous and the involved part may be cyanotic and cold, the periarticular edema has spread, and blood flow is not as great though a tendency to vasodilatation still exists; and during the *third* stage, a lack of objective evidence of vasodilatation. The main hindrance to the acceptance of this view is the variability in the nature and degree of trophic and vascular phenomena (including skin temperature and oscillometric examination) reported by other authors. Although increased blood flow to the causalgic extremity has been confirmed by others, it may vary in a normal extremity a hundred fold under a variety of conditions, including pain of any kind. In a study of 114 cases of causalgia, Freeman (1947) observed that in early stages "vasomotor changes were quite variable . . . . and that skin temperature and oscillometric readings were usually within normal limits." Also de Takats' view does not take inactivity sufficiently into account. On this point, Lewis (1942) commented that in causalgia the trophic disturbances in the skin are "no doubt, partly though not wholly, due to disuse."

Non-causalgic Pain

Pain variously described by the patient but lacking the burning quality of causalgia may also occur following incomplete interruption of a nerve. Such pain is encountered most frequently in the cutaneous fields of supply of the median and tibial nerves with the ulnar and common peroneal nerves not far behind. The pain is restricted to the field of the affected nerve and is invariably superficial, i.e., in the skin. It usually begins when the period of shock or concussion wears off, and is almost always continuous, although it may be reduced when the attention is diverted. The pain tends to be worse at night. Some patients refer to the pain as pricking, cutting, tingling, piercing, or throbbing. Others compare the pain to that induced by pressure; they state, for instance, that the foot feels as though someone were constantly standing on it. Nathan (1947), who referred to these sensations as "pins and needles pain," noted them in 23 of 160 patients. (Causalgia was complained of in 22 and "deep pain" in 15.) This is an incidence of 14.4 per cent, which compares favorably with that cited by other authors, namely between 15 and 20 per cent. (See also Zülch, 1942b.)

The pain usually disappears spontaneously after a month or two, but occasionally persists unabated for several months or even years, causing grave behavioral disorders and insomnia. In contrast to the conditions under which causalgia occurs, there is frequently an associated fracture, widespread damage to soft tissues, or wound infection. Unlike causalgia, this type of pain does not respond to sympathectomy. (Zülch, 1942a and b.)

Neuralgiform pain without a paresthetic quality which follows nerve injury is frequently due to pressure exerted on a nerve by an aneurysm or by local changes in a nerve produced by scarred connective tissue. This type of pain, which rarely if ever occurs in severe nerve injury, is an indication for exploration. Zülch (1942b) described this form of pain as "cutting-piercing" and persistent, though subject to paroxysmal exacerbations.

Over-response in a partially re-innervated cutaneous field is a disorder which occurs some weeks or months after injury of a nerve which has undergone regeneration either spontaneously or after suture. The over-response consists of an exceedingly disagreeable, spreading, tin-

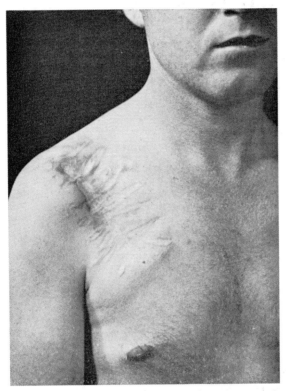

FIGURE 146.   *Cutaneous Scar Following Superficial Wound by Shell Fragment.* Intense paresthesia occurred over the region of distribution of the supraclavicular nerves upon minimal stimulation of the surface of the scar. Recovery followed resection of the scar. (W.R.)

gling sensation induced by light touch or pin prick. The condition is difficult to treat inasmuch as neurolysis or even resection followed by suture often fails to help. Gradual spontaneous improvement is, however, the rule. Similar reactions may occur in the region of *large cutaneous scars* when the part is brought into contact with an object. These reactions vary considerably—from intense pain to an annoying sensation bordering on pain. The reaction may be eliminated by resection of the scar (Fig. 146).

Neuroma may also be painful. Sharp radiating pain may be produced by tapping or pressing upon a neuroma. The pain may also originate spontaneously from a neuroma, or it may be precipitated by cold. The occurrence of the pain bears no relation to the degree of nerve interruption. The most common sites of painful neuromas are in the digital nerves (Fig. 147). Neuromas-in-continuity with preservation of motor

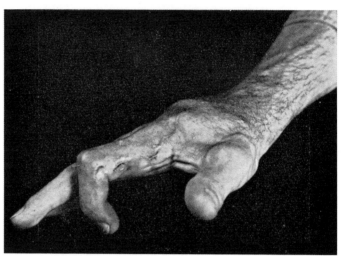

FIGURE 147.   *A Case of Digital Neuroma Involving Branches of the Median Nerve in the Vicinity of the Amputated Index Finger.* On percussion over the palm and web space, pain characteristic of neuroma is induced. The scar on the analgesic radial aspect of the third digit is due to a cigarette burn. (W.R.)

and sensory conduction may present an exceedingly difficult therapeutic problem if in the procaine-block test the pain is not abolished (Woodhall, 1952b).

Painful sole occasionally develops after incomplete interruption of the tibial nerve or of the tibial nerve component of the sciatic nerve. The sole of the foot is extremely sensitive to deep pressure, so that the patient has great difficulty in standing or walking. Even moderate pressure exerted by a finger may precipitate a violent pain reaction. Cutaneous stimuli have no exaggerated effect, nor does the pain occur spontaneously. To spare the sole in getting about, the patient usually walks on his heel or on the outer side of the sole. In milder cases the pain comes on only after a hundred yards or so have been negotiated. The disorder is apparent from the start and tends to persist unabated for many months. Injection of alcohol into the lumbar sympathetic chain frequently has a curative effect. (Hirschmann, 1943a.)

Pain of Amputees

Pain occurring in amputation stumps may be due to pathological changes in the skin, bone or soft parts of the stump, but exclusive of these sources may be subdivided into (1) intermittent pain and (2) continuous pain.

Intermittent pain may occur in the stump, in the phantom part, or in both. It is frequently severe, episodic in nature and of short duration and is usually compared to a discharge of electricity. In most cases it is accompanied by synchronous jactitations of the stump. Each attack is similar to the previous one both as to site and type of pain and is localized to the whole or a part of the region of distribution of a peripheral nerve. The pain is commonly associated with a tender neuroma at the termination of a nerve in the stump, so much so that when the pain commences in the stump the patient points directly to the region of a neuroma as the site of origin of the pain.

Continuous pain varies as to type. It is diffuse either in the stump or the phantom part, or in both. This continuous pain (continuous in the sense that it remains of the same intensity for hours, days or even years) may be tingling, burning, cramping, crushing, bursting, etc., in character.

Pain either intermittent or continuous may affect the stump or the phantom part or both. When intermittent and continuous pains occur, they are separable into distinct entities.

The time of onset of pain following amputation may be immediate or delayed for even months or years. Continuous pain usually has an early onset after amputation and intermittent pain a late onset.

One rather uncommon pain syndrome referable to the stump deserves separate mention. The syndrome has three main characteristics: (1) the pain is severe and (2) diffuse, and (3) is accompanied by vasomotor and trophic disorders in the stump. This condition is benefited by infiltration of the sympathetic nerve supply to the part or by sympathectomy. By contrast, pain occurring in a phantom part is not likely to be influenced by interruption of the sympathetic nerve supply to the part. (Bradley, 1953; see also Weir Mitchell, 1872, White, 1944, Leriche, 1950, Stone, 1950, Thurel, 1951.)

"Functional" Palsies

Disabilities of so-called functional nature often come into consideration in the differential diagnosis of nerve palsies. Hirschmann (1943b), for instance, has observed the disorder in 46 of 700 cases of peripheral nerve injury. The term "functional" does not imply an hysterical reaction, nor does it include simulation but may be explicable on the basis that the habit of guarding a limb against pain induced by movement ("paralysis due to protection") has become so ingrained that after the pain has disappeared the patient has forgotten how to use this or that group of muscles harmoniously in a given movement ("paralysis due to habitual disuse"). Slight neural injury with evanescent reduction in neural function doubtless is an important factor in some of the cases. The functional aberration may also occur after fracture, soft tissue wounds, etc., in which nerves are not significantly damaged.

In "functional" palsies, the usual complaint is that voluntary movement of the affected part has been impossible since the time of injury. The patient may also experience numbness in the region of distribution of a nerve and complain that the part is overly sensitive to cold or that a scarred area becomes painful when pressed on or that the joints are painful when bent.

The affected muscles show little if any atrophy (though exceptions have been cited), and alterations in muscle tone are minimal or absent. Highly significant is the retention of normal direct and indirect electrical irritability of the muscles and nerves without significant alteration in the threshold of irritability. As a rule, the hand, fingers or other part takes on an abnormal position which always remains the same, as though the part has been set in a mold. The upper limbs are more often affected than the lower. Following median nerve involvement from a missile wound in the region of the elbow the index finger and thumb may remain in a position of extension despite lack of atrophy of muscles of the thenar eminence and despite integrity of electrical irritability. The same may be true of sciatic nerve injuries in which the peroneal subdivision may be functionless even though electrical irritability is intact.

The involved part may be cyanotic or pale, hot or cold, dry or moist, covered with an exanthematous rash and pigmented, and the finger or toe nails may be hard or brittle and lusterless. Such changes might be contingent to a degree on immobilization.

Following trauma to the lower limb, a "functional" disorder may be noted in the gait. Thus, the patient may walk stiff-kneed or imitate the gait of a hemiplegic. Here, again, one will recognize the discrepancy between the patient's performance and the physical examination, i.e., the lack or paucity of isolated muscle atrophy, the presence of a play, or dance, of tendons of the dorsum of the foot when they are put on stretch (e.g., by having the patient stand on his heels), the lack of changes in the deep and superficial reflexes, and the absence of alterations in electrical irritability. Sensory change, if present, will almost always be of glove or sock distribution or extend to the most proximal part of the entire circumference of a limb, findings inappropriate for an organic nerve lesion; the reported spread of sensory loss after some nerve injuries should, however, not be overlooked. The testing of motor function will reveal widespread reduction or loss in motor power, not restriction to any one muscle group. Characteristic is the lack of automatic dorsiflexion of the hand when the patient is requested to make a fist.

Certain maneuvers will assist further in diagnosis and even open the way to treatment.

The examiner may, for instance, elevate the patient's "functionally paralyzed" arm and then direct his attention suddenly to the exposed axilla, giving the patient the impression that the causative lesion had just been found there; while the patient tries to look into his axilla to see the lesion, the examiner lets go the arm, and soon afterward, to his astonishment, the patient finds that he is supporting his own arm in that position. Or, in regard to a leg which the patient claims that he is unable to flex at the knee—the examiner has him lie on his back and then asks him to turn over on his belly, meantime supporting the leg in a flexed position; taken by surprise by the request to turn over, the patient is not immediately aware that at the end of the maneuver the examiner had let go his leg and that he is now keeping it flexed by himself. Such preservation of tonic innervation and loss of locomotor innervation not infrequently occurs despite retention of electrical irritability and indicates that psychotherapy is in order. (Foerster, 1918; Hirschmann, 1943b; Bodechtel, Krantzum and Kazmeier, 1951.)

Another aspect of the problem is the loss of function in muscle groups adjoining those obviously paralyzed by a neural lesion, for instance, inability to flex the fingers or hand in the presence of a bona fide radial nerve palsy. The electrical reactions establish that the flexor muscles are normally innervated. Under such circumstances one may conclude either that the patient is consciously or unconsciously protecting the injured part by not using his flexors or that the nerves concerned with flexion had originally suffered concussion and that during the postconcussion state the patient had not become aware that his flexors could be used. Here, energetic suggestive therapy, in which the patient should be shown how normal are the electrical reactions and that his nerve is again in operation, is in order.

Peripheral Nerve Injury in Fractures and Dislocations

Injury to a nerve may go unrecognized when all attention is focused on the care of a fractured or dislocated bone. All too often a nerve injury is discovered only after a plaster cast or splint has been removed. Bone and nerve may be simultaneously damaged by a missile, or splinters from a fractured bone may compress or lacerate an adjacent nerve, or, again, a nerve may be injured during manipulation of a limb in setting the fracture; such nerve injuries are referred to as "primary," in contradistinction to "secondary injury" brought about by inclusion of the nerve in scar tissue or callus. Approximately 21.7 per cent of all peripheral nerve injuries are associated with bone injuries of such severity that the repair of both bone and nerve become a combined orthopedic-neurosurgical problem (see Lyons and Woodhall, 1949). The incidence of nerve injury in fracture of long bones is given in Table 5.

The *radial nerve* is the one most commonly involved in fractures, the incidence according to Lewis (1936) being 57.6 per cent and according to Gurdjian and Smothers (1945), 60.4 per cent. The nerve is considerably more often involved primarily than secondarily, and may be implicated by fractures particularly of the humerus (most often its

TABLE 5   *The Incidence of Nerve Injury in Association with Fracture of the Long Bones, Based on 290 Cases of Combined Bone-Nerve Injury* (Spurling, 1945)

EXTREMITY AND PERCENTAGE OF INJURY	BONE	NERVE	PERCENTAGE OF INJURY
Upper 74	Humerus	Radial	70
		Median	8
		Ulnar	22
	Radius and/or ulna	Radial	35
		Median	24
		Ulnar	41
Lower 20	Femur	Complete sciatic	60
		Peroneal component	20
		Tibial component	20
	Tibia and/or fibula	Peroneal	70
		Tibial	7
		Both nerves	23

supracondylar part), and occasionally by anterior dislocation of the head of the radius with or without fracture of the ulna.

The *ulnar nerve* is injured in about 25 per cent of fractures of the upper extremity, most commonly in connection with fractures of the medial condyle of the humerus and the olecranon process of the ulna. This nerve is particularly subject to *delayed palsy* after fracture in the region of the elbow. The damage sustained is due either to its inclusion in the developing callus in the region where it passes posterior to the medial epicondyle or to angulation of the nerve brought about by the cubitus valgus deformity of the elbow. The nerve may be similarly affected at the elbow by recurrent dislocation of the nerve, by a neuroma developing as a consequence of pressure applied to this region in connection with occupational activities, by arthritis involving the elbow joint, or by local sepsis, e.g., following resolution of cellulitis due to puncture wounds (Richards, 1945).

Median nerve involvement in fractures and dislocations is uncommon.

FIGURE 148.   *Comminuted Fracture of the Humerus Associated with Radial Nerve Palsy Resulting from Missile Wound.* Roentgenogram of compound, comminuted fracture of right humerus secured five hours after shotgun injury, .12 gauge deer load. Immediate onset of radial nerve paralysis. Operation two months after injury disclosed multiple neuromas-in-continuity in the radial nerve segment caused by fragments of lead and bone. (Case C-46596; DUH.) (From B. Woodhall in Surg. Clin. N. America *31:* 1369–1390, 1951.)

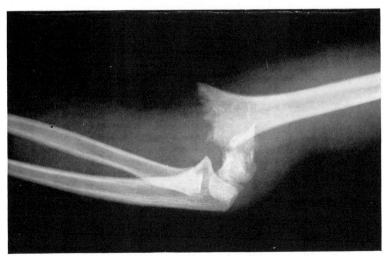

FIGURE 149.   *Fracture of the Lower End of the Humerus with Severe Laceration of the Median Nerve.* Pre-reduction roentgenogram of closed fracture-dislocation of lower end of right humerus. Immediate onset of median nerve paralysis following fall from oil drum. Exploration six months later disclosed complete division of median nerve. (Case D-10402; DUH.)

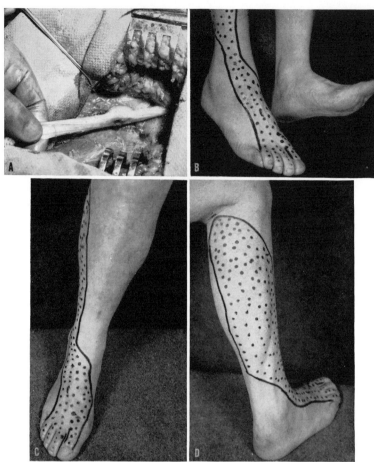

FIGURE 150.   *Delayed Common Peroneal Nerve Palsy from Injury of the Sciatic Nerve.* A piece of glass penetrated the buttock as a consequence of an automobile accident in 1929. Foot drop gradually developed over a period of one year, and was present on examination in August, 1944. Also there was anesthesia and analgesia in the region of distribution of both superficial and deep peroneal nerves. All reflexes were normal. From the middle of September, 1944, onward, the patient noticed a burning "pins-and-needles" sensation gradually spreading up the posterolateral surface of the calf, and after a month it had reached the gluteal fold. Exploration in December, 1944, disclosed the piece of glass lodged between the common peroneal and tibial components of the sciatic nerve (*A*). Neurorrhaphy was performed. By April, 1945, when photographs *B*, *C*, and *D* were taken, considerable tactile sensibility had returned, but analgesia persisted. Foot drop persisted, as is evident in *B*, in which the patient is endeavoring to dorsiflex both feet. The Hoffmann-Tinel sign indicated regeneration of the nerve 50 cm. below the site of the injury. (W.G.H.)

the incidence being about 5 per cent. The nerve may be implicated in fractures of the humerus (Fig. 149) and in dislocations of the elbow and wrist joints. Primary injury of the median nerve from fracture of the lower end of the radius is rare, whereas secondary and delayed injury to the nerve, due to pressure and friction against projecting fragments of the malunited radius, is fairly common; acute palmar flexion maintained by a splint may also lead to median nerve palsy through pressure exerted on the nerve in the region between the transverse carpal ligament and the anterior border of the lower end of the radius (Abbott and Saunders, 1933). Carpal lunate bone dislocation anteriorly is also a fairly common cause of median nerve palsy.

Sciatic nerve damage due to fractures in the region of the hip joint is uncommon. The nerve may be injured in association with fracture of the femur or upward and posterior dislocation of the head of the femur. Gurdjian and Smothers (1945) have alluded to delayed sciatic nerve palsy occurring eleven years after gunshot injury to the hip region.

Common peroneal nerve involvement is fairly frequent in connection with adduction injuries of the knee and in fracture of the head of the fibula. Either stretching or laceration of the nerve may occur. An example of *delayed common peroneal nerve palsy* from injury to the sciatic nerve is illustrated in Figure 150.

Plaster Casts, Splints, Bandages and Tourniquets

Splintage by whatever means is an important element in the outcome of peripheral nerve injuries. Splinting should always be done in such a manner as not to stretch denervated muscles, for, as Highet (1942b) has emphasized, the stretching of paralyzed muscles accelerates disintegration of muscle fibers and their replacement by fibrous tissue.

Constant or intermittent pressure on a nerve can readily be exerted by a poorly fitting splint or plaster cast. An excessively tight plaster cast is as likely to compress a nerve as is one so fitted that its ends deeply indent the skin when movements are performed. A body cast improperly fitted at the armpit may give rise to axillary nerve palsy. Nerves near the skin are most apt to be thus affected—the common peroneal, for instance, from pressure against the head of the fibula (Fig. 151) and the ulnar by being pressed against the medial epicondyle of the humerus. A flexion splint applied to the forearm and hand which buckles at the wrist may compress the median nerve.

Not only do casts or splints directly injure nerves but when applied continuously to the forearm and hand region they often lead to severe fixation of finger, thumb and wrist joints.

Tightly applied bandages may do as much harm; for instance, the ulnar or median nerve, or both, may suffer from compression when the adducted and flexed arm is held against the chest by a tight bandage. Tourniquets applied for too long a time are equally dangerous; when

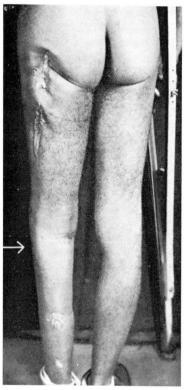

FIGURE 151.   *Delayed Common Peroneal Palsy due to Pressure of a Plaster Cast.* The patient sustained multiple wounds of the left thigh and compound fractures of the femur as the result of penetrating machine gun bullets. Common peroneal nerve palsy ensued a considerable time after application of a plaster cast to the thigh. The transverse scar in the popliteal space marks the region, confirmed at operation, where the edge of the cast compressed the common peroneal nerve. (W.R.)

used above the elbow they are most likely to injure the ulnar and median nerves. The basic cause of paralysis in all these procedures is neural or more widespread ischemia.

Blood Vessel Injury and the Development of Gangrene

Gangrene of an extremity may develop as a consequence of missile injuries to arteries, but the incidence of this grave complication has been reduced by the early application of vessel grafts. Should circulatory embarrassment be sufficiently severe, i.e., should collateral circulation be blocked completely, gangrene of the distal part will supervene (Fig. 152), but more often after arterial injury there is merely the threat of gangrene which, at the crucial period, is withdrawn. In his Hunterian Lecture on ischemic contracture, Griffiths (1940) pointed out that if arterial blockage is incomplete, but too severe or too prolonged for complete recovery of the limb, then necrosis develops in the tissues having the greatest circulatory requirements. According to Makins (1919), the

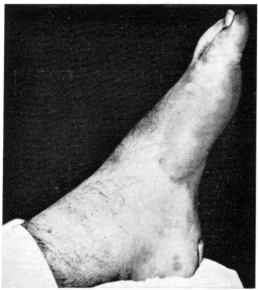

FIGURE 152.   *The Foot in a Case of Interruption of the Tibial and Common Peroneal Nerves, Left, Associated with Severance of the Posterior Tibial Artery.* One week after a missile wound in the region of the popliteal fossa. Early gangrene is evident. (W.R.)

statistics show that the incidence of gangrene following ligation of the main arteries from all causes varies from 6 to 12 per cent, but is somewhat higher in missile wounds. This was found to be true especially for wounds of the femoral and popliteal arteries, gangrene having developed in 46 of 205 cases, or 22.4 per cent.

Blood Vessel Injury and Aneurysm Formation

Since, with few exceptions, all arteries are accompanied by nerve trunks, both artery and peripheral nerve are apt to be affected simultaneously by the same inflicting force. Damage to either or both may be due to concussion, contusion, or laceration. In some 6,300 cases of peripheral nerve injury requiring nerve suture, associated major vascular injuries were found in approximately 13 per cent (Woodhall, 1952b).

Some of these vascular injuries result in aneurysm formation. Considering the subject the other way around, aneurysm formation may or may not be complicated by involvement of peripheral nerves. The incidence of involvement of nerves by aneurysms is considerably higher in the upper than in the lower limb. In cases in which peripheral nerve injury due to missiles is slight, signs and symptoms of such injury may have completely resolved by the time repair of the aneurysm is indicated.

Contusion or laceration of an artery by a missile or other penetrating object may weaken the wall to such a degree that a "true aneurysm" develops. By definition a true arterial aneurysm is one in which the arterial endothelium is continuous into the aneurysm. The great major-

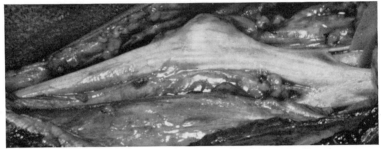

FIGURE 153.   *Aneurysm of the Brachial Artery Compressing the Median Nerve.*
A week or two after stab wound in the axilla a prickling sensation developed in the lateral (radial) aspect of the palm and corresponding fingers. Two months later hypesthesia in this region became evident. Operation disclosed compression of the median nerve by an aneurysm of the brachial artery. (DUH, C-99401.) (From B. Woodhall in Surg. Clin. N. America *31:* 1369–1390, 1951.)

ity of missile-induced arterial aneurysms are "false." These are formed as the result of the escape of blood from a damaged artery, followed by clot formation about the vessel orifice and the envelopment of the hematoma by fibrous connective tissue, or "sac." Either form of aneurysm may develop gradually and in due time compress an adjacent previously normal nerve, and thus induce neural ischemia. In such instances the nerve becomes flattened (Fig. 153) and even eroded (Lyons and Woodhall, 1949). The nerve is so closely adherent to the aneurysmal wall that attempts to separate the two at operation often result in profuse hemorrhage. Associated injury of an adjacent vein, occurring at the time of the injury or secondarily, provides the background for development of an arteriovenous aneurysm, or fistula (Fig. 154). The artery and vein may communicate either directly (Fig. 155) or through the medium of a false sac. In a study of 450 traumatic aneurysms, Elkin (1946) observed that 340 were of the arteriovenous type, and that 110 were false arterial aneurysms.

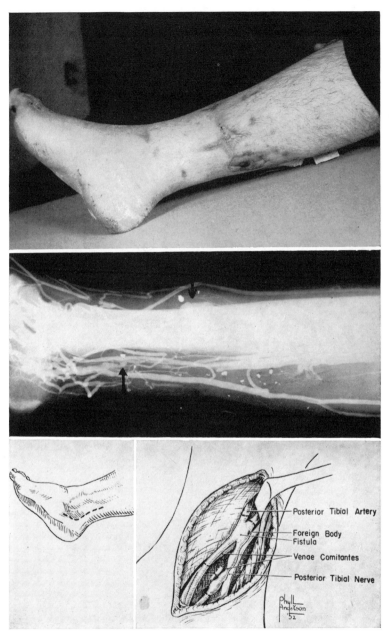

FIGURE 154.   *Arteriovenous Aneurysm and Arterial Aneurysm Complicating Missile Wounds of the Lower Leg.* The leg and foot were wounded by grenade fragments on September 9, 1951, in Korea. Débridement was done the next day. By October 3, a diagnosis of aneurysm of the anterior tibial artery and arteriovenous aneurysm of posterior tibial artery and vein was made on the basis of a constant thrill and bruit. Roentgenograms revealed many metallic fragments but no fracture. The photograph of the leg and foot was made on November 5 and the arteriogram on November 9. The aneurysm was resected on January 24, 1952. An aneurysm of the right anterior tibial artery was resected on February 11, 1952. Recovery was uneventful. (W.R.)

The presence of a well developed aneurysm is often betrayed by a rounded elevation of the skin (Fig. 156). While still small, an aneurysm may be detected by auscultation, a procedure which should be routine in battle casualties. Elkin (1946) has pointed out that arteriovenous aneurysms are usually characterized "by a continuous vibratory thrill

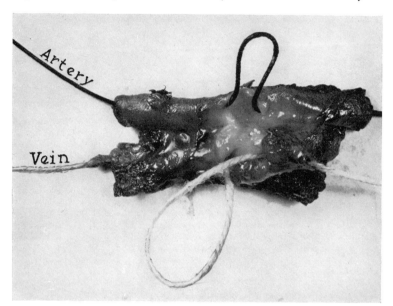

FIGURE 155.   *Arteriovenous Aneurysm Involving the Brachial Artery and Vein.*
The black string has been passed through the artery, and the white string through the vein. The artery and vein have grown together and the lumina of the two are continuous with each other. The patient received a missile wound in the lower arm on June 13, 1944. Shortly thereafter severe causalgia developed in the region by distribution of the median nerve. A few weeks later the causalgia was replaced by dysesthesias. Two weeks after the injury the patient noticed a slight swelling in the antecubital region which "purred like a cat" when felt. A harsh bruit, audible throughout the pulse beat, could be heard up into the axilla and down along the forearm into the wrist. Obliteration of the aneurysm by pressure resulted in reduction of pulse rate from 84 to 72 (a positive Branham's sign). The blood pressure in the brachial artery was 90/60, and after obliteration of the fistula, 90/68. The aneurysm was removed on September 29, 1944. (A.G.H.)

and a loud, rough, *continuous* murmur with systolic intensification, whereas in the false aneurysm, there is a distinct pause between the systolic and diastolic phases and often the murmur is heard only in systole." As a rule in arteriovenous aneurysm the murmur is transmitted for a distance along the course of the involved vessels, while in an arterial aneurysm the murmurs can be heard only in the immediate region of the aneurysm. Neuralgiform pain brought about by compression of an adjacent nerve is frequently complained of. Rhythmic contractions of muscles supplied by the compressed nerve have been noted in occasional instances.

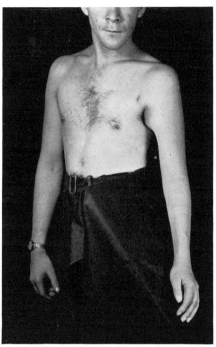

FIGURE 156.   *Arteriovenous Aneurysm Involving the Axillary Artery and Vein.* In February, 1950, a bullet entered the inferior aspect of the left axilla. An incomplete brachial plexus paralysis resulted. The photograph was taken in November, 1951, and the aneurysm was removed a few days later. On examination in July, 1952, both the brachial and the radial pulse were weak. Blood pressure readings could scarcely be obtained. (W.R.)

Several distinct vessel-nerve syndromes due to aneurysm and nerve injury have been recognized (Table 6). (Elkin and Woodhall, 1944; Elkin, 1945).

Traction, or Stretch, Paralysis

Traction paralysis may be the most serious of nerve injuries or the most benign. Actual rupture of a nerve may occur. Regardless of the cause of the traction, the paralysis is the consequence of reparative scarring of the nerve secondary to damage of neurilemmal sheaths and intraneural blood vessels.

Traction applied in the longitudinal axis of the upper limb most commonly damages the brachial plexus (Figs. 157, 158), and when there

TABLE 6.   *Vessel-Nerve Syndromes Due to Aneurysm and Nerve Injury*

SITE OF ANEURYSM	NERVES INJURED
Carotid Artery and Jugular Vein	Lower four cranial nerves
Vertebral Artery	Lower four cranial nerves
Occipital Artery	Accessory and occipital nerves
Internal Maxillary	Glossopharyngeal and hypoglossal nerves
Vertebral	Roots of cervical plexus
Subclavian or Axillary	Brachial plexus
Brachial	Median or ulnar nerve
Cubital	Median nerve
Femoral	Saphenous nerve
Gluteal	Sciatic and gluteal nerves
Popliteal	Peroneal or tibial nerve

is associated dislocation of the shoulder the axillary nerve is frequently involved. The long thoracic and accessory nerves are less apt to be im-

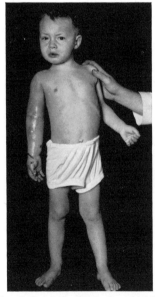

FIGURE 157.   *Traction Paralysis of the Right Brachial Plexus and Rupture of the Axillary Vein, Photographed Forty-eight Hours after Automobile Accident in Which Child Was Thrown from Vehicle.* Complete paralysis of right arm below C5 with incomplete Horner's syndrome. (Case D-5568; DUH.) (From B. Woodhall in Surg. Clin. North America *31:* 1369–1390, 1951.)

plicated. Fractures or dislocations may in themselves induce traction palsies, e.g., the ulnar nerve in fracture of the medial condyle of the humerus, the axillary nerve in dislocation of the shoulder, the common peroneal nerve in dislocation of the knee, and the sciatic nerve in dislocation of the hip. In hip dislocation there is often the added factor of sciatic nerve compression. (Platt, 1940; Highet and Holmes, 1943.)

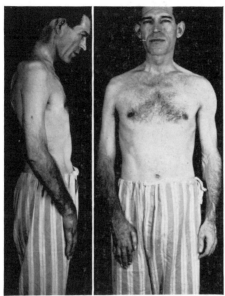

FIGURE 158.   *Stretch Paralysis of Entire Right Brachial Plexus.* This man was struck on top of the right shoulder and received a glancing blow on the right parietal area when the boom of a crane fell on him. Consciousness was lost for forty minutes, after which the right arm was found totally paralyzed. The photograph was taken fifteen months after the accident. In addition to paralysis of all arm muscles, sensibility from C6 to C8, inclusive, was completely lost and that from T1 and T2 partially. Subjectively, sensations of burning and coldness resembling "bee stings" were frequently felt in the hand and forearm. (DUH, C-79675.)

Tendon and Muscle Injuries

In approximately 4.5 per cent of all peripheral nerve injuries there is associated soft tissue injury of sufficient severity to require plastic operation for its repair (see Lyons and Woodhall, 1949). In wounds in certain locations, tendons as well as nerves are apt to be severed. In the vicinity of the wrist, for instance, the flexor tendons and the ulnar or median nerve may be divided simultaneously. An example is illustrated in Figure 159. The disability occasioned by a severed tendon or by one fixed in a cutaneous scar may simulate a funicular palsy. Painstaking examination will, however, clarify the nature of the injury, as sensory change is lacking and the contractile power of adjacent muscles supplied by the same nerve is undiminished. An example of funicular palsy associated with tendon fixation is illustrated in Figure 160. Severe flexion-contraction of the fingers and hand may occur as a result of laceration of flexor tendons (Fig. 161) or inclusion of the tendons in the developing scar (Fig. 162). When doubt exists as to the structures damaged, electrical examination may be employed to advantage: a tendon is certain to have been severed if, on galvanic stimulation, its muscle contracts briskly but fails to produce movement.

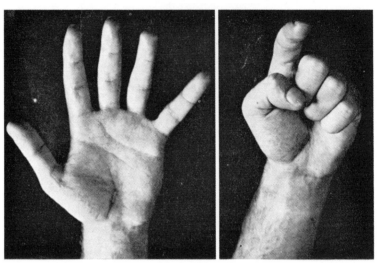

FIGURE 159.   *Shell Fragment Wound of the Palm of Hand with Injury to the Median Nerve.* The distal phalanx of the index finger cannot be flexed although nerve injury lies distal to innervation of flexor digitorum profundus. A severance of the flexor tendon of the index finger was noted at operation. (W.R.)

What has been said of tendons applies equally to muscles. Missiles which penetrate fleshy parts inevitably damage muscle bundles, and thus give rise to impaired motor function. Suppuration in connection with muscle injury adds to the motor loss because of the damage incurred by the muscle and its sheath and by the intramuscular nerve fibers. As a consequence, the electrical irritability of the muscle is reduced and deep reflexes dependent on the muscle concerned may be decreased or lost.

Rupture of muscle may also give rise to impaired motor function by virtue of the inclusion of a nerve trunk in the ensuing scar formation. Muscles tend to be ruptured by indirect violence when they are in a state of contraction. Under such conditions the muscle belly may be torn across or the musculotendinous junction separated. Some of the literature on this type of injury has been reviewed by Girard and Childress (1939).

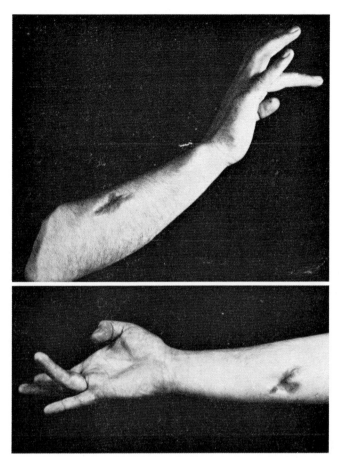

FIGURE 160.   *Palsy of the Posterior Interosseus Branch of the Radial Nerve with Involvement of Branches to the Extensor Pollicis Longus and to the Extensor of the Fourth Finger.* The preoperative clinical diagnosis was that of double funicular palsy. At operation funicular palsy of the extensor pollicis longus was confirmed, but involvement of the extensor of the fourth finger was found to be due to fixation of the muscle in the cutaneous scar of the dorsal aspect of the forearm. Normal function of the fourth finger was restored by resection of the scar. (W.R.)

Contractures

Muscle contracture is a dreaded complication of wounds of the extremities and occurs under a variety of conditions.

Myostatic Contractures

Normally an equilibrium exists between agonist and antagonist muscles, but when a muscle or a muscle group is paralyzed as a consequence of nerve injury the unopposed antagonists undergo a contraction which

pulls the affected part in their direction. The ensuing adaptive shortening of the antagonists gives rise to contracture, referred to as "myo-
static contracture." Eventual fibrotic changes in joint capsules lead to
bony fixation, or ankylosis.

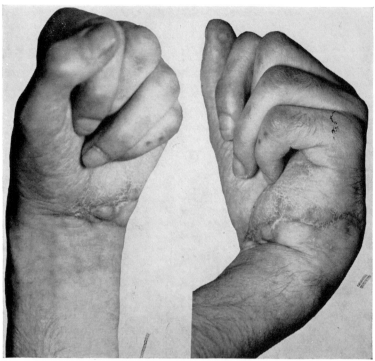

FIGURE 161.   *Deformity of the Hand and Wrist Secondary to Laceration of the
Flexor Tendons and Wrist.* The soldier received the injury to the
wrist in combat in Italy in October, 1943. The photograph was
taken six months later. There is extreme flexion-contraction of
the fingers and wrist brought about by the action of the atrophic
long flexor muscles. No nerves were implicated. (F.A.H.)

Reflexly Induced Contractures

Another basis of muscle contracture is inclusion of a nerve in scar
tissue. Contractures occurring under such circumstances are believed
to be reflexly induced by irritation incident to gradual stretching of the
nerve fibers by the enveloping scar. Sometimes a tremor develops in the
affected part. In involvement of a digital nerve in this manner or occasionally as a consequence of a neuroma, the finger may gradually become flexed until extreme flexion-contracture ensues. During this time
any effort at extension, active or passive, is very painful. Similar involvement of the lateral cutaneous nerve of the forearm may lead to
flexion-contracture at the elbow; here the forearm is in supination for

this is the position in which the nerve is least stretched. Flexion-pronation contracture may develop in connection with inclusion of the posterior cutaneous nerve of the forearm in scar tissue, and adduction of the arm with similar involvement of the medial cutaneous nerve of the

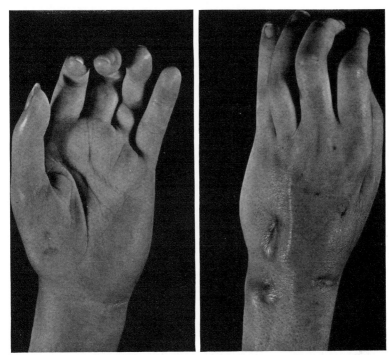

FIGURE 162.   *Deformity of the Hand Due to Median Nerve Palsy, Comminuted Fracture of Third and Fourth Metacarpals, and Adhesions of Flexor Tendons in Forearm Scar.* The soldier was wounded in action in January, 1945. The median nerve was injured in association with compound comminuted fracture of the distal one third of the ulna. The photographs were taken in November, 1945. The ring finger is shortened because of loss of a part of the metacarpal bone and there is flexion-contracture of the index, middle and ring fingers due mostly to adhesion of the flexor tendons to the forearm scar. As a result of capsulotomy of the index and middle metacarpophalangeal joints and freeing of the flexor tendons (June, 1946), the flexion-contractures disappeared and flexor function of the fingers was restored. In the meantime, median nerve function was almost completely recovered. (N.D.B.)

arm. Extension of the forearm is the characteristic posture when the ulnar nerve is included in scar tissue in the region just above the region of the elbow, and moderate or extreme flexion-contraction of the fourth and fifth fingers and sometimes the third when this nerve is involved in the region of tendons or muscle bellies of the forearm.

The same is true for the lower extremity: flexion contracture of the toes from plantar nerve involvement by scar tissue, causing the patient to walk on his heel or on the side of his foot; contracture of the foot in dorsal flexion and inversion through involvement of the superficial peroneal nerve in the region of the lower one third of the leg or foot, as the result of which the patient often walks on his heel; and plantar flexion and abduction at the ankle (with flexion at hip and knee) in involvement of the sural nerve. When the sciatic nerve is thus implicated flexion-contracture at the knee may develop. The patient may continuously hold his fully flexed leg against his chest, guarding it against the least movement. Such contractures may gradually lessen, but full functional restoration requires many months. Neurolysis is often necessary to relieve the disorder. (Foerster, 1918.)

Dupuytren's Contracture

This is a condition characterized by contracture of the palmar fascia in association with flexion-contracture of the fingers. This form of contracture has occasionally been noted in median nerve palsy.

Ischemic Contracture (of Volkmann)

Involving hand and forearm more often than the lower limb, ischemic contracture may occur under a variety of conditions in which blood flow to the part is reduced for too long a time. Arterial occlusion produced through the intermediation of the trauma or by ligation is a recognized precipitating cause, and it has been suggested that traumatic arterial spasm may have the same effect (Griffiths, 1945). Venous occlusion may also be responsible (Albert and Mitchell, 1945). Meyerding (1930) expressed the opinion that ischemic contracture results from extrinsic or intrinsic pressure in which both the arterial and the venous circulation are impaired, practically shutting off the latter, and that these conditions, together with immobilization, hemorrhagic infiltration and fibrosis result in scarring and contracture of the normal tissue. Regardless of the precipitating cause, the factor of perhaps greatest importance in the development of ischemic contracture is obstruction of the collateral circulation. According to Parker (1945), such obstruction may be due to (1) spasm of collateral arteries, (2) thrombosis, or (3) obstruction by swelling, with or without external constriction.

Fracture is a frequent inciting cause. In 128 cases of this kind reported by Meyerding (1930) there was fracture of the humerus in 55, the radius and ulna in 19, the radius in 17, the radius and humerus in 6, the ulna in 3, the clavicle in 3, metacarpal bones in 3, the tibia and fibula in 3, and miscellaneous in 19. Supracondylar fractures of the humerus are among the most important, and in such cases, as in many others, the flexor muscles of the forearm tend to suffer most, presumably through extension of arterial spasm or thrombosis to these muscles, thus isolating them from collateral circulation (Parker, 1945). Vascular obstruction by an arterial or arteriovenous aneurysm is occasionally the basis of ischemic contracture. Partial vascular occlusion due to cicatrix formation or a reduction in blood flow from splints, casts or bandages has also been cited as a cause (Meyerding, 1930). The condition may also be due to copious local hemorrhage or suppuration.

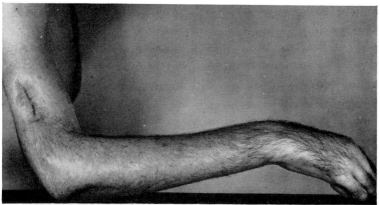

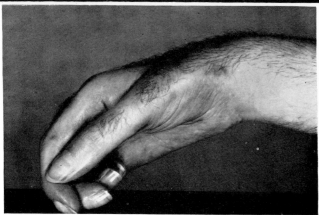

FIGURE 163.   *Ischemic Contracture of the Hand Unassociated with Primary Traumatic Nerve Injury.* Note the relatively minor muscle atrophy. (H.H.)

Following relatively severe ischemia, the involved muscles often undergo patchy or total necrosis. Under such conditions the nerves in the affected region become degenerated and ultimately a widespread, striking increase in endoneurial collagen occurs, leading in some cases to complete collagenous replacement of nerve bundles. Affected nerves have occasionally been found completely necrotic. Ischemic fibrosis of a nerve may sometimes be limited to the region of arterial insult, beyond which wallerian degeneration develops. In such cases satisfactory neural regeneration is likely to occur.

The signs of ischemic paralysis are usually readily detectable. The pulse of peripheral arteries is usually undetectable for at least several days, after which it is exceedingly weak and often remains so for

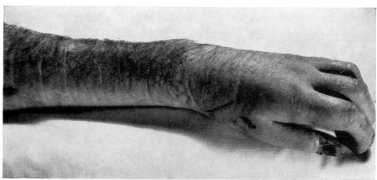

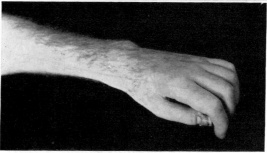

FIGURE 164.   *Ischemic Contracture.* In August, 1943, the soldier incurred a severe compound, comminuted fracture of the middle one third of the humerus together with extensive wounds of the medial aspect of the left axilla, arm and upper forearm as a result of penetration of bullets fired from a rifle at close range. Dry gangrene of the tips of the left thumb and index and little fingers developed. Three months later no pulsation of the radial artery could be felt. Muscles supplied by the median and ulnar nerves were paralyzed and there was glove distribution of sensory loss, i.e., up to 2 inches above the wrist. The upper photograph was taken four and three-quarter months after the injury. Eleven months after injury the median nerve was found at operation to be completely severed, and the ulnar the seat of a neuroma. Following neurolysis, there was some return of function of ulnar-innervated muscles. Loss of median nerve function persisted. The entire anterior compartment of the left forearm contained fibrotic muscles. The lower photograph was taken eight and one half months after injury. Thanks to persistent physiotherapy, the fingers show only a moderate degree of ischemic contracture. (W.G.H.)

months. The impairment of the circulation is also evident by oscillometry and in arteriograms. The onset of the condition is marked by profound swelling of the part and frequently by severe pain. Where there has been arterial ligation or fracture, paralysis of the distal or the more proximal muscles, or both, tends to set in within an hour or two, presumably because of secondary neural ischemia, but where severe hemorrhage is responsible the onset of paralysis, if it occurs, may be delayed eight to ten hours. Sensory deficit becomes apparent more slowly than motor paralysis and is first evident in the digits and spreads centripetally, ultimately assuming a glove or sock distribution. Fibrous tissue gradually replaces normal muscle and encompasses tendon

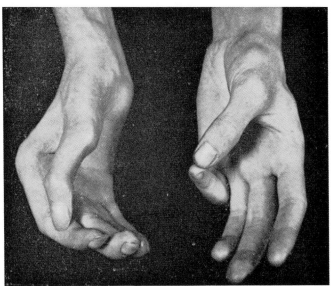

FIGURE 165.   *The Hand in a Case of Combined Neural and Vascular Injury.* A bullet penetrated the medial aspect of the middle third of the right arm, severing the ulnar and median nerves and lacerating the brachial artery and vein. The latter were ligated and for a while there was a threat of gangrene of the tips of the fingers. Eight months after the injury, when the photograph was taken, there was fixation at all joints, severe atrophy and trophic changes. The attempt to oppose thumb and little finger is futile. (A.G.H.)

sheaths, aponeuroses, and eventually immobilizes the joints. The involved muscles become shrunken, noncontractile, hard and cordlike, not soft and yielding as in uncomplicated atrophy. Flexors of the forearm being the muscles most implicated in ischemic contracture, they undergo shortening and as a consequence the hand becomes "frozen" in a claw-like position, with the terminal digits sharply flexed (Figs. 163, 164). The hand tends to remain pronated and in later stages is frequently hyperextended. Intrinsic muscles of the hand may or may not undergo contracture. When the examiner attempts to straighten the fingers and wrist, the atrophied fibrous bands of flexor muscles of the forearm stand out in relief. Only when the hand is flexed can extension of the fingers be induced. When the fingers are straightened and then the hand is hyperextended at the wrist the fingers undergo sharp flexion, with the result that they cut deeply into the hand of the examiner. Being atrophic, cold, cyanotic and often sloughed or ulcerous, the hand appears lifeless.

Direct nerve injury occurring in association with the trauma which induced the ischemia may be diagnosed on the basis of the distribution of the motor and sensory changes (Figs. 165, 166).

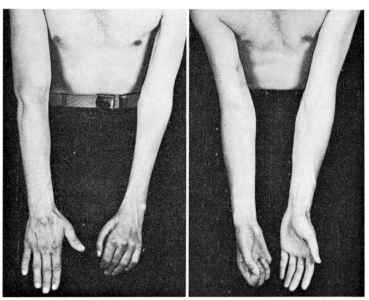

FIGURE 166.   *Two Cases of Gunshot Wound of the Arm in Which the Median and Ulnar Nerves Were Interrupted and the Brachial Artery Lacerated.* Soon after injury the brachial artery in each instance was ligated. The left and right hands, respectively, show the characteristics of the "frozen" hand described in the text. (W.R.)

In early stages the muscles respond to both faradic and galvanic current. Subsequently those which have undergone necrosis fail to respond either to mechanical or to electrical stimulation, whereas denervated muscle exhibits merely the reaction of degeneration. Percutaneous electrical stimulation of nerves may, however, be unreliable, for muscles relatively unaffected by ischemia may fail to respond because of impaired circulation and associated edema of the subcutaneous tissue. Also there may be a total lack of response from muscles which have undergone patchy necrosis; here the true state of affairs may be determined by electromyography. (Holmes, Highet and Seddon, 1944; Pollock, 1944; Parkes, 1945; Lyons and Woodhall, 1949.)

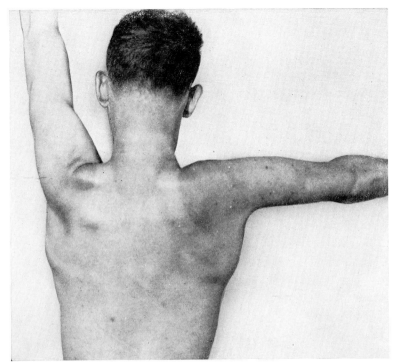

FIGURE 167.   *Loss of Abduction of Arm above 90 Degrees Following Gunshot Wound of Shoulder.* The electrical reactions were normal. The disability is due to ankylosis of the glenohumeral joint. The supplementary abduction is achieved through scapular rotation. (A.G.H.)

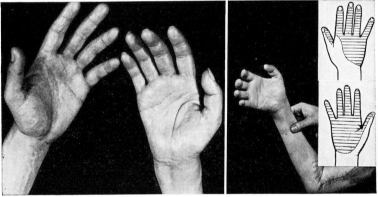

FIGURE 168.   *Combined Median and Ulnar Nerve Palsy, Right, with Relatively Little Deformity Owing to Early Institution of Physiotherapy.* Manipulation of the hand was started soon after injury to the middle third of the right arm by shell fragments. Seven months later the thenar and hypothenar eminences are somewhat atrophied, and wrist movements are weak. The fingers are slightly extended at the metacarpophalangeal joints and somewhat flexed at the interphalangeals. The sensory loss in the fields of the median and ulnar nerves is more extensive than ordinarily encountered. (W.R.)

Ankylosis

In ankylosis of whatever cause one should be on his guard not to misinterpret limitation of movement. When any part of a limb is immobilized for a sufficient length of time the muscles waste and the joints stiffen, greatly restricting movement even though nerve supply is intact (Fig. 167). Under such conditions, normally innervated muscles usually reveal their potential power by contracting when movements are attempted. In cases in which the nature of the disability is in doubt the electrical examination will usually tell whether the disability has a mechanical or a neural basis. Ankylosis frequently does not develop when physiotherapy is begun early (Fig. 168).

CHAPTER 9

Tests Employed
in the Diagnosis or
Prognosis of Nerve Injuries

SPECIAL TESTS have their place when information as to the degree of nerve damage or more precise localization is desired. They may also yield valuable information on the status of regeneration.

Hoffmann-Tinel's Sign, and the Recovery of Function of an Injured Nerve

Hoffmann-Tinel's sign* consists of the occurrence of tingling in the region of distribution of an injured nerve when the part of the nerve distal to the site of the injury is tapped gently by a single finger. Stronger percussion or firmer pressure is necessary in testing deeper nerves. Tingling merely at the spot percussed is not to be construed as a positive Hoffmann-Tinel's sign. The peripheral reference of the sensation differs from that which may be elicited by striking a normal nerve in that it is induced with greater ease and persists longer (ten to fifteen seconds) after cessation of the stimulus. Reaching the conclusion that vibration of the percussion wave is transmitted through soft tissues to the site of the nerve lesion, Napier (1949) advocated that the sign should not be considered as irrefutably positive until it can be elicited 10 cm. below the site of the injury.

The sign of Hoffmann-Tinel first becomes evident about four to six weeks after suture or injury, although it has been induced as early as the twentieth day (Boring, 1916). The sign is taken as evidence of the presence, at the site stimulated, of regenerating, still unmyelinated sensory axons. As a rule, not much more than about 30 cm. of a nerve is at any one time sensitive to percussion for when regenerating axons have advanced over that distance their proximal part has become myelinated though not yet necessarily functionally mature. At early stages the test does not provide information as to the quality of the ensuing

---

* In the German literature the sign is often referred to as "Hoffmann's sign," whereas in the literature of other countries it is usually called "Tinel's sign." Hoffmann's papers on the subject appeared in 1915, and Tinel's in 1915 and 1917— hence our use of both names.

regeneration, for tingling to percussion may occur when only a few axons are growing down their intended route, too few to provide satisfactory functional recovery. Henderson (1948) has dwelt on the hazards of interpretation of the test under such conditions, and has advocated that in earlier stages of regeneration a comparison be made of the intensity of the tingling induced by tapping the distal part of the nerve and that induced by tapping the neuroma or the site of end-to-end suture. If the tingling in both is of much the same intensity, but not stronger in the region of the neuroma or suture than over the distal segment of the nerve, it is likely that many axons are regenerating, but that if distal tingling on tapping the nerve is slight, very few axons are regenerating. Hence the test is quantitative rather than qualitative. According to Henderson, three or four months after injury or suture are requisite before the degree of regeneration as determined by the Hoffmann-Tinel test can be unequivocally assessed in a superficial nerve and four to six months in a deep nerve. Henderson's decision as to whether or not to operate hinged on the results of the test after these periods of time.

Certain points should be kept in mind in comparing the sensation induced by tapping a neuroma and that provoked by tapping the distal segment of a nerve. As pointed out above, pain induced by tapping a neuroma may be quite independent of the distal tingling which occurs when the distal segment of the nerve is tapped. Moreover, the distal tingling brought about by tapping a neuroma frequently persists after the sign is no longer elicitable from the rest of the nerve. As Napier (1949) has emphasized, distal tingling becomes more intense as the tapping finger approaches a neuroma and less intense again as the neuroma is passed, a procedure of special localizing value in cases in which multiple injuries have occurred and in which the sites of nerve injury are in doubt.

The rate of advance of regenerating axons, as manifested by Hoffmann-Tinel's sign, varies not only with the nature of the lesion but also with the lapse of time and with the level of the nerve affected. There is evidence that under highly favorable conditions the rate of growth increases progressively. Pollock and Davis (1933) have reported a rate of growth of 2 cm. in the first month after the sign was initially elicited, 3 cm. in the second month, and 4.5 cm. in the third month—rates of growth which closely parallel those illustrated in Figure 169. However, in a detailed study of a large series of peripheral nerve injuries, Sunderland (1947) found that the process of functional restoration—preceded by a positive Hoffmann-Tinel's sign in the cases in which the sign was elicitable—diminishes progressively over the whole period of recovery. The distal advance of regeneration, as detected by Hoffmann-Tinel's sign, was more rapid the closer the nerve lesion was to the spinal cord, then slowed down as the periphery was approached. In the presence of an injury in proximal parts of the limbs in which axons were disrupted but in which endoneurial tubules and other elements of the nerve were intact, the rate of advance of functional restoration in the upper part of the arm and thigh was estimated to be approximately 3 mm. per day,

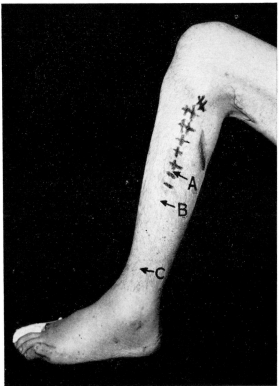

FIGURE 169.   *Elicitation of Hoffmann-Tinel's Sign in a Case of Palsy of the Common Peroneal Nerve.* Complete interruption of the nerve occurred as the result of a gunshot wound in the region of the knee. On June 2, 1944, four and one-half months after the injury, Hoffmann-Tinel's sign was positive for a distance of 100 mm. below the head of the fibula (*A*). On June 30, 1944, the sign was obtained at a point 150 mm. below the head of the fibula (*B*), and on August 22, 1944, 240 mm. below this landmark (*C*). Thus, Hoffmann-Tinel's sign indicated a regeneration of 140 mm. of the nerve over a period of eighty days, a growth averaging 1.75 mm. per day. During this time there had been no restoration of function. This case is illustrated also in Figure 262. (W.R.)

and subsequently in distal parts about 0.5 mm. per day. In cases in which the injury was located distally, the rate of recovery was only about 0.5 mm. per day from the start. Sunderland and Bradley (1952) have observed that the initial rate of growth may be as much as 8.5

mm. a day. Henderson (1948) remarked that after a delay of one or two months regenerating nerve fibers grow at the rate of about 8 cm. a month. It is generally conceded that the rate of growth is slower after nerve suture than in spontaneous nerve regeneration.

The rate of descent of Hoffmann-Tinel's sign was considered by Napier (1949) as a valuable indication of the degree of functional recovery to be expected. Rates of the order of 2 to 3 mm. per day were found to be associated with good functional restoration, and a rate of 1 to 2 mm. or less per day an indication that satisfactory spontaneous recovery was unlikely and hence called for immediate exploration of the nerve. Henderson (1948), on the other hand, considered relative intensity of tingling from percussion of the site of injury and distal segment of the nerve as decisive.

Retardation of advance of the sign of Hoffmann-Tinel or fixation along the path of expected regeneration indicates that the fibers have met an impasse, such as an adhesion, a local scar, a neuroma, or a generalized fibrosis such as occurs in funicular injury (third degree injury).

Retardation in the advance of Hoffmann-Tinel's sign may also be observed in the presence of completely divided nerves. In a study of 45 cases of complete division, Napier (1949) observed preoperatively that Hoffmann-Tinel's sign was positive in 21. At operation, manifest anatomical gaps of 1.0 to 10 cm. were found in 14 of these, and subsequent histological studies showed regenerated axons bridging the gap in 6. It is possible, though rare, for the Hoffmann-Tinel sign to advance rapidly and progressively in cases of complete division of a nerve in which the tissue gap is small, but under such circumstances functional recovery is minimal. Zülch (1942b) described a case in which the sign was positive over the entire ulnar nerve, and yet at operation the nerve was completely severed, with the stumps held together by scar tissue.

As to the ultimate fate of Hoffmann-Tinel's sign, Napier (1949) reported that of 48 cases observed by him three and one half years after injury the sign was no longer present in 18, was fading in 20, and was still clear-cut in the remaining 10 cases. The fading was centrifugal in 80 per cent and centripetal in the remainder. The earlier the sign disappeared, the better was the ultimate recovery. In Napier's experience (242 nerve lesions), recovery of sensory function was preceded by a positive and migratory Hoffmann-Tinel's sign in all lesions of a degenerative nature, with the exception of 5 instances in which the nerves concerned were relatively inaccessible to stimulus. Other workers have had considerably less success in eliciting the sign. Thus, despite recovery in function, Spurling and Woodhall (1946) were unable to induce the sign in 8 of 59 cases of late primary suture, and Woodhall and Lyons (1946) had the same experience in 115 of 456 cases.

Test for Sweating

A dependable test for sweat secretion is that devised by Guttmann (1940). As a preliminary measure the patient is given 5 to 10 grains of aspirin, followed by a cup or two of hot coffee or tea. The area of skin to be investigated is then dusted with powder containing sodium chinizarin 2–6 disulfonate.* The arm or other part being examined is placed beneath a hot air cradle or in a radiant heat chamber. Within fifteen to thirty minutes, profuse sweating occurs, and the powder, previously light grey, takes on a deep red-purple color. The cutaneous areas rendered anesthetic remain uncolored (Fig. 139). In performing the test, care should be taken not to allow sweat to run into adjacent areas. The degree of sweating will vary with the region tested, and where the skin is thick or hyperkeratinized, sweating tends to be minimal.

Prostigmin has occasionally been found to produce sweating where the usual tests have been negative or faintly positive. This response has been ascribed to increased sensitivity of the autonomic system, analogous to the heightened sensitivity of sensory fibers during regeneration (Götze, 1942).

Procaine Nerve Block

Procaine block of peripheral nerves, nerve roots and sympathetic ganglia is widely used as a preoperative test to determine whether surgical measures are indicated in painful disorders. A 2 per cent solution of procaine with adrenalin or one of the longer lasting agents such as 1 per cent xylocaine may be used as the blocking agent. The order of loss of function in a peripheral nerve following procaine or xylocaine block is well established: namely, vasodilatation, loss of sweating, hypalgesia, and finally analgesia, anesthesia and motor paralysis. If pain is not relieved by this measure, it is generally considered to be psychogenic. (Highet, 1942a.)

Procaine sympathetic block has also been employed as a procedure for the diagnosis of interruption of peripheral nerves. The vasodilatation in the fingers occurring in connection with stellate block and that in the toes following lumbar ganglion block is associated with a rise in temperature of 8 to 10° C., but in the anesthetic area of an interrupted nerve the skin temperature fails to rise. This test is only of value during the first two weeks after injury, as only during this time is there paralytic vasodilatation. (Philippides, 1942a; White, Smithwick and Simeone, 1952.)

* The composition of the powder is as follows: sodium chinizarin 2–6 disulfonate, 28 gm., anhydrous sodium bicarbonate, 24 gm., and rice starch, 48 gm. The bicarbonate is included in order to prevent moistening of the powder during storage, and the starch serves merely as a base.

Procaine block is also of value in the study of anomalous innervation and in the unmasking of trick movements.

Skin Resistance

A series of studies by Richter and his associates has shown that a sympathectomized area of skin is highly resistant to the passage of a minute direct current. This is true regardless of the site at which sympathetic fibers are interrupted, whether in ganglia, plexus components, or peripheral nerves. By means of the measurement of cutaneous resistance, called *dermometry*, the area of increased skin resistance, which corresponds closely to that of sensory loss, can be outlined with precision.

The instruments and technique employed in dermometry are as follows (Richter, 1953): The dermometer consists of a galvanometer (microammeter), a 1000-volt potential divider, a 90-volt battery, a jack switch, a reversing switch for changing the direction of the testing current, a telephone plug, and two electrodes (one for use on the ear, the other on the area of skin to be tested). Full insertion of the plug in the jack switch makes the contact and allows the current from the battery to flow through the subject. The potential divider regulates the amount of the current. The instrument is fairly rugged; care must be taken, however, to prevent contact between the electrodes. It is light in weight, portable, and highly practicable in clinical use. It gives only outlines of areas of high and low resistance, not the actual resistance of these areas in ohms. The latter is determined by means of another simple instrument, designed by Dr. Frederick Whelan, of Baltimore. With this instrument the testing current can be kept constant at 2 microamperes at all ranges of skin resistance. It reads up to 45 million ohms. This instrument, like the dermometer, is equipped with the same type of telephone socket so that the electrodes can readily be connected to either instrument. A machine is in use which incorporates both instruments in one, thus eliminating the necessity of having to shift the telephone plug from one instrument to the other.

The disc of the ear electrode is covered with electrode jelly and then clipped to the ear lobe. The skin electrode, which consists of a small nickel-plated bronze disc, or a metal roller, is then touched to any part of the body with probably normally innervated skin in order to adjust the current by means of a potential divider so that the indicator moves a few divisions across the microammeter dial. Preliminary exploration of the areas of low resistance, indicated by greater deflection of the pointer, and the areas of high resistance, marked by decreased or minimal deflection, will allow adjustment by means of the potential divider so that maximal differences between areas of low and high resistance may be elicited. The transition zone between areas of low and high resistance is relatively small, measuring only ⅛ of an inch or less. By recording on the skin the successive points of demarcation between areas of low and high resistance, the area of altered cutaneous innervation may be rapidly outlined.

Patients can be tested at room temperature and the contrast between normal and abnormal areas may be enhanced by the use of aspirin or hot tea. But testing under such conditions is not as satisfactory as in a cold room and in a heat cabinet. Cold external temperatures increase the resistance on all normally innervated areas of skin, but not on areas of sympathetic hyperactivity, which help to give an objective record of the presence and distribution of pain. High external temperatures decrease the resistance on all normally innervated areas of skin, but not on

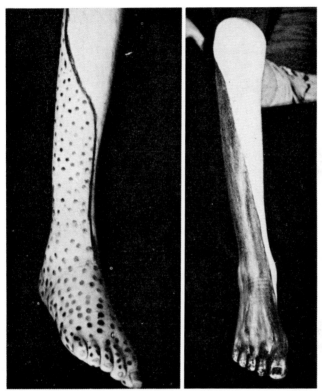

FIGURE 170.   *A Comparison of the Field of Sensory Deficit with That of Increased Skin Resistance in a Case of Interruption of Tibial and Common Peroneal Nerves.* The area of sensory loss (in dots) is virtually the same as that of skin resistance (in solid black). (W.R.)

denervated areas. By means of this technique it is possible to outline areas of complete denervation and of varying degrees of partial denervation.

The skin resistance method has also proved useful in outlining areas of skin having defective circulation because of peripheral vascular disease of various kinds. Knowledge of the presence of such areas is often important in evaluating skin resistance changes produced by the peripheral nervous system.

Dermometry may be used to supplement sensory examination. The changes from normal skin resistance correspond closely to the area of sensory impairment (Fig. 170) and may be used to differentiate complete and incomplete nerve division. Regeneration of autonomic fibers in injured peripheral nerves may be recognized by a progressive shrinkage of the customary patterns of high skin resistance (Fig. 171). (Rich-

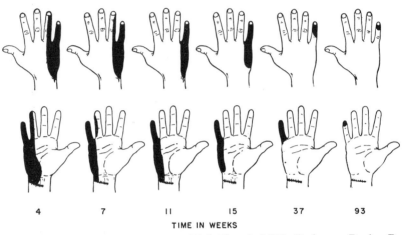

ULNAR NERVE REGENERATION

(SHADED AREAS-HIGH ELECTRICAL SKIN RESISTANCE)

| 4 | 7 | 11 | 15 | 37 | 93 |

TIME IN WEEKS

FIGURE 171.   *Changes in Pattern of High Electrical Skin Resistance During Regeneration of the Ulnar Nerve.* The time (in weeks) after severance and suture of the nerve is indicated. (Courtesy of Dr. Curt P. Richter, from J. Neurosurg. *3:* 188, 1936.)

ter and Woodruff, 1942, 1945; Richter and Katz, 1943; Richter, 1946; Herz, Glaser, Moldaver and Hoen, 1946.)

Electrical Examination

A number of electrodiagnostic methods may be used to supplement or refine the information obtained through a study of sensory or motor function. For the most part, these methods demand apparatus not usually available to the casual student. The commonest electrical test is the simple percutaneous stimulation of the nerve trunk at the point where it is close to the skin. Any one of a variety of stimulators may be used. In *faradic* stimulation of a healthy muscle or a motor nerve, a tonic contraction ensues; it persists until the current is shut off. In *galvanic* excitation a brief contraction of the muscle occurs only at the moment the circuit is closed or when it is broken, but not while the current is passing. Normally, when the *kathode* is the source of the stimulus the contraction occurs in more muscle fibers on closing (or "making") than on opening (or "breaking") the circuit; however, by using a strong current the same degree of muscle contraction can be obtained with the *anode*. To put it in the terms generally employed: K.C.C. (kathodal closing contraction) >*A.C.C.* (anodal closing contraction). In testing with either type of current, the electrodes must be applied at the point of entry of the nerve into the muscle. These, known as "motor points," are illustrated in Figures 172 and 173.

When any part of the lower motor neuron is damaged, changes in excitability to both faradic and galvanic currents occur. Toward the end of one week after nerve injury, the muscle concerned ceases to respond to faradic stimulation of its motor point. For about ten days after an injury, excitation with the galvanic current produces a normal contraction but after that time the response changes. Instead of the usual prompt twitch there is a sluggish, lingering, vermicular contraction of the muscle which starts at the point stimulated; a stronger current is required for its elicitation than normally. Moreover, the phenomenon of "polar reversal" occurs, the anodal closing contraction being more pronounced than the kathodal closing contraction (A.C.C.> K.C.C.), although at times the two are equal (A.C.C. = K.C.C.). These changes, of which the phenomenon of polar reversal is the least significant, are spoken of as the *reaction of regeneration* (R.D.).

Reaction of degeneration is said to be *complete* when the muscular contraction is vermicular. Faradic excitation is no longer present and polar reversal is in evidence, but these changes are not as important or as constant as the vermicular contraction. The reaction is said to be *partial* when faradic excitability is reduced and when the polar response is modified but not reversed. Usually in complete division of a nerve the reaction of degeneration is evident in ten days after the injury. If after three weeks the response of a muscle to faradism still persists, the interruption may be regarded as incomplete. Neither response gives information regarding the nature of the interruption, whether anatomical or physiological.

The faradic response becomes normal only after function has been restored. It may be absent, however, even after voluntary contraction of the muscles has been completely reestablished.

A portable direct current stimulator devised by Golseth and Fizzell (1947) provides a steady monophasic, relatively painless current, delicate current strength control, and time control of duration of stimuli and interval between stimuli. Accurate current strength measurement permits a comparison of examinations done at successive time periods.

Intraneural Stimulation

The neuromuscular response may be tested not only percutaneously but also by the introduction of fine needles directly into nerve trunks.

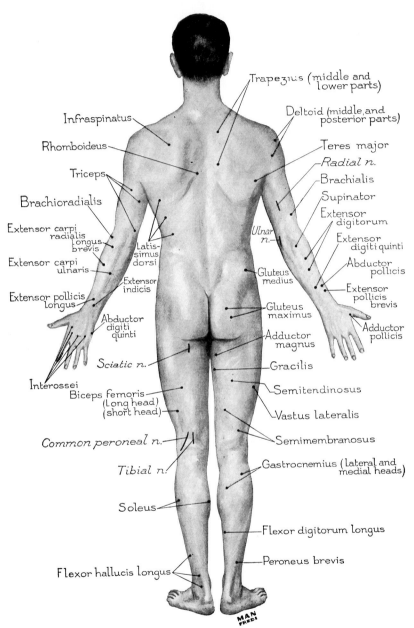

FIGURE 172.   *Motor Points of the Neck, Trunk and Limbs from the Posterior Aspect.* These are the points at which electrical stimulation normally produces maximal muscular contraction.

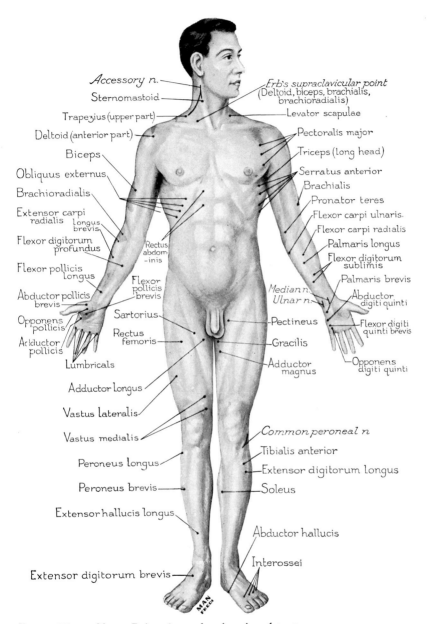

Accessory n.
Sternomastoid
Trapezius (upper part)
Deltoid (anterior part)
Biceps
Obliquus externus
Brachioradialis
Extensor carpi radialis longus brevis
Flexor digitorum profundus
Flexor pollicis longus
Abductor pollicis brevis
Opponens pollicis
Adductor pollicis
Lumbricals
Rectus abdom-inis
Flexor pollicis brevis
Sartorius
Rectus femoris
Adductor longus
Vastus lateralis
Vastus medialis
Peroneus longus
Peroneus brevis
Extensor hallucis longus
Extensor digitorum brevis

Erb's supraclavicular point
(Deltoid, biceps, brachialis, brachioradialis)
Levator scapulae
Pectoralis major
Triceps (long head)
Serratus anterior
Brachialis
Pronator teres
Flexor carpi ulnaris.
Flexor carpi radialis
Palmaris longus
Flexor digitorum sublimis
Palmaris brevis
Abductor digiti quinti
Flexor digiti quinti brevis
Opponens digiti quinti
Median n.
Ulnar n.
Pectineus
Gracilis
Adductor magnus
Common peroneal n
Tibialis anterior
Extensor digitorum longus
Soleus
Abductor hallucis
Interossei

FIGURE 173.   *Motor Points from the Anterior Aspect.*

Through this method the exact point of stimulus can be ascertained and the results of stimulation of the exposed nerve at operation duplicated. A simple apparatus for this purpose is that devised by Lewey and Nulsen (1947). The test is particularly valuable for the study of both spontaneous and postoperative regeneration.

Galvanic Tetanus Ratio

The passage of a strong galvanic current through muscle produces prolonged excitation and a continuous or tetanic contraction of the muscle, persisting as long as the current passes. This phenomenon is known as *galvanic tetanus*. The ratio between the rheobase, or the threshold current necessary for a minimal visible contraction, and the threshold current required to produce tetanus is the *galvanic tetanus ratio*. It is determined by dividing the strength of the galvanic current (in milliamperes) producing the tetanic response by that of the current producing the minimal visible contraction. In normal muscle with an intact nerve supply, the galvanic tetanus ratio varies between 3.2 and 9.5, whereas in denervated muscle it approaches unity. During regeneration, there is a considerable rise in the rheobase, a high threshold amperage for tetanus, and a high tetanus ratio (as high as 20). The Golseth-Fizzell stimulator or any other reliable instrument may be used for this purpose. (Pollock et al., 1948.)

Chronaxia

Chronaxia represents a comparison of the intensity of a current with its time of passage or of current strength versus current duration. In its determination, the rheobase is first measured: this is the minimum voltage conducive to perceptible muscle contraction when the galvanic current flows for an indefinite period of time. Currents of briefer duration are then used and the strength of current necessary for perceptible contraction is recorded. As current duration is diminished, the effective current strength must be increased. Chronaxia may be defined as the minimal time required for adequate stimulation of a neuromuscular unit by a current strength which is twice that of rheobase.

Determination of the chronaxia gives a convenient index of the state of denervation. Chronaxia below 1 msec. may be construed as being within the range for innervated muscle. The chronaxia for each muscle and nerve is constant. Values between 1 and 10 msec. denote partial innervation. Chronaxia values above 15 msec. indicate complete denervation, and such values may rise as high as 40 to 60 msec. In general, a fall in chronaxia appears to lag behind functional recovery, and in re-innervation voluntary power may be present while the chronaxia is still markedly elevated. (Pollock et al., 1948.)

Electromyography

The electromyogram is an essential tool in the investigation of peripheral nerve injuries. Its use is restricted primarily by the demands of instrumentation. It is capable, however, of yielding precise information as to the state of the neuromuscular unit. Normal muscles at rest show no electrical activity, but with volitional contraction they exhibit a series of action potentials of varied size, frequency, and number. The normal pattern of electrical activity varies in different muscles depending on their size; however, no absolute correlation exists between the electrical potentials of a given muscle and the strength of its contraction.

Two to three weeks after complete interruption of the nerve supply to a muscle, spontaneous discharges (fibrillations) occur at rest and no additional potentials are noted with attempts at volitional contraction. In occasional cases of "physiological block" neither fibrillations nor voluntary motor action potentials are encountered, but normal-appearing action potentials occur with needle movement. Such electromyographic observations suggest the possibility of spontaneous recovery. The number and size of the fibrillation potentials are unimportant.

In partial nerve lesions, a combination of fibrillations and small isolated potentials with volitional contraction is seen. As the process of regeneration commences, fibrillation gradually subsides and large areas of muscle are found which appear "silent," without effort potentials. Eventually, with continuing regeneration, most of the spontaneous activity in the muscle ceases and the only potentials present are those occurring with volitional contraction.

The potential amplitude in normal muscle ranges between 6.0 to 15.0 millivolts. That in re-innervated muscle may show a wide variation ranging between 15 to 500 millivolts. The appearance of spontaneous potentials does not necessarily mean that regeneration will continue until voluntary motor movement is achieved. (Denny-Brown and Pennybacker, 1938; Bauwens, 1944; Harvey and Kuffler, 1944; Ritchie, 1944.)

Injuries of Plexuses
and Peripheral Nerves

IN CONTRAST WITH Chapter 5, which deals with diagnosis of acute nerve injuries, this section is concerned with diagnosis after sufficient time has elapsed for the atrophy, the sensory changes and the other tell-tale marks of injury to have become unequivocally established. In the description of each injury, considerable emphasis has been placed on the means by which the level of nerve injury may be detected. In this connection the reader will find the diagrams of the nerves highly useful for they illustrate a serial order of the branching which is fairly constant from individual to individual. Also of help in locating the level of an injury is the rule—which has few exceptions— that the order in which motor branches enter muscles corresponds with the order in which they arise from the parent nerve trunk, as has been emphasized on page 44. A knowledge of this order is a *sine qua non* not only to the localization of nerve injury but also the recognition of the extent of nerve regeneration.

CHAPTER 10

Injuries of the Cervical Plexus

COMPONENTS OF the cervical plexus are involved infrequently in war wounds. For this reason only the essentials of anatomical distribution of this plexus and some of the clinical consequences of injury are dealt with in the ensuing paragraphs.

Anatomy

The cervical plexus is composed of anterior primary rami C1, C2, C3 and C4 (Fig. 174). It is situated for the most part beneath the sternomastoid muscle. Part of the plexus consists of a number of anastomotic loops which give off branches to skin and muscles; other parts, predominantly muscular in distribution, are made up of individual nerves not joined by anastomoses. Closely associated with the plexus are the accessory and hypoglossal nerves.

The distribution of the cutaneous branches is indicated in Figures 27 to 30 inclusive. The lesser occipital, the great auricular and the anterior cutaneous nerve of the neck are each derived from spinal segments C2 and C3; the supraclavicular nerves from C3 and C4. Since the greater and the third occipital nerves are parts of posterior primary rami they are not included in Figure 174.

The muscular components of the plexus consist of lateral and medial branches. The lateral branches go chiefly to the sternomastoid (C2), the trapezius (C3, C4), the levator scapulae (C3, C4 [and C5]), and the medial and anterior scaleni (C3, C4), whereas the medial branches extend to the diaphragm (C3, C4 [and C5]) via the phrenic, the geniohyoid muscles (C1, C2, C3) by means of the ansa hypoglossi, and to the prevertebral muscles (C1–C4).

The *accessory nerve* arises from cells of the lateral part of the base of anterior horns of cervical segments 1–4. The root fibers emerge from the lateral aspect of these segments and unite to form a common ascending trunk which enters the intracranial cavity through the foramen magnum. Within the skull the trunk is joined by the bulbar rootlets of the vagus nerve, and on passing out of the intracranial cavity through the jugular foramen it leaves the vagus nerve, and descends into the neck to supply, as mentioned, the sternomastoid and the upper third or half of the trapezius. In its extracranial course, the nerve lies at first (together with the vagus and glossopharyngeus) in the interval between the internal jugular vein and internal carotid artery, then passes obliquely downward and lateralward beneath the posterior belly of the digastric muscle to reach the deep part of the sternomastoid muscle. After giving off a branch to this muscle and receiving branches from cervical segments 3 and 4 (Fig. 174), the accessory nerve appears at the posterior border of the sternomastoid at about the level of the

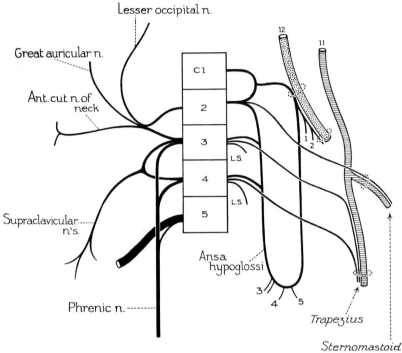

FIGURE 174.   *Diagram of the Cervical Plexus.* The relations of branches of the plexus to hypoglossal (*12*) and accessory (*11*) nerves are indicated. The numbered branches of the ansa hypoglossi innervate the following muscles: *1*, thyrohyoid; *2*, geniohyoid; *3*, omohyoid; *4*, sternothyroid; *5*, sternohyoid. *L.S.* Refers to the levator scapulae.

upper border of the thyroid cartilage. From here it extends obliquely downward through the posterior triangle of the neck, courses under the trapezius, and then penetrates and supplies this muscle.

Injuries

Any of the nerves of the cervical plexus may be injured by penetrating missiles. Division of cutaneous branches can usually be detected in the sensory examination. The area of sensory change following interruption of the great auricular nerve, for instance, is illustrated in

Figure 175. Damage inflicted on branches to cervical muscles may or may not give rise to weakness of movement. With interruption of the accessory nerve, however, the trapezius muscle always suffers and if the interruption is sufficiently high, the sternomastoid is also affected.

Missile wounds in the region of the base of the skull may involve nerves in various combinations, for instance, cranial nerves IX, X, XI and XII (*syndrome of Collet and Sicard*), and if the wound is in the retroparotid region the sympathetic trunk may also be injured, thus giving rise to

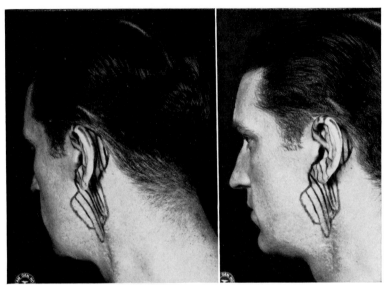

FIGURE 175.   *Region of Sensory Loss Following Severance of the Great Auricular Nerve.* The nerve was damaged during the course of excision of a neurinoma situated in the region of the left carotid sheath. The recurrent branch of the vagus was also damaged, resulting in complete paralysis of the left vocal cord. (R.G.H.)

Horner's syndrome as well. A missile wound or fracture which implicates the region of the foramen lacerum is likely to damage nerves IX and XI with or without X (*Vernet's syndrome*), and wounds similarly located may involve the laryngeal and palatal branches of the Xth nerve (*syndrome of Avellis*). Another syndrome (*Tapia's*) consists of paralysis of the XIIth nerve and of the recurrent laryngeal branch of the Xth, the latter being involved below the level where its branches are given off to the soft palate and pharynx; the XIth and sympathetic trunk may or may not be affected. And finally there is the syndrome of the posterior retroparotid space (*Villaret*), characterized by paralysis of the XIIth, Xth (either above or below the level where it gives off branches to the pharynx and soft palate), the cervical sympathetic, and occasionally the VIIth. Since Villaret published his article on the subject, subsequent authors have added XIth and IXth nerve involvement to the syndrome (Pollock, 1920; Elkin and Woodhall, 1944).

The Sternomastoid

The sternomastoid muscle receives its motor supply mainly, if not wholly, from the accessory nerve. The branch reaching it from the cervical plexus is afferent. Among other actions, the muscle turns the

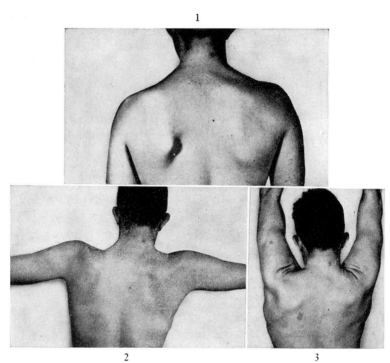

FIGURE 176.   *Trapezius Palsy, Left.* The patient sustained an oblique penetrating wound of the right side of the neck. After seven months, at the time the first two photographs were taken, there were upward and lateral displacement of the scapula, atrophy of the superior third of the left trapezius and flaring of the vertebral border of the scapula. Abduction of the arm was not possible above 90 degrees. Four months later, after spontaneous regeneration of the accessory nerve had occurred, abduction of the arm can be well performed although some lateral displacement of the scapula is still evident. (A.G.H.)

head to the opposite side, a movement which is somewhat weakened when the muscle is paralyzed. In unilateral sternomastoid palsy there is no abnormality in the position of the head. Weakness in rotating the head to the opposite side is experienced, and when flexion of the neck is attempted the chin turns slightly to the paralyzed side by reason of the unopposed action of the normal contralateral sternomastoid. In due time the sternomastoid muscle undergoes complete atrophy.

The Trapezius

As mentioned, the trapezius alone may be affected if the accessory nerve is interrupted below the level where the branch to the sterno-mastoid muscle is given off. The accessory nerve courses superficially through the posterior cervical triangle, making it peculiarly susceptible to injury during operative interventions (Woodhall, 1952), including

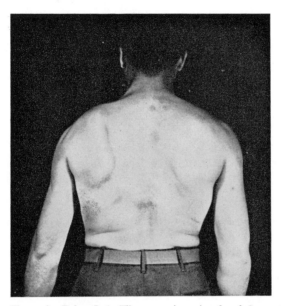

FIGURE 177.   *Trapezius Palsy, Left.* The posterior triangle of the neck was pene-trated by a bullet. Subsequently the patient became unable to shrug the left shoulder or to raise the left arm above the horizontal plane. The upper one half of the trapezius is atrophic. An attempt to abduct the arm leads to flaring of the vertebral border and to lateral displacement of the scapula. (A.G.H.)

incision at the angle of the jaw for the removal of suppurating lymph nodes (Bodechtel et al., 1951).

The trapezius muscle derives its motor supply from two sources: the upper one third or one half of the muscle is supplied by the accessory nerve, and the remainder by elements of the cervical plexus (C3 and C4). Some of the cervical plexus components passing to the trapezius are probably afferent.

Accessory nerve palsies are illustrated in some detail because of their relative frequency in the war-wounded. When, in trapezius palsy, the shoulder girdle is at rest, the scapula is somewhat higher than that of the normal side and is rotated so that its flared inferior angle is closer to the spine than the superior angle (Fig. 176). This position is due to the action of the levator scapulae and rhomboids on the scapula at the acro-

mioclavicular joint. The scapular position in trapezius palsy is accentuated when the arm is moved laterally against resistance (Figs. 177, 178),
but on forward flexion the flaring of the inferior angle virtually disap-

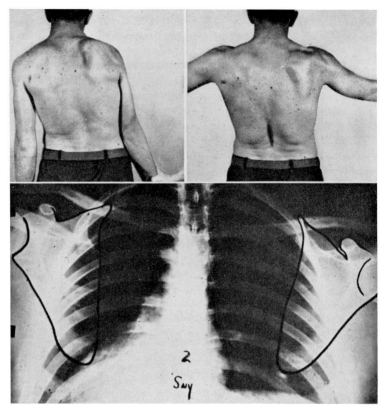

FIGURE 178.   *Trapezius Palsy, Right.* A shell fragment penetrated the region of
the right supraspinatus muscle four months previously. Attempted
abduction of the arm from the resting position against resistance
leads to flaring of the vertebral border of the scapula. With
abduction limited to the horizontal plane, the same phenomenon
occurs and the scapula is rotated downward and forward. This
characteristic flaring of the vertebral border in trapezius palsy is to
be compared with the equally characteristic winging of the inferior
angle caused by serratus anterior palsy (Fig. 194).

A roentgenogram of the scapulae in another case of trapezius
palsy, right, illustrates again the characteristic downward and lateral
displacement of the scapula during an effort to carry out abduction. (A.G.H.)

pears because of serratus anterior muscle action (Fig. 179). The upper
one third or one half of the trapezius is, as a rule, completely paralyzed,
while the remainder is relatively normal. Despite elevation of the scapula
brought about by the action of the levator scapulae—as a consequence

of which the levator undergoes hypertrophy—a slight sagging of the affected shoulder is of common occurrence and can be demonstrated by having the patient extend his arms in front of him and slightly downward with the palms touching each other. The fingertips of the affected side extend beyond those of the normal side. Because of the shoulder

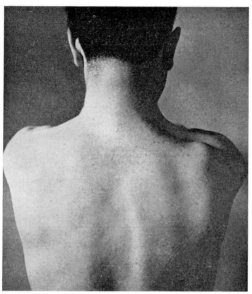

FIGURE 179.   *Trapezius Palsy, Right.* Elevation of the arms in the forward plane of the body, i.e., flexion, causes lateral displacement of the scapula. Note atrophy of the superior third of the trapezius muscle and the firm approximation of the inferior angle of the scapula to the chest wall. Compare with illustrations of serratus anterior palsy (Figs. 193, 194). (B.G.H.)

sagging a deep-seated nagging pain in the arm is often complained of (Wartenberg 1953).

The Levator Scapulae

This muscle is supplied by branches of primary rami C3 and C4 and by a component of the brachial plexus, the dorsal scapular nerve, which arises from undivided anterior primary ramus C5. The levator scapulae and the rhomboids have the action of rotating the scapula so that its inferior angle moves medially and backward (medial rotation). These muscles thus serve as antagonists to the serratus anterior.

The Rhomboid Muscles

The main innervation of the rhomboid muscles is derived from the dorsal scapular nerve (C5), a component of the brachial plexus. These muscles probably receive no motor supply from C4 or higher. Adduction of the shoulder can be accomplished to some degree by the combined action of the rhomboids, latissimus dorsi, and the upper part of the trapezius.

The Scaleni

The medial, posterior and anterior scalenes are innervated by twigs given off anterior primary rami C3 to C8 inclusive. They are lateral flexors of the vertebral column and aid in respiration by elevating the first and second ribs. They are seldom involved in war wounds.

The Diaphragm

The fibers of the phrenic nerve are derived constantly from segment C4 and variably from C3 and C5. The roots of the nerve emerge from the more proximal parts of undivided anterior primary rami. As the nerve descends vertically, it passes in front of the scalenus anterior and then traverses the mediastinum to gain and innervate the diaphragm.

The phrenic nerve is occasionally interrupted by missiles entering the medial supraclavicular region. Unilateral interruption of the phrenic is often manifested by dyspnea, and there may be radiating pains in the shoulder region and vague gastric complaints, especially when the left phrenic nerve is affected. Fluoroscopy usually reveals on the involved side an elevation of the diaphragm, paradoxical movements of the diaphragm with respirations, and great reduction in the movement of the lower part of the lung. The occasional absence of paralysis of the diaphragm has been ascribed to anastomosis of the phrenic with the subclavian nerve (Foerster, 1929).

CHAPTER 11

Injuries of the Brachial Plexus

Composition of the Plexus

THE BRACHIAL plexus is composed of anterior primary rami of spinal segments C5, C6, C7, C8 and T1 (Fig. 180). Its components are the following:

(1) undivided anterior primary rami
(2) trunks—upper, middle, lower
(3) divisions of the trunks—anterior and posterior
(4) cords—lateral, posterior and medial

The *undivided anterior primary rami*, which issue from the region just distal to the series of intervertebral foramina, are situated between the scalenes. Ramus C5 may occasionally receive an accession from ramus C4, and T1 frequently from T2. From undivided primary rami there arise two nerves of consequence: the long thoracic and the dorsal scapular.

The *trunks* of the brachial plexus are three in number: the *upper*, which contains fibers of spinal segments C4, C5 and C6; the *middle*, which is a continuation of undivided anterior primary ramus C7, and the *lower*, which includes fibers from C8, T1 and sometimes from T2. The trunks are situated mainly in the supraclavicular fossa, all three commencing just distal to the scalenes. The upper trunk gives origin to the suprascapular and subclavian nerves.

The *divisions* are the means by which fibers of the trunks reassemble to gain the ventral and the dorsal aspects of the limb; those reaching ventral parts cross through the *anterior* divisions, those destined for dorsal parts extend through the *posterior* divisions. The divisions are situated deep to the middle third of the clavicle and they extend distally to a point just beyond the lateral border of the first rib.

Variations in the pattern of the divisions of the trunks occur with some frequency. One of the most common variants consists of an additional anterior division which joins the middle trunk to the medial cord. When this connection exists, an injury of the middle trunk may lead to disability in the field of distribution of the ulnar nerve.

The only peripheral nerve arising from brachial plexus divisions is the lateral anterior thoracic (Fig. 180). This nerve is derived from the anterior divisions of the upper and middle trunks (cervical segments 5, 6, 7).

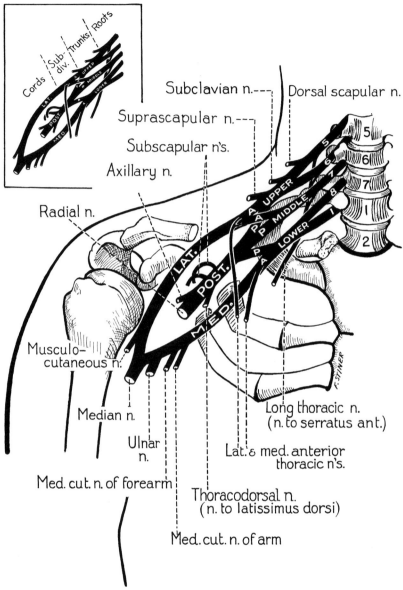

FIGURE 180.   *Diagram of the Brachial Plexus Showing Its Various Constituents.*
For purposes of clarity the components of the plexus have been
separated and drawn out of scale. It will be noted that peripheral
nerves arise from various components of the plexus: *undivided
anterior primary rami* (indicated by [C] 5, 6, 7, 8, and [T]1), *trunks*
(upper, middle and lower), *divisions* (anterior and posterior) and
cords (lateral, posterior and medial). The median nerve arises from
the heads of the lateral and medial cords. Not infrequently an
anterior division of the middle trunk connects with the medial cord.

The *cords*, which are situated in the axilla, are formed by the union of divisions. The *lateral* (outer) cord is derived from the anterior divisions of the upper and middle trunks, the *medial* (inner) cord from anterior division of the lower trunk and frequently also from the middle one, and the *posterior* cord from posterior divisions of all three trunks. The three cords give off the majority of the peripheral nerves: ·thus, from the *lateral* cord issues the musculocutaneous nerve and the lateral head of the median nerve; from the *medial* cord, the medial anterior thoracic nerve, the ulnar nerve, the medial cutaneous nerves of forearm and arm, the medial head of the median nerve, and a branch to the intercostobrachial nerve (the last-named is not shown in Fig. 180); from the *posterior*. cord the axillary, the radial, the thoracodorsal, and the two subscapular nerves.

Certain components of the plexus are in close relation with blood vessels. The lower trunk is immediately behind the subclavian artery. All cords are near the axillary artery: the *medial* lies at first behind, then medial to this artery, the *lateral* remains lateral to it, and the *posterior* shifts from a lateral to a posterior position in relation to it (Fig. 189).

Sympathetic fibers are present in all parts of the plexus; they consist of postganglionic fibers derived from the sympathetic ganglionated chain. The only preganglionic fibers in the brachial plexus are those coursing distally in undivided anterior primary ramus T1.

Pre- and Post-fixation

In the *pre-fixed plexus* all components are shifted upward approximately one segment. Such a plexus possesses a contingent from ramus C4 as well as an implemented ramus C5; T1 contributes little. The *post-fixed plexus*, characterized by a shift of all components downward, has a scanty supply of fibers from C5. T1 is unusually strong and there is almost always a branch from T2.

Injuries

The position of the missile tract gives some indication of what components of the brachial plexus are likely to have been injured. If the wound is above the clavicle, the upper and middle trunks and their emergent nerves are most likely to have suffered; if below the clavicle, cords and their derivatives will be the structures most subject to damage. Blood vessels are more likely to be damaged by axillary than by supraclavicular or infraclavicular wounds.

In the examination of a patient who has been wounded in the region of the brachial plexus, it is of utmost importance to take into account the possibility of injury to bones, joints, muscles and blood vessels, for such injuries may in themselves so interfere with the performance of movements that the degree of damage to nerve trunks is difficult to assess. Another point is that the explosive force of a missile may temporarily affect all components of the plexus although the missile may actually have penetrated only one component. Under such circumstances the examination gives little reliable information as to the scope of the injury until the period of total paralysis—usually one to three weeks—is past.

INJURIES OF SPINAL ROOTS

Injuries of individual nerve roots by the common missiles of war are rare. Due to the other physical hazards of training and combat, closed

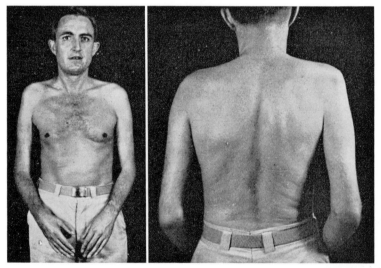

FIGURE 181.   *Upper Brachial Plexus Palsy.* A missile penetrated the base of the right side of the neck nine months previously. The brachial plexus was explored and undivided anterior primary rami C5 and C6 sutured end-to-end. Atrophy of deltoid, biceps brachii and the spinati is visible. The triceps is not affected. Note the normal appearance of the hand. (W.R.)

neck injuries are common; of these, *rupture of a cervical intervertebral disc* deserves brief comment. The onset of pain in the neck, shoulder, scapular region, anterior chest and/or arm (of radicular distribution) may occur spontaneously or after trauma to the neck. Compression of the head and pressure exerted over the affected spinous processes will initiate the pain. The head may be tilted to the opposite side. Weakness of the triceps and biceps muscles is common, deep reflexes are usually lost, and characteristic dermatomal sensory deficits develop (Fig. 14; p. 21). The cervical discs most commonly ruptured are those between vertebrae C5 and C6 and C6 and C7, compressing spinal roots C6 and C7 respectively.

Injuries of the Most Proximal Part of the Plexus

Paralysis of serratus anterior is indicative of an injury either of the nerve to this muscle (the long thoracic) or of the undivided anterior primary rami through which its fibers course. The same applies to the levator scapulae and rhomboids, for the nerve to these muscles (the

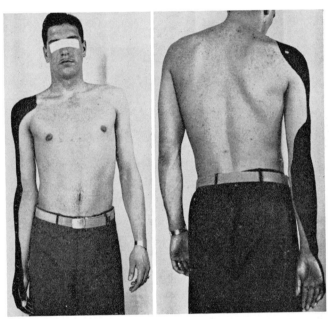

FIGURE 182.   *Injury of Proximal Components of the Brachial Plexus.* The patient received a severe blow to the right clavicular region. The sensory loss is in the region of distribution of C4 (distal part), C5, C6, C7, C8 (dorsum of hand only), and T1. The flexion contraction of the little finger also indicates involvement of T1. The brunt of the injury fell on the undivided anterior primary rami of the plexus. (B.G.H.)

dorsal scapular) also emerges from an undivided anterior primary ramus; however, since each of these muscles receives accessions from the cervical plexus, damage to the brachial plexus component is more likely to cause weakness than paralysis.

Injuries sustained by undivided anterior primary rami alone are manifested by segmental distribution of the disability, motor as well as sensory.

When the upper part of the plexus is damaged the shoulder and upper arm are chiefly affected (Fig. 181). Not infrequently the sensory changes outweigh the motor disability (Figs. 182, 183). In lower plexus injuries the hand and forearm suffer most.

Should undivided anterior primary ramus T1 be interrupted, Horner's syndrome will be apparent; if a lesion of this ramus is irritative,

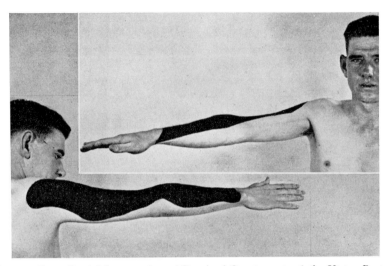

FIGURE 183.   *Partial Interruption of Proximal Components of the Upper Part of the Brachial Plexus Injury, Right.* The shoulder was injured in a jeep accident. Examination reveals weakness of movements performed by deltoid, supraspinatus and biceps muscles. The segmental distribution of sensory deficit (C4 [partly], C5 and C6) suggests strongly that lesion is in proximal components of the plexus. (B.G.H.)

as occasionally it is, pupillary dilatation and widening of the palpebral fissure will be manifest.

INJURIES OF ROOTS AND TRUNKS

Here, too, the motor and sensory changes tend to take on segmental distribution. Three types of syndrome may be distinguished: upper, lower, and middle.

The Upper Type (of Duchenne-Erb)

When well developed, the syndrome of the upper type of brachial plexus palsy is easily recognized (Fig. 181). The muscles affected are those innervated by spinal segments C5 and C6: a list of these can be seen at a glance by referring to Table 1 (p. 34). The position of the limb is characteristic: limp at the side, adducted, and medially rotated. When the arm is passively supinated it quickly returns to its position of medial rotation. Because of the weight of the arm, the shoulder girdle is lowered and the capsule of the shoulder joint is stretched, as a result of which a diastasis of the joint space occurs. Movements dependent on forearm and hand muscles are intact, whereas those at shoulder and elbow joints are greatly restricted: the patient is unable to elevate his arm either in forward flexion or in abduction (*deltoid, supraspinatus*) —nor, when the arm is placed in a position of medial (internal) rotation, can he rotate it laterally (*infraspinatus, teres minor*). He is unable to flex the forearm at the elbow (*biceps, brachialis, brachioradialis*) and, when the forearm is placed in a position of pronation he is unable to supinate it (*supinator*). The movements by which a glass is lifted to the

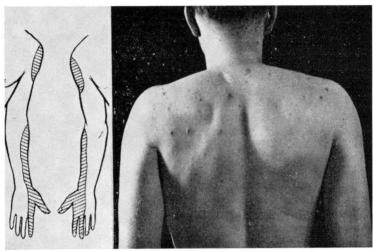

FIGURE 184.   *Injury of the Suprascapular Nerve and of the Upper Trunk of Brachial Plexus, Left.* Shell fragments penetrated the left supra-clavicular region. Four months later the suprascapular nerve was repaired and neurolysis of the upper trunk of the brachial plexus performed. One year after the injury there are sensory deficits in the fields of the axillary, musculocutaneous, median and radial nerves, and atrophy of the infraspinatus and deltoid. (W.R.)

lips are considerably impaired. Wartenberg (1953) has pointed out that German students referred to this impairment as paralysis of the "nervus poculomotorius," *poculus* meaning "drinking cup." The consequences of interruption of the upper trunk of the plexus and of the suprascapular nerve are illustrated in Figure 184.

Sensibility is in large measure preserved, the only deficit being in the region of the deltoid and along the course of the musculocutaneous nerve. Interruption of components from C6 often leads to greater sensory change than does interruption of those from C5.

The distribution of the disability differs when the plexus is post-fixed or pre-fixed: the brunt of the injury falls on deltoid and spinati when the plexus is *post-fixed*, and includes pronator teres and radial extensors when *pre-fixed*.

The Lower Type (of Klumpke)

This type of brachial plexus palsy is most often encountered as the result of forceful upward pull of the shoulder during birth. It may occur in adults as a consequence of being dragged by the arm. Since the muscles affected are supplied by spinal segments C8 and T1 the chief disabilities are in finger and wrist movements, with the flexors of the hand and fingers being most affected—as in combined median and ulnar nerve palsy. The extensors of the forearm (radial nerve) may also be implicated, particularly the abductor pollicis longus, but their degree of involvement is comparatively slight.

Sensory deficit is to be noted along the ulnar side of the arm, forearm, and hand. If sympathetic fibers traversing the proximal part of undivided anterior primary ramus T1 are damaged, ptosis of the eyelid and miosis of the corresponding side will also occur.

Where the plexus is pre-fixed or post-fixed the distribution of the disability is accordingly shifted up or down. In injury of the *pre-fixed* plexus the small muscles of the hand are only slightly affected and the sensory deficit usually is evident in the region of T2 and perhaps also in a part of T3; in injury of the *post-fixed* plexus the flexors of hand and forearm are likely to be included in the paralysis, and the distribution of sensory loss extends no lower than the level of T1 or C8.

The Middle Type

Interruption of the middle trunk, or of the corresponding undivided anterior primary ramus, involves chiefly the fibers extending to the radial nerve. Extensors of arm and forearm are weakened; however, the brachioradialis is not affected since it is supplied chiefly from spinal segment C6. Sensory deficit is minor and restricted: it consists usually of a narrow strip of hypesthesia on the back of the forearm and on the radial aspect of the dorsum of the hand.

Total Plexus Palsy

As has been pointed out (p. 212), missile wounds of the brachial plexus produce a temporary loss of function of the entire limb. Only after the acute phase of the injury has passed can the degree of damage be accurately determined. Since the brachial plexus is relatively widespread, damage to all its components by a missile is rare. Total plexus palsy occurs most commonly in connection with a fall from a moving motorcycle or other vehicle.

The arm hangs limp. All muscles of the upper arm, forearm, hand and fingers are paralyzed and undergo atrophy—most of the shoulder musculature likewise (Figs. 157 and 158). Sensory deficit varies: it may be evident as far proximally as the shoulder girdle (Fig. 190), but as a rule extends proximally only to the middle third of the upper arm (which it completely encircles), the deficit reaching more proximally on the medial side of the arm than on the lateral.

Injuries of Cords

Injuries of cords of the brachial plexus give rise to fairly simple patterns of impaired function, as may be gathered from a study of Figure 180. *Lateral cord* injuries implicate the fields of distribution of the

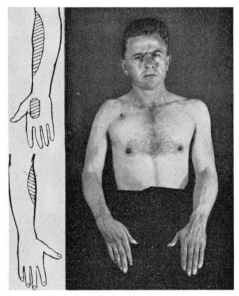

FIGURE 185.   *Pistol Wound of Right Infraclavicular Region, Involving the Lateral Cord of the Brachial Plexus and Radial Nerve.* The site of the through and through wound will be noted. The German prison surgeon regarded the extremity as useless and for one month there was complete paralysis, whereupon rapid resolution of the neural defect set in. Nine months after the injury, when the photograph was taken, there is slight atrophy of the biceps and of the extensors of the forearm. The deformity of the hand suggests combined median and ulnar paralysis, but all movements can be performed and sensory loss in the field of the median nerve is minimal. The deformity is the result of an irritative nerve lesion and prolonged immobilization. (W.R.)

musculocutaneous and the lateral head of the median nerve—the latter (Fig. 208) supplying all median-innervated muscles except for intrinsic muscles of the hand. Injuries of this cord are manifested chiefly by weakness of flexion and pronation of the forearm. Sensory deficit can usually be detected on the radial aspect of the forearm but its field is small. An example of interruption of the lateral cord and the radial nerve is illustrated in Figure 185. Occasionally this cord may be injured in dislocation of the humerus. *Medial cord* injuries affect the ulnar, the medial head of the median (which supplies intrinsic muscles of the thumb and index finger), and the medial cutaneous nerves of the arm and forearm. Thus, the clinical picture simulates that of combined ulnar and median palsy (Fig. 186). Sensory loss is to be found along the medial border of the limb. This cord is also commonly affected by dislocation of the humerus. In *posterior cord* injuries the disability is apparent in the fields of distribution of radial, axillary, sub-

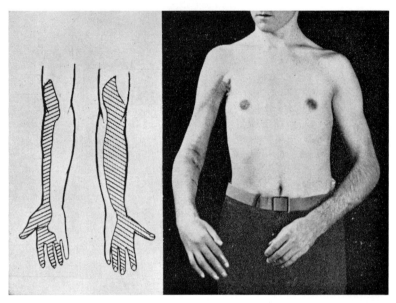

FIGURE 186. *Injury of the Radial Nerve and the Medial Cord of the Brachial Plexus.* A bullet wound of the right axilla was incurred four months previously. Radial nerve injury is indicated by the wrist drop and the site of sensory deficit; damage of the medial cord of the plexus, by palsy of the median and ulnar. The musculocutaneous nerve also is affected. (W.R.)

scapular and thoracodorsal nerves; the disability consists of weakness of the extensors, difficulty in elevating the limb, and impairment of medial rotation of the arm at the shoulder. An instance is illustrated in Figures 187 and 188.

INJURIES OF THE MEDIAN, ULNAR AND RADIAL NERVES AT THE AXILLARY LEVEL

Injuries involving the median, ulnar and radial nerves jointly in the region of their emergence from the brachial plexus give rise to paralyses closely simulating those due to plexus injuries inasmuch as in early stages the entire arm is affected. These nerves lie close together in the distal part of the axilla (Fig. 189), and therefore are apt to be simultaneously involved by a penetrating missile. Occasionally the musculocutaneous nerve may be secondarily affected, as may also the medial cutaneous nerves of the arm and forearm. Other nerves supplying muscles of the shoulder retain their functional integrity.

Hemorrhage from adjacent vessels is a common accompaniment, and if as a result of vessel damage there is generalized ischemia of the limb—a point which can be gauged by the presence or the absence of the

FIGURE 187.   *Interruption of Upper Trunk and Posterior Cord of Brachial Plexus.* Shell fragments penetrated the left supraclavicular region eleven months previously. Interruption of the posterior cord of the plexus is indicated by atrophy of triceps (*radial n.*), deltoid (*axillary n.*), latissimus dorsi (*thoracodorsal n.*) and the teres major (*lower subscapular n.*). Injury of the upper trunk is evidenced by atrophy of the biceps (*musculocutaneous n.*), and the pectoralis major (*lateral anterior thoracic n.*). On lateral elevation of the arm the muscle bellies of the posterior wall of the axilla are not visible (cf. Fig. 61). Figure 188 illustrates the same case from the posterior view. (W.R.)

radial pulse—nerves otherwise little damaged will suffer further functional loss. Such loss is, however, usually evanescent.

In early stages of the full-blown syndrome, the clinical examination shows that all three nerves are affected in their entirety, though sometimes the upper branch to the triceps is spared (Fig. 190). But as weeks pass by, spontaneous restoration of function, with the degree of restitution differing in the different nerves, usually becomes evident. This early involvement of all three nerves and the subsequent partial functional restoration occurring at a different tempo in the nerves is the chief

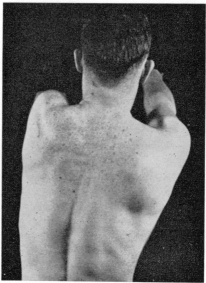

FIGURE 188.   *Interruption of the Upper Trunk and Posterior Cord of the Brachial Plexus.* This is the same case illustrated from the anterior aspect in Figure 187. Supra- and infraspinatus muscles (supplied by the suprascapular nerve) are atrophic. On forward flexion of the arms the trunk bends away from the affected side, as may also be noted in the front view; this trunk movement aids abduction of the arm in deltoid paralysis. (W.R.)

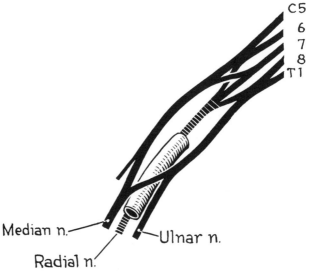

FIGURE 189.   *Diagram of the Brachial Plexus and the Relationship of the Median, Ulnar and Radial Nerves to the Axillary Artery.*

characteristic of the syndrome under discussion. In contrast to lower root injuries, Horner's syndrome is absent.

The symptoms are, in general, no different than those resulting from other nerve injuries. Illusions are, however, commonly complained of. For instance the patient may for several hours after the injury have the

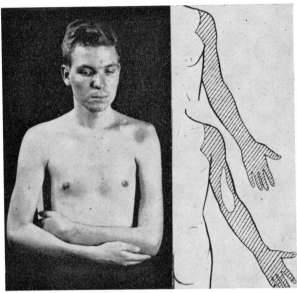

FIGURE 190.   *A Case of Total Brachial Plexus Palsy.* The injury occurred three months previously when a jeep overturned. The arm is incapable of voluntary movements. The descent of the head of the humerus is due not only to paralysis of all the muscles involved in normal fixation of the humerus in the glenoid fossa, but also to stretching of the articular capsule by the weight of the dependent arm. Sensory loss is total, except in the region of the arm supplied by branches of the radial nerve. Six months after injury a return of triceps function was noted. The supraclavicular nerves also have suffered. (W.R.)

impression that his arm has been torn away, an impression not much lessened when he repeatedly looks at his arm. Some patients find during the first two or three months that when they attempt to grasp or scratch the painful, paralyzed limb with the normal hand they do not find the limb in the place where they supposed it to be. (Vogel, 1941.)

CHAPTER 12

Injuries of Peripheral Nerves
Derived from the Brachial Plexus

IN THE ENSUING pages the peripheral nerves are presented seriatim in accordance with the parts of the plexus from which they spring. Those arising from proximal parts of the plexus and extending to shoulder muscles are considered first.

The Long Thoracic Nerve*

ANATOMY

The long thoracic nerve arises from undivided anterior primary rami C5, C6 and C7 shortly after they emerge from intervertebral foramina. It traverses the neck behind the cords of the brachial plexus, enters the medial aspect of the axilla, and then continues downward on the lateral wall of the thorax to reach the serratus anterior muscle (Fig. 191). Muscle slips of the serratus are supplied, in turn, by individual branches of the descending nerve trunk: in general, innervation of the upper part of the muscle is derived from spinal segment C5, the middle part from segment C6, and the lower part from segment C7.

INJURIES

Because of its straight course and fixation by the scaleni and muscle slips of the serratus anterior, the long thoracic nerve is subject to undue stretching. Serratus palsy occurs not infrequently, for instance, in furniture movers. Because of its exposed position, the long thoracic nerve is sometimes injured during removal of the contents of the axilla in radical breast operations. Isolated serratus palsy due to penetrating missiles is of rare occurrence. The long thoracic nerve may, however, be affected along with other nerves by wounds involving the most proximal part of the brachial plexus.

Appearance of the Shoulder

In total paralysis of the serratus anterior relatively little change is apparent when the arms are at rest at the sides of the body. Careful inspection will, however, reveal (1) that the shoulder girdle is displaced

* This nerve is known also as the *posterior thoracic nerve*, the *external respiratory nerve of Bell*, and the *nerve to the serratus anterior*.

slightly backward, as is also the acromial end of the clavicle, (2) that the lower part of the scapula has undergone slight winging, and (3) that, owing to the action of the rhomboids and levator scapulae, the scapula is medially rotated so that its lower part is closer than usual to the vertebral column (Fig. 192).

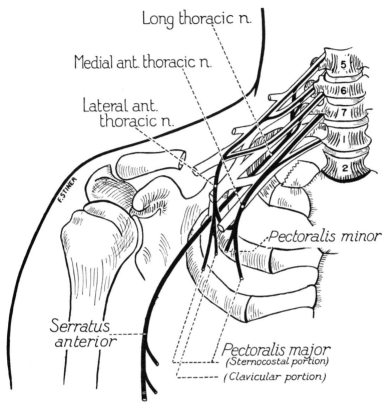

Long thoracic n.

Medial ant. thoracic n.

Lateral ant. thoracic n.

Pectoralis minor

Serratus anterior

Pectoralis major
(Sternocostal portion)

(Clavicular portion)

FIGURE 191.   *The Course and Distribution of the Long Thoracic and Anterior Thoracic Nerves.* The names of the muscles supplied by each of these nerves are italicized.

Motor Power

Normal movement of the shoulder girdle is accomplished by individual motor and fixator muscles which function synchronously during successive phases of movement. The serratus anterior contributes significantly to this synchronization. In forward movement of the shoulder (abduction of the scapula) and in pushing movements the serratus anterior keeps the scapula close to the thoracic wall, and when the arm is raised in forward flexion or in abduction this muscle is largely responsible for rotating the scapula so that its inferior angle moves laterally and forward.

When, in serratus anterior palsy, any of these movements is attempted, the scapular shift produces a striking deformity of the shoulder girdle.

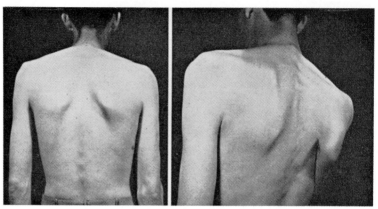

FIGURE 192.   *Serratus Anterior Palsy, Right.* The patient injured his neck while demonstrating a commando hold. The findings at that time suggested an ill-defined cervical disc syndrome. One year after injury the inferior angle of the scapula is slightly winged when the arm is at rest, but when the outstretched arm is thrust forward the winging is sharply accentuated. Abduction of the arm above 90 degrees was not significantly impaired. (A.G.H.)

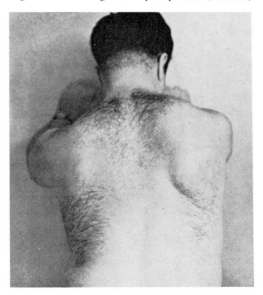

FIGURE 193.   *Serratus Anterior Palsy, Right, Incomplete.* Winging of inferior angle of scapula is minimal. Abduction of the arm was not impaired. (A.G.H.)

On forward movement of the shoulder, which can be carried out fairly well by the pectoralis major and levator scapulae, elevation of the shoulder occurs simultaneously, but more striking is the dorsal and lateral displacement of the vertebral border of the scapula, especially its inferior angle (winging). A pushing movement has the same effect (Fig. 193), as does also elevation of the arm over the head. Winging of the

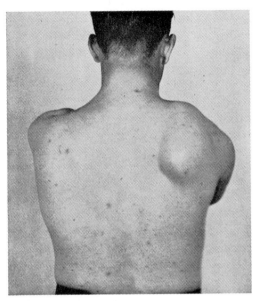

FIGURE 194.   *Winging of the Scapula in Serratus Anterior Palsy.* When elevation of the arm is attempted the scapula becomes winged and moves upward and laterally. Abduction of the arm was not impaired. (H.G.H.)

scapula is more pronounced during forward flexion of the arms (Figs. 192, 194) than during abduction, the reason being that during forward flexion the lower part of the serratus anterior is largely responsible for turning the scapula round the vertical and frontal axis, whereas during abduction the middle part of the trapezius goes into activity and turns the scapula in the sagittal axis. During abduction of the arm (in the presence of anterior serratus palsy), the scapula is strongly adducted by means of the trapezius and rhomboids so that its vertebral border is pressed against the thorax. Furthermore, during this movement the lower part of the trapezius and the pectoralis minor are capable of rotating the scapula laterally and upward and thus, through this *supplemental movement*, sometimes permitting the arm to be elevated somewhat above the horizontal plane.

The illustrations of paralysis of the serratus anterior should be compared with those of trapezius palsy (Figs. 177–179); the differential diagnosis may be further clarified by a study of the illustrations of combined trapezius and serratus palsies (Figs. 195–197).

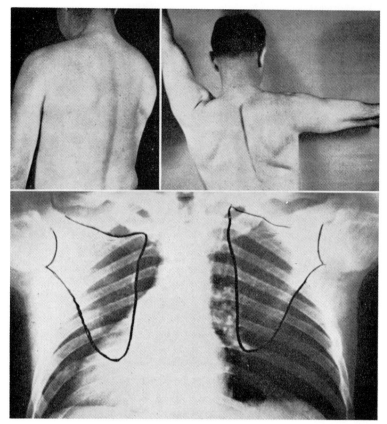

FIGURE 195.   *Incomplete Trapezius and Serratus Anterior Palsies, Right.* This
patient was thrown from a vehicle and landed on his right shoulder.
Eight months after injury, a distinct winging of the inferior angle
of the right scapula could be induced. Electrical studies showed
paresis of the serratus anterior and of the middle and lower thirds
of the right trapezius. Note the medial shift of the scapula, the lack
of fixation, and the absence of rotation during efforts to complete
abduction. The roentgenogram of the scapular shift should be compared with that of isolated trapezius palsy (Fig. 178). (W.R.)

The Anterior Thoracic Nerves

There are at least two anterior thoracic (or "pectoral") nerves, the
medial and the lateral. The *medial anterior thoracic nerve*, derived from
spinal segments C8 and T1, arises from the most proximal part of the
medial cord of the plexus, whereas the *lateral anterior thoracic nerve*,
from segments C5, C6 and C7, emerges from the anterior divisions of
the upper and middle trunks (Figs. 180 and 191). They both descend,
communicating en route by means of an anastomotic loop which partly
encircles the axillary artery.

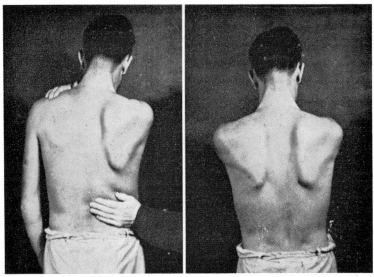

FIGURE 196.   *Bilateral Serratus Anterior Palsy Associated with Bilateral Paresis of Middle and Lower Thirds of the Trapezius, and Unilateral Vocal Cord and Diaphragmatic Palsies, Developing in the Course of an Obscure Meningoradiculo-encephalitis.* Forward thrust of the flexed arms causes almost complete dorsal dislocation of the scapulae. Abduction is limited bilaterally to 90 degrees. (A.G.H.)

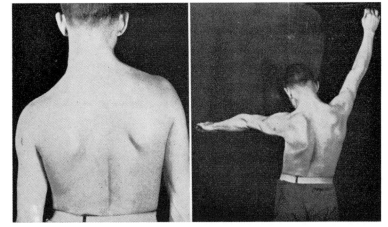

FIGURE 197.   *Isolated Complete Trapezius and Serratus Anterior Palsies, Left.* A shell fragment penetrated the left posterior cervical triangle and coursed down and posteriorly. The resulting deformity represents a classical combined palsy of these muscles (supplied by the accessory and long thoracic nerves). At rest, the left shoulder droops and there is minimal flaring of the entire vertebral border of the left scapula. There is some compensatory elevation of the right shoulder girdle with a tendency for the head to rotate to the opposite side. Abduction is severely compromised and is possible to 90 degrees only in the forward plane of the body. At this point, or with thrust of the flexed arm, a severe winging of the inferior angle of the scapula develops. (W.R.)

The nerves are distributed to the pectoralis major and minor in the following fashion: the medial anterior thoracic nerve, joined by anastomotic fibers from the lateral nerve (from segment C7), supplies the pectoralis minor and the more inferior part of the sternocostal portion of the pectoralis major. The lateral anterior thoracic is distributed to the clavicular as well as to the (more superior) sternocostal portion of the pectoralis major, but not to the pectoralis minor. Thus, the pectoralis minor is innervated by segments C7, C8 and T1, the clavicular portion of the pectoralis major by C5 and C6, and the sternocostal part by C5, C6, C7, C8 and T1.

The anterior thoracic nerves are of relatively little clinical importance. Atrophy of the pectoralis major will tend to corroborate other localizing signs of injury to the brachial plexus (Figs. 186, 187). The shoulder may be higher or lower than that of the normal side and it may be displaced slightly backward. Paralysis of the pectoralis minor and the lower part of the pectoralis major is betrayed by weakness on the patient's part in lowering the shoulder; however, he is fully capable of moving it forward and upward. On elevating the patient's shoulders on the two sides by exerting upward pressure on the axillae, the examiner will notice that the shoulder of the affected side rises higher than that of the normal side. When the patient raises his two arms before him, the one on the affected side tends to deviate laterally. Moreover, because of paralysis of the pectoralis major there is considerable weakness in adduction of the arm.

The Dorsal Scapular Nerve

The dorsal scapular nerve is one of the few derived from the proximal part of the brachial plexus (Fig. 198). It arises mainly from spinal segment C5, extends through the corresponding anterior spinal root and, on emerging from the undivided primary ramus, courses downward behind the brachial plexus to reach the medial border of the scapula. En route it innervates the levator scapulae, the rhomboid major, and the rhomboid minor. The levator scapulae is supplied also from segments C3 and C4, and the rhomboids from C5 and C6.

The rhomboids are small muscles, but normally their contraction can be seen and felt when the patient "squares" (adducts) his shoulder against resistance (Fig. 54) or lowers his arm from the elevated position. In addition to adducting the scapula, these muscles together with the levator scapulae rotate the scapula so that its inferior angle moves medially. Thus, these muscles are antagonists of the serratus anterior.

Following total interruption of the dorsal scapular nerve, which causes paralysis of the rhomboids and paresis of the levator scapulae, the vertebral border of the scapula, especially its lower part, is displaced dorsally, forming a prominence under the skin. Frequently the scapula is also shifted laterally. When the patient attempts to "square" or to elevate his shoulders, which can be well performed by the intact trapezius and other shoulder elevators, the scapula of the affected side

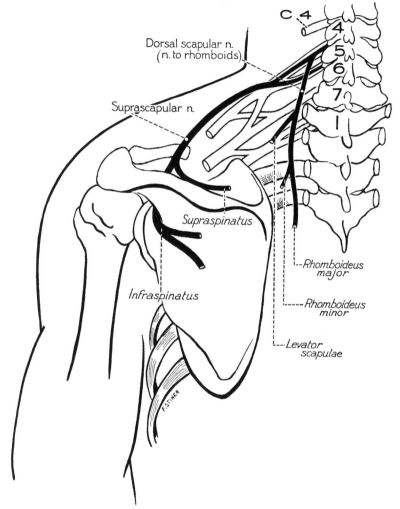

FIGURE 198.   *Diagram of the Course and Distribution of the Dorsal Scapular and Suprascapular Nerves.* Neither has cutaneous branches. The muscles supplied are indicated in italics.

assumes a somewhat oblique position, the upper part of its vertebral border moving medially and the lower part laterally. During this movement, which occurs at the acromioclavicular joint, the inferior angle of the scapula is brought against the rib cage. The dorsal displacement of the lower part of the scapula also disappears when the arm is elevated over the head, but reappears again when the arm is lowered. (Foerster, 1929.)

The Subclavian Nerve

The subclavian nerve, derived from spinal segments C5 and C6, emerges from the upper trunk of the brachial plexus (Fig. 180). It descends in the posterior triangle of the neck in front of the third part of the subclavian artery to reach the subclavian muscle.

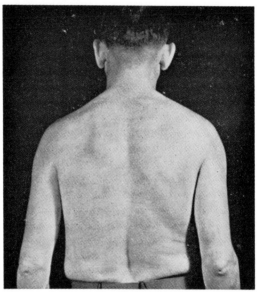

FIGURE 199.   *Isolated Involvement of the Suprascapular Nerve in Obscure Infection.* There is atrophy of the supra- and infraspinatus muscles, manifested clinically by paresis of external rotation of the arm. (A.G.H.)

The subclavius muscle serves as a depressor of the lateral end of the clavicle. It also draws the clavicle medially toward the sternum, and thus steadies the clavicle and prevents luxation at the sternoclavicular joint during movements of the shoulder girdle. Paralysis of the subclavius is usually manifested by slight forward displacement of the lateral end of the clavicle. There is no noteworthy functional disturbance.

The Suprascapular Nerve

After its fibers have traversed undivided anterior primary rami C5 and C6, the supraclavicular nerve emerges from the upper trunk of the brachial plexus (Fig. 198). In the proximal part of its course it is situated superficial to cords of the plexus. Proceeding downward, it passes through the suprascapular notch, then on to the back of the scapula. After giving off a branch to the supraspinatus muscle, the nerve passes through the spinoglenoid notch to reach and supply the infraspinatus.

Involvement of the suprascapular nerve alone in missile wounds is rare, as it was observed by Foerster (1929) in only 16 of 2907 cases of missile wound. Isolated palsy has been noted in gymnasts. Atrophy above and below the spine of the scapula is evident even though obscured by the overlying trapezius (Fig. 199). When at rest, the arm assumes a position of slight medial (internal) rotation, most noticeable in the region of the scapulohumeral joint. The position of the shoulder is, however, not altered. Lateral rotation of the humerus, a movement in which the infraspinatus is concerned, is considerably weakened despite the assistance of the teres minor, which is supplied by the axillary nerve. Elevation of the arm is not affected, though a slight subluxation of the head of the humerus dorsally may occur on elevation of the arm in the lateral plane.

Foerster (1929) remarked that he was able on many occasions to confirm certain observations made by Duchenne on suprascapular nerve palsy. Among these was the inability to scratch the back of the head or to unlock a door with arm outstretched. Also such patients were unable to write a long series of words one after another from left to right without shoving the paper to the left while doing so.

The suprascapular nerve is affected most frequently in injuries of the upper plexus which involve undivided primary rami of segments C5 and C6. Since both the infraspinatus and the teres minor are affected in lesions at this site, lateral rotation of the humerus is very difficult. An instance of interruption of the suprascapular and axillary nerves is illustrated in Figure 200. Other examples of palsy involving the suprascapular nerve are shown in Figures 181, 184 and 188.

The Thoracodorsal Nerve

The thoracodorsal nerve (known also as the "long subscapular nerve" and as the "nerve to the latissimus dorsi") emerges from the brachial plexus in close association with the subscapular nerves (Fig. 201). It originates from spinal segments C7 and C8 and frequently also from C6. Its fibers traverse the three trunks of the plexus—upper, middle and lower—then pass through the posterior divisions of the trunks to gain the posterior cord.

After emerging from the posterior cord of the plexus and then passing behind the medial cord, the thoracodorsal nerve takes a downward course in the axilla (between the two subscapular nerves) to reach the latissimus dorsi.

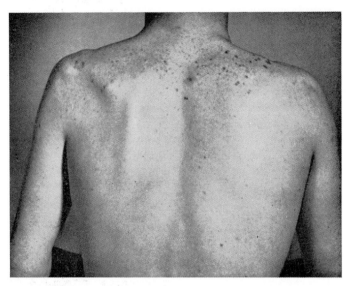

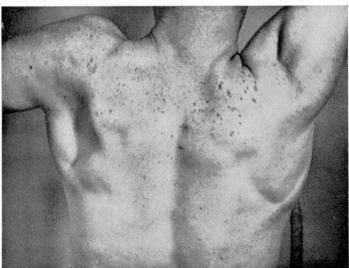

FIGURE. 200.   *Combined Suprascapular and Axillary Nerve Palsy. Left.* A missile penetrated the neck just above the center of the left scapula. Subsequently the brachial plexus was explored and neurolysis of lateral cord and suprascapular nerve performed. The affected shoulder shows atrophy of supraspinatus, infraspinatus and deltoid. Elevation of the arm in abduction is performed with difficulty and is supplemented by rotation of the scapula and the vertebral axis.

Interruption of the thoracodorsal nerve usually is associated with lesions of the posterior cord or more proximal parts of the plexus. Palsy of the latissimus dorsi leads to little deformity; sometimes there is a winging of the inferior angle of the scapula owing to weakness of the part of the muscle that crosses over the angle. In latissimus palsy the only

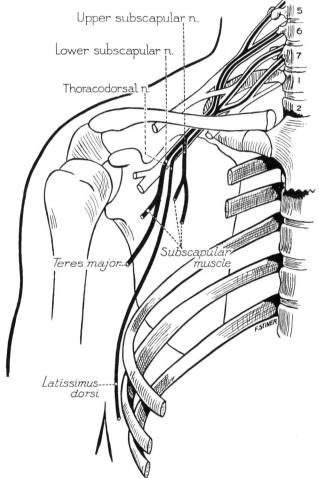

FIGURE 201.   *Diagram of the Course and Distribution of the Thoracodorsal and Subscapular (Upper and Lower) Nerves.* The muscles supplied by each of these nerves are indicated in italics. None of the nerves has cutaneous distribution.

movement compromised is that of strong adduction at the shoulder when the arm is moved medially behind the back. Since the latissimus dorsi tends to lower the shoulder, the shoulder may move upward when the extended arm is pushed forward strongly against a stationary object.

Paralysis of the latissimus dorsi is illustrated in Figures 187 and 188.

The Subscapular Nerves

The fibers of the two subscapular nerves arise from spinal segments C5 and C6, traverse the corresponding anterior roots and undivided anterior primary rami, merge in the upper trunk of the plexus, and then pursue their course through the posterior division of this trunk to reach the posterior cord (Fig. 201). Here they leave the plexus as two separate nerves. The *upper subscapular nerve* passes downward to supply the subscapular muscle. The *lower subscapular nerve* pursues a more lateral course, innervating chiefly the teres major but sending a branch also to the subscapular muscle.

Subscapular nerve palsies usually are encountered in brachial plexus injuries that involve the more proximal part of the posterior cord. In total subscapular nerve interruption the resting arm is somewhat laterally (externally) rotated because of paralysis of the subscapular muscle. Involvement of this muscle also accounts for weakness of medial (internal) rotation of the arm at the shoulder. This movement is weakened rather than lost because other muscles assist in its performance, namely the pectoralis major and the anterior fibers of the deltoid and to a less degree the latissimus dorsi. Scratching of the lower part of the back is exceedingly difficult. Paralysis of the teres major seems to have no clinical import.

The Axillary Nerve

ANATOMY

The axillary (or "circumflex") nerve is derived from spinal segments C5 and C6. Leaving the distal part of the posterior cord of the brachial plexus, the axillary nerve passes laterally through the armpit, then bends round the back of the surgical neck of the humerus to gain and innervate the deltoid muscle and the overlying skin. En route it sends a branch to the teres minor muscle (Fig. 202).

INJURIES

The exposed position of the axillary nerve as it winds round the lateral aspect of the humerus makes this nerve especially liable to injury. It may be compressed or torn in dislocation of the shoulder joint, in fractures of the surgical neck of the humerus, and occasionally in fractures of the scapula. In war injuries, axillary nerve palsy usually forms only a part of a wider lesion of the brachial plexus. Such palsy is an inevitable consequence of interruption of the posterior cord and also occurs in upper trunk injuries (Figs. 181, 183, 187).

A well developed axillary nerve palsy can be recognized on inspection: because of atrophy of the deltoid, the contour of the upper arm is flattened or is slightly concave and the shoulder "squared" (Figs. 203, 204). Disordered movement at the shoulder is equally noticeable. Under normal conditions the middle fibers of the deltoid assisted by the supraspinatus abduct the arm to the horizontal plane, the anterior fibers

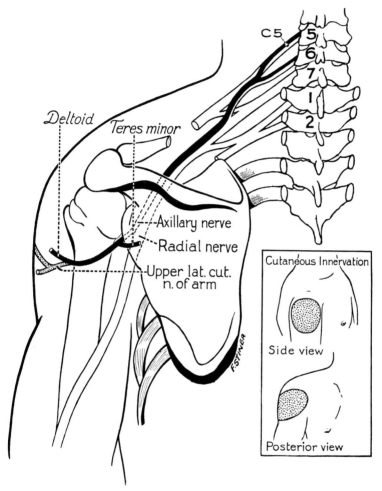

FIGURE 202.   *Diagram of the Course and Distribution of the Axillary (Circumflex) Nerve.* The muscles supplied are indicated in italics. The cutaneous branch of the axillary (i.e., the upper lateral cutaneous nerve of the arm) is stippled, as is also its cutaneous field of distribution.

help to bring the arm forward and the posterior ones aid in drawing the arm backward. Successful abduction of the arm to the horizontal plane is contingent, however, on the action of the lateral rotators of the humerus (infraspinatus and teres minor). In paralysis of the deltoid the attempt to abduct the arm to the horizontal plane may be partly success-ful: in the attempt to get his arm up, the patient shrugs the shoulder and tilts his trunk to the other side, thus raising the arm with the help of the rib cage (Fig. 188). The fault is serious since other muscles contributing to this movement (supraspinatus, serratus anterior, infraspinatus, teres minor, trapezius and pectoralis major) ordinarily give little material aid

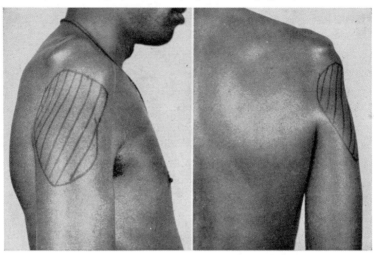

FIGURE 203.   *Axillary Nerve Palsy.* A dislocation of the shoulder occurred when a truck in which the patient was riding, overturned. There is marked atrophy of the deltoid muscle. The area of sensory deficit is indi-cated. (R.G.H.)

to the deltoid. Elevation of the arm by forward or by backward flexion is compromised to about the same degree.

Occasionally, in paralysis of the deltoid, the patient is able to abduct the arm actively through 90 degrees, and in combined deltoid and supra-spinatus palsy through 45 degrees. During the excursion, in which only a trace of forward flexion occurs, the head of the humerus is fixed in the glenoid fossa, presumably by the long head of the biceps and coracobrachialis, while the trapezius externally rotates the scapula, thus carrying the arm away from the side. The manner in which the movement occurs may be detected by observing the lateral motion of the inferior angle of the scapula while palpating the deltoid, supraspinatus and trapezius for evidence of contrac-tion (Sunderland, 1944b). This *supplementary movement,* i.e., abduction of the arm through 95 degrees, may also be induced by the supraspinatus (Foer-ster, 1929) and possibly by the long head of the biceps (Highet, 1942).

Elevation of the arm in deltoid or in deltoid and supraspinatus palsy may be even more successful when it is performed in a plane midway between abduction and forward flexion.

Paralysis of the teres minor is not reflected clinically since other mus-cles (e.g., infraspinatus) aid it in lateral (external) rotation of the arm at the shoulder.

Disturbances of cutaneous sensibility over the deltoid are almost always encountered in complete division of the nerve (Fig. 203).

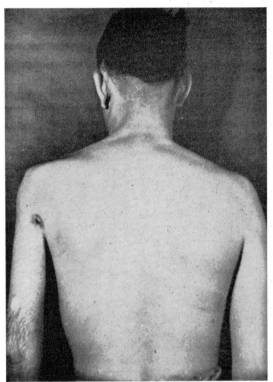

FIGURE 204.   *Deltoid Paralysis. Left.* A shell fragment penetrated the posterior portion of the left shoulder, destroying the axillary nerve. The typical deformity is obvious. During a twelve-month period of observation, the arm could be abducted only 15 degrees. (A.G.H.)

The Musculocutaneous Nerve

ANATOMY

The musculocutaneous nerve arises from spinal segments C5, C6 and C7. Its fibers traverse the upper trunk, then proceed through the anterior division of this trunk to reach the lateral cord (Fig. 205). On emerging from the plexus the musculocutaneous nerve crosses the axilla in company with the median, pierces the coracobrachialis, and then extends downward between biceps and brachialis to the bend of the elbow. Here it is not far removed from the radial nerve. After emerging from the deep fascia over the front of the elbow, it descends as the lateral cutaneous nerve of the forearm.

The musculocutaneous nerve supplies the biceps (both heads) and the brachialis. On occasion the last-named muscle also receives a supply

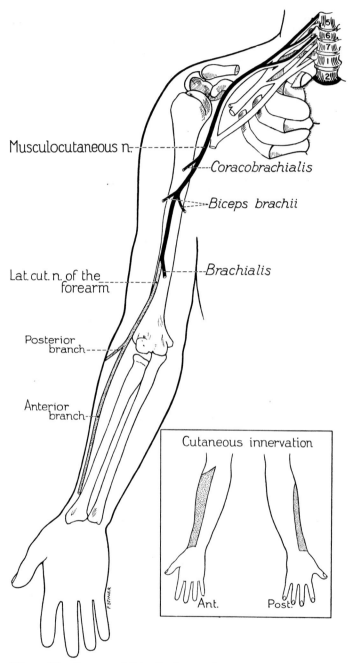

Musculocutaneous n.

Coracobrachialis

Biceps brachii

Lat. cut. n. of the forearm

Brachialis

Posterior branch

Anterior branch

Cutaneous innervation

Ant.   Post.

FIGURE 205.   *The Course and Distribution of the Musculocutaneous Nerve.* The names of the muscles supplied by this nerve are in italics. The cutaneous distribution is indicated in the inset.

from the radial nerve. A separate branch (from spinal segments C6 and C7), partly embodied in the musculocutaneous nerve, innervates the coracobrachialis. Not infrequently an anastomotic branch of the musculocutaneous nerve joins the median. Variations in the field of supply of the musculocutaneous nerve are illustrated in Figure 209.

INJURIES

War injuries seldom involve the musculocutaneous nerve alone. Usually the palsy is a feature of injury of the lateral cord of the upper trunk of the brachial plexus, as in Figure 206.

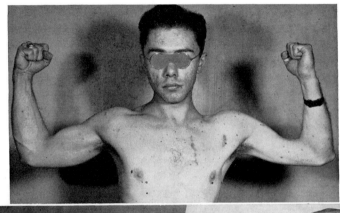

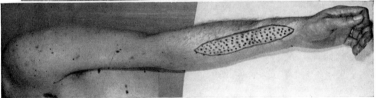

FIGURE 206.   *Complete Musculocutaneous Nerve Palsy.* Note the pronounced atrophy of the biceps brachii and the smallness of the upper arm as compared to the forearm. There was also weakness of abduction and external rotation of the arm. Anesthesia in the field of distribution of the anterior branch of the musculocutaneous nerve is indicated. The wound was due to a high velocity projectile which entered the infraclavicular region and took exit from the supraspinous region of the scapula. (E.G.H.)

Appearance of the Upper Arm

In palsy of the musculocutaneous nerve which has persisted for some time, the atrophy of the biceps and brachialis is made obvious by a flattening of the contours of the flexor surface of the upper arm (Figs. 206, 207). Sometimes, owing to paralysis of the coracobrachialis and of the long head of the biceps and associated muscles, the head of the humerus falls slightly from its socket (Fig. 190).

Motor Power

Flexion of the forearm at the elbow is weakened but the disability usually is not severe since the brachioradialis and pronator teres muscles take part in producing the movement (Fig. 207). These muscles, chiefly the former, are responsible for the pronation that invariably occurs when flexion at the elbow is attempted. If the forearm is placed in a

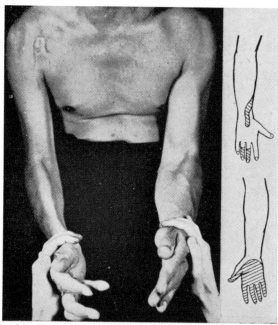

FIGURE 207.　*Interruption of Musculocutaneous and Median Nerves Following a Missile Wound of the Infraclavicular Region.* The site of the injury is visible. The palsy is of fourteen months' standing. The deltoid and biceps brachii are somewhat atrophied. The brachioradialis (supplied by the radial nerve) contracts vigorously when flexion at the elbow is resisted. The sensory map indicates also an involvement of the ulnar nerve. The hands of this patient are shown in Figure 210. (W.R.)

position of supination, flexion at the elbow is virtually impossible. Active supination of the forearm is considerably weakened since this is one of the actions of the biceps. The loss of coracobrachialis function (which under normal conditions aids in adduction of the arm, and to a less degree in medial rotation) is difficult to detect.

Sensibility

Reduced sensibility usually is to be found along the lateral border of the forearm. Its extent is considerably less than the anatomical limits of the cutaneous field.

The Median Nerve

Origin and Course

Fibers of the median nerve are derived from spinal cord segments C6, C7, C8 and T1, and in some cases also from C5. They traverse each of the three trunks and, in turn, their anterior divisions, to reach the lateral (outer) and medial (inner) cords of the brachial plexus. From these cords are given off two bundles of fibers which unite in the uppermost part of the arm to form the median nerve proper (Fig. 208).

The median nerve descends the inner side of the arm in close association with the brachial artery. At first the median nerve lies lateral to this artery but in the middle third of the arm it crosses the artery, and thereafter lies medial. In the proximal half of the arm the median nerve is close to the ulnar.

After reaching the hollow of the elbow, where it is under cover of the bicipital aponeurosis, the median nerve extends into the forearm between the two heads of the pronator teres muscles. (At this level the anterior interosseous nerve branches from the median, and soon finds its way to the ventral surface of the interosseous membrane, on which it descends.) The median nerve then passes downward in a plane between the superficial and deep flexors; it gains the wrist where in company with flexor tendons it passes deep to the flexor retinaculum. Emerging from the latter it divides into terminal branches.

Usual Distribution

The median nerve gives off no branches until it reaches the elbow. Flexors and pronators are its chief destinations. The muscular and cutaneous branches of the median nerve are as shown on page 244, Table 7.

Variations in Distribution

Some of the muscles listed may be supplied by other nerves. The pronator teres not infrequently receives anastomotic branches from the musculo-cutaneous nerve, and on occasion the flexor carpi radialis and some of the long flexors of the hand and fingers are innervated from the same source. The flexor digitorum profundus receives its innervation from both the median and the ulnar and the muscular slips of the third and fourth fingers are often innervated from both these sources. Occasionally the slip to the fifth finger is also doubly innervated and rarely may be supplied solely by the median. Vice versa, the ulnar may overshadow the median by supply-

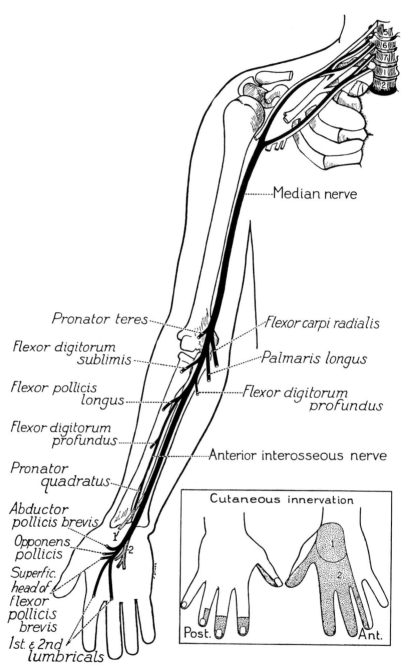

Median nerve

Pronator teres

Flexor digitorum sublimis

Flexor pollicis longus

Flexor digitorum profundus

Pronator quadratus

Abductor pollicis brevis

Opponens pollicis

Superfic. head of flexor pollicis brevis

1st & 2nd lumbricals

Flexor carpi radialis

Palmaris longus

Flexor digitorum profundus

Anterior interosseous nerve

Cutaneous innervation

Post.

Ant.

FIGURE 208.   *Diagram of the Course and Distribution of the Median Nerve.* The muscles supplied are indicated in italics. In the hand the cutaneous branches are marked by stipple, as is also the field of cutaneous innervation (see inset). The nerve indicated by 1 is the palmar cuta-

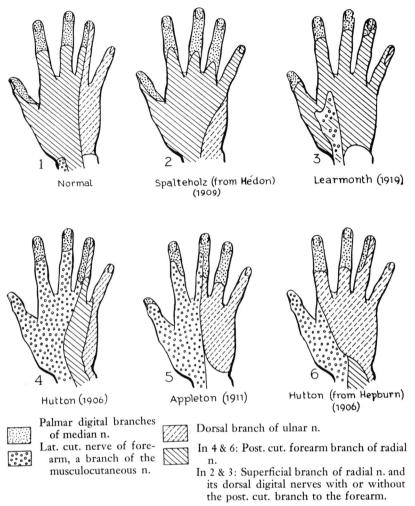

1   Normal

2   Spalteholz (from Hédon)
(1909)

3   Learmonth (1919)

4   Hutton (1906)

5   Appleton (1911)

6   Hutton (from Hepburn)
(1906)

	Palmar digital branches of median n.		Dorsal branch of ulnar n.
	Lat. cut. nerve of forearm, a branch of the musculocutaneous n.		In 4 & 6: Post. cut. forearm branch of radial n.

In 2 & 3: Superficial branch of radial n. and its dorsal digital nerves with or without the post. cut. branch to the forearm.

FIGURE 209.   *Variations in Innervation of the Dorsum of the Hand and Fingers.*

ing most or even all the muscles of the thenar eminence. Variations in sensory distribution of the median nerve are indicated in Figure 209.

When in the presence of median nerve injury certain movements ordinarily dependent on an intact median nerve can still be performed, the question will arise as to whether the nerve supply of those muscles is anomalous or whether the nerve injury is incomplete. This problem can be resolved by means of *procaine block*.

neous branch of the median nerve; and those by 2, the palmar digital nerves. The corresponding areas of cutaneous innervation are indicated in the inset. In some individuals the region of innervation of the dorsal aspect of the fingers is somewhat more proximal than indicated in this drawing.

TABLE 7   *Distribution of the Median Nerve*

MUSCULAR BRANCHES

In Forearm

From Median Nerve Proper
  Pronator teres
  Flexor carpi radialis
  Flexor digitorum sublimis
  Palmaris longus
  Flexor pollicis longus (frequently)
  Flexor digitorum profundus (frequently)

From Anterior Interosseous Nerve
  Flexor pollicis longus
  Flexor digitorum profundus
    (lateral half)
  Pronator quadratus

In Hand

Abductor pollicis brevis
Opponens pollicis
Flexor pollicis brevis (superficial, or outer, head)
1st & 2d lumbricals

CUTANEOUS BRANCHES

Palmar branch (sometimes absent)
Palmar digital nerves

INJURIES

Appearance of the Hand

SIMILARITIES TO THE SIMIAN HAND   In the simian hand the palmar
aspect of the thumb lies in the same plane as the rest of the palmar sur-

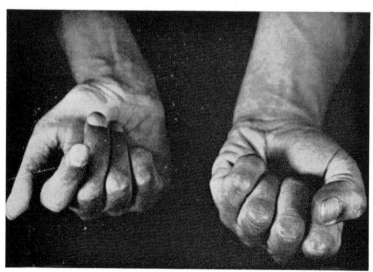

FIGURE 210.   *A Case of Median Nerve Palsy Illustrating the Attempt to Make a
Fist.* The thumb remains extended and adducted. Only the little
finger is capable of full flexion. Muscles of the thenar eminence are
considerably atrophied. The arms of this patient are illustrated in
Figure 207. (W.R.)

face. There is a tendency for this attitude to develop in median nerve palsy by reason of the unopposed action of the extensor pollicis longus (supplied by the radial nerve) and the adductor pollicis (supplied by the ulnar).

BENEDICTION ATTITUDE   The index finger is often totally incapable of flexion and the middle finger partially so, and thus when the patient

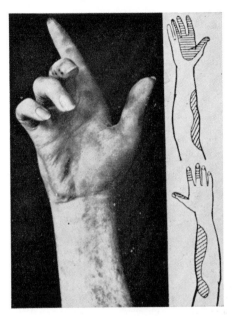

FIGURE 211.   *Attempted Flexion of the Fingers in a Case of Median Nerve Palsy.*
A bullet wound was incurred in the region of the right elbow, injuring the median and musculocutaneous nerves above the level of innervation of the flexor digitorum profundus. An attempt to make a fist reveals complete paralysis of the flexor digitorum profundus component to the index finger and partial paralysis of that to the third finger. The thumb fails to flex because of paralysis of the flexor pollicis longus and flexor pollicis brevis. Failure of flexion at the metacarpophalangeal joints is ascribed to faulty sublimis action. The patterns in the inset indicate areas of sensory deficit. The median nerve was repaired three months after injury and the photograph was taken one month later. (W.R.)

raises his arm before him the outstretched index finger and serial flexion of other fingers give the hand the appearance of that of a clergyman in saying benediction (Fig. 212).

HOLLOWING OF THE THENAR EMINENCE   Owing to the atrophy of the abductor pollicis brevis and opponens pollicis much of the thenar eminence is sunken (Fig. 210). In longstanding cases the contour of the underlying first metacarpal bone may be visible. On occasion, atrophy of the thenar eminence is completely lacking because of a variation of innervation (Fig. 73; p. 88).

Motor Function

LOSS OF ABILITY TO FLEX THE INDEX FINGER   When an effort is made to bend the index finger, the response at the different joints varies (Figs. 211, 212, 213). As a rule the patient is able to flex somewhat at the metacarpophalangeal joint because of contraction of interosseous muscles, which are innervated by the ulnar. Flexion of the distal phalanx, dependent entirely on the median nerve, is always lost when the

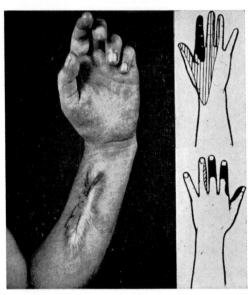

FIGURE 212.   *The Hand in a Case of Median Nerve Palsy.* The position of the hand and fingers is similar to that of a clergyman's in benediction. The inability to flex is most pronounced in the thumb and two radial fingers. The thenar eminence shows mild atrophy. The scar on the forearm is the result of a bullet wound sustained eleven months previously. In the maps the black area indicates anesthesia; the lined, hypesthesia. (W.R.)

interruption is above the level at which branches are given off to the flexor digitorum profundus.

LOSS OF FLEXOR ACTION OF THE DISTAL PHALANX OF THE THUMB Active flexion of the distal phalanx of the thumb is brought about by the flexor pollicis longus. Its nerve comes off the median trunk in the upper one third of the forearm (Fig. 208). When this muscle is paralyzed, the distal phalanx is incapable of flexion when the movement is tested (1) with the thumb adducted to, or inside of, the radial margin of the index finger and (2) with the wrist in a neutral position. If the thumb assumes the position of radial abduction and if, at the same time, the hand is dorsiflexed, the tendon of the affected flexor pollicis longus is stretched as it passes along the palmar surface of the thumb, causing flexion of the distal phalanx (*a supplementary movement*) (Sunderland, 1944b). Loss of flexion of the thumb is illustrated in Figures 211 to 214 inclusive.

Loss of Other Thumb Movements   *Palmar abduction of the thumb* is a movement in which the thumb is brought straight out from the base of the index finger at a right angle to the palm (Fig. 78). The movement is dependent on the abductor pollicis brevis, the flexor pollicis brevis (both heads), and, to a limited degree, the opponens pollicis. Since the branches supplying these muscles are given off in the hand,

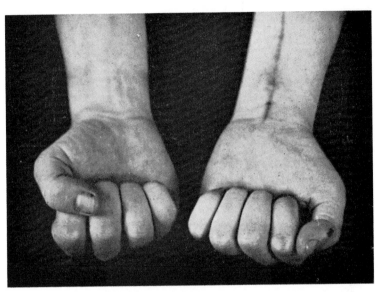

FIGURE 213.   *A Case of Partial Median Nerve Palsy, Left, in Which the Thumb Fails to Oppose or Flex Fully in the Closure of a Fist.* The nerve was injured at a level somewhat above the wrist, distal to the site where branches are given off to the flexor digitorum profundus and flexor digitorum sublimis. (W.R.)

interruption of the median nerve in the region of the wrist or at more proximal levels will involve them. In median nerve palsy, palmar abduction of the thumb usually cannot be performed. Occasionally, however, the movement can be carried out to a limited degree, presumably by the deep head of the flexor pollicis brevis (supplied by the ulnar nerve) or by the entire flexor pollicis brevis when it receives its innervation solely from the ulnar. There are instances also in which the supply of the superficial head of the flexor pollicis brevis from unaccustomed sources (musculocutaneous and radial nerves) is responsible for the movement. *Radial abduction of the thumb* may have a limited range owing to action of the abductor pollicis longus (supplied by the radial nerve). The palsy may be demonstrated by having the patient raise his hands in

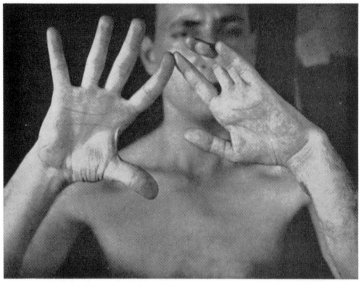

FIGURE 214.   *A Sign of Median Nerve Palsy.* The patient is able to separate widely the thumb and index finger of the normal (right) hand but is unable to do so on the affected side. "Griffe" is moderately severe. (W.R.)

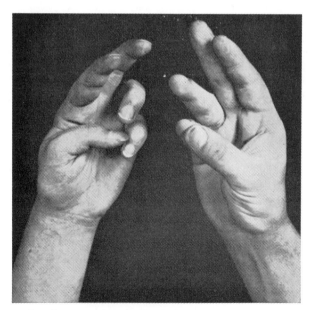

FIGURE 215.   *Pseudo-opposition of the Thumb in a Case of Median Nerve Palsy, Left.* The thumb, incapable of rotation, advances across the palm to meet the side of the flexed little finger. (W.R.)

front of him with palms forward (as in the position used by Moslems for prayer), and then having him attempt to separate thumb and index finger of both hands: the thumb of the normal side abducts fully, that of the palsied side slightly or not at all (Fig. 214).

In cases of median nerve palsy in which the flexor pollicis brevis is active, palmar abduction of the thumb may be carried out by this muscle and the abductor pollicis longus, but the range of the movement is only about half of normal.

Opposition of the thumb is a movement in which the thumb advances across the palm in a wide arc, rotating en route, so that at the end of

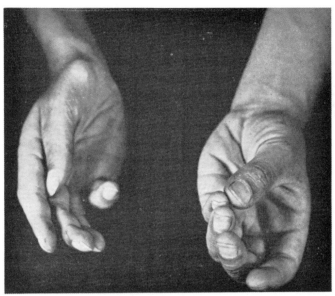

FIGURE 216. *An Attempt to Oppose Little Finger and Thumb in a Case of Median Nerve Palsy.* The movement is performed fairly well by the little finger but the thumb, unable to rotate, is moved inward along the palm ("pseudo-opposition"). This movement of the thumb is contingent on the adductor pollicis and the deep head of the flexor pollicis brevis, both of which are innervated by the ulnar. (W.R.)

the movement the palmar surface of the thumb comes in contact with the palmar surface of the ulnar side of the hand. Under normal conditions opposition of thumb and little finger is such that, with both extended, their tips meet, the two digits forming a vertical arch over the palm. When the opponens pollicis is paralyzed, the deep head of the flexor pollicis brevis and the adductor of the thumb (both having ulnar innervation) are brought into action and usually a makeshift opposition of the thumb occurs: the thumb, *bent at an angle*, usually meets the *side* of the distal phalanx of the advancing little finger (Fig. 215). This is spoken of as "pseudo-opposition." In longstanding cases the degree of pseudo-opposition may be restricted (Fig. 216). Rotation of the thumb (an opponens pollicis action) may be performed when both heads of the flexor pollicis brevis are supplied by the ulnar nerve.

ATTEMPT AT MAKING A FIST   The motor deficits resulting from total interruption of the median nerve above the elbow are such that in the patient's attempt to make a fist only the ring and little fingers follow out the movement intended, but even their action is not complete because function of the flexor digitorum sublimis is lacking. As emphasized, the index finger is often incapable of flexion. The ability of the middle finger to flex varies considerably; it may flex only slightly if innervated by the median or almost completely when innervated by the ulnar (Figs. 210, 211, 212).

LOSS OF PRONATION OF THE FOREARM   Care must be taken in testing pronation of the forearm lest the movement occur passively through the influence of gravity (p. 68). When the conditions for the test are correct, pronation cannot be performed.

FAULTY FLEXION AT THE WRIST   Flexion at the wrist usually is weakened because of paralysis of the flexor carpi radialis and the palmaris longus, but it still can be performed by the flexor carpi ulnaris and the abductor pollicis longus (the former of ulnar innervation, the latter of radial). The *supplementary movement* of flexion is frequently accompanied by ulnar deviation of the hand.

PARALYSIS OF DISTAL PHALANGES OF THE INDEX AND THIRD FINGERS WITH ABILITY TO FLEX AT THE MIDDLE PHALANGEAL JOINTS   The distal phalanges remain extended, the middle flexed. This is due to interruption of the median nerve below the level of flexor digitorum sublimis and above the region where the anterior interosseus nerve is given off (Fig. 208). Thumb movements are also abnormal when there is interruption at this level.

Sensibility

In complete interruption of the median nerve at a level above the lower third of the forearm there is total sensory loss of the tip of the index finger. The adjoining area of hypesthesia conforms more or less with the anatomical distribution of the nerve (Figs. 211, 212). With interruption of the median nerve distal to the level at which the palmar cutaneous branch (*1* in Fig. 208) is given off, sensibility is preserved over the more proximal part of the dorsal surface of the hand. In median nerve palsy, sensibility of the joints of the thumb and the index finger may be lost. These remarks are subject to modification when variations exist in the field of supply of the median nerve (Fig. 209).

The Ulnar Nerve

ANATOMY

Origin and Course

Components of the ulnar nerve are derived from spinal segments C8 and T1. They traverse the lower trunk of the brachial plexus and, in turn, the anterior division of this trunk, then enter the medial cord (Fig. 217).

In a considerable number of cases the ulnar nerve receives fibers also from the seventh cervical segment. These may reach the ulnar nerve by way of the lateral cord of the plexus or through the lateral root of the median nerve, or at times via a connection from the middle trunk to the medial cord.

The ulnar nerve issues from the brachial plexus in the upper axilla, and, gaining the upper arm, comes to lie medial to the brachial artery a few millimeters from the median nerve. As the nerve reaches the distal half of the arm, it leaves the brachial artery to enter the groove between the medial epicondyle of the humerus and the olecranon.

In the upper part of the forearm the ulnar nerve passes between the humeral and ulnar heads of the flexor carpi ulnaris muscle. Approaching the wrist, it becomes superficial and comes to lie near the ulnar artery. A short distance above the pisiform bone the ulnar nerve gives off a *palmar branch* (*1* in Fig. 217) which innervates the skin of the more proximal part of the ulnar aspect of the hand, and a *dorsal branch* (*2* in Fig. 217) which supplies the ulnar part of the back of the hand and parts of the dorsum of the little and ring fingers. At the inner aspect of the pisiform bone the ulnar nerve divides into terminal branches, which extend into the hand. These branches are the *superficial terminal* (*3* in Fig. 217), which is cutaneous in distribution, and the *deep terminal* (*4* in Fig. 217), the source of supply of muscles, which passes beneath the flexor digiti quinti brevis, rounds the hook of the hamate bone, courses laterally along the deep palmar arch and under cover of the deep flexor tendons, finally reaching the thenar eminence.

Usual Distribution

The ulnar nerve is distributed only to the forearm and hand (Fig. 217). The muscular and cutaneous branches are listed in Table 8 (p. 253).

Variations in Distribution

Figure 217 illustrates what is customarily regarded as the cutaneous supply of the ulnar nerve. For variations in the sensory distribution of the ulnar nerve, see Figure 209.

Occasionally the 2d lumbrical, and rarely the 1st, is innervated by the ulnar rather than by the median. Conversely, the 3d lumbrical may receive its supply from the median nerve. The flexor digitorum profundus, though it usually is supplied partly by the ulnar and partly by the median, may in

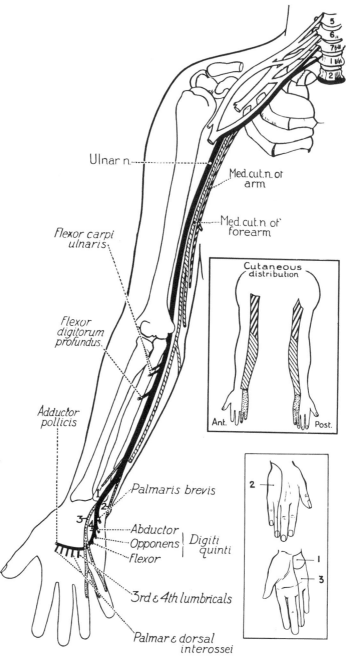

FIGURE 217.   *The Origin and Distribution of the Ulnar Nerve, the Medial Cutaneous Nerve of the Forearm and the Medial Cutaneous Nerve of the
Arm.* The muscles supplied are indicated in italics. The patterns of
the different nerves are duplicated in the inset. The numbered
nerves are the following: *1,* palmar branch, *2,* dorsal branch; *3,*
superficial terminal branch; *4,* deep terminal branch. The fields of
innervation of cutaneous branches 1, 2, and 3 are illustrated in the
inset.

some instances be innervated wholly by the median, p. 241). On occasion the flexor carpi ulnaris also is supplied by the median.

The flexor pollicis brevis usually is supplied by both the ulnar and the median nerve; on occasion, however, both heads of this muscle are innervated solely by the ulnar, and even more rarely by the musculocutane-

TABLE 8   *Distribution of the Ulnar Nerve*

MUSCULAR BRANCHES

To Forearm

Flexor carpi ulnaris
Flexor digitorum profundus (medial half)

To Hand

Adductor pollicis	Palmaris brevis
Interossei	Abductor digiti quinti
3rd and 4th lumbricals	Opponens digiti quinti
Flexor pollicis brevis (deep,	Flexor digiti quinti
or inner, head)	

CUTANEOUS BRANCHES

Dorsal branch
Palmar branch
Superficial terminal branch

ous or by the radial. Occasionally all thumb muscles receive their nerve supply from the median, as may be noted in Figure 73 (p. 88). For other variations, see pages 241 and 243.

INJURIES

Some months after complete interruption of the ulnar nerve above the elbow the chief alterations are as follows:

Appearance of the Hand

"GUTTERING"   The spaces between the tendons, particularly the interval between index finger and thumb, are converted into hollows (Figs. 218, 219). This "guttering" reflects atrophy of the interossei, the 4th and 3d lumbricals and the adductor pollicis.

FLATTENING OF THE HYPOTHENAR EMINENCE   This change in contour is due to atrophy of the palmaris brevis and of muscles of the little finger.

SEPARATION OF LITTLE AND RING FINGERS   The position of abduction of the little finger is characteristic of ulnar palsy (Figs. 220, 221). The position is due to loss of adduction function of the 4th palmar interosseous muscle together with unopposed action of the radial nerve-supplied extensor digiti quinti and a slip of the extensor digitorum (Wartenberg, 1939). In delayed ulnar palsy which is slowly progressive one of the first signs is the tendency of the little finger to drift away from the other digits and to take a position of slight flexion. Moreover, abduction of this finger may persist long after functional restoration is

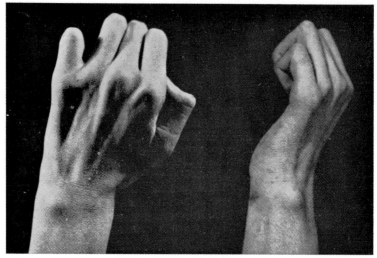

FIGURE 218.   *The Dorsum and Medial Border of the Hand in a Case of Ulnar Palsy.* There is atrophy of the hypothenar eminence and of the dorsal interossei. The abduction of the little finger, due chiefly to unopposed action of the extensor digiti quinti, is characteristic of ulnar palsy. In contrast to the normal hand, in which the dorsum presents a rounded contour when the fingers are clenched, in this case the knuckles are relatively straight across. This straightening of the dorsal metacarpal arch, which is even more evident when opposition of fifth finger and thumb is attempted, is illustrated also in Figures 225 and 226. (W.R.)

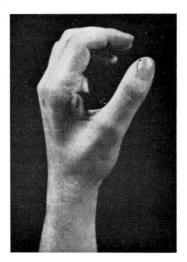

FIGURE 219.   *Severe Atrophy Between First and Second Metacarpals in a Case of Ulnar Palsy.* The depression is due to atrophy of first dorsal interosseous muscle and the adductor pollicis. (W.R.)

otherwise complete (Fig. 220). The abduction position can best be demonstrated when the fingers are extended.

ULNAR CLAW-HAND   The fifth and fourth fingers are overextended at the metacarpophalangeal joints and are flexed at the interphalangeal joints; the third and index fingers, owing to intact 3d and 2d lumbricals, are much less affected (Figs. 221, 222). This position has

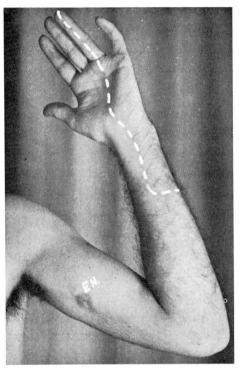

FIGURE 220.   *Residual Ulnar Palsy.* The site of entrance (*EN*) of a missile is indicated. Abduction and slight flexion of the little finger is the only remaining evidence of ulnar palsy. Hypesthesia is apparent in the field of the ulnar nerve as well as that of the medial cutaneous nerve of the forearm. (B.G.H.)

been likened to that of a hand in the act of playing a piano and is such that the patient is unable to place his fingers into a position for writing. The overextension at the metacarpophalangeal joints is due to unopposed action of the extensor digitorum, and the flexion at the interphalangeal joints is ascribed to compensatory pull on the long flexor tendons. The 4th and 3d lumbricals and the interossei are also concerned since under normal conditions they aid materially in flexion at the metacarpophalangeal joints and extension at the interphalangeal joints. The net result is the so-called "ulnar claw-hand," or partial *main*

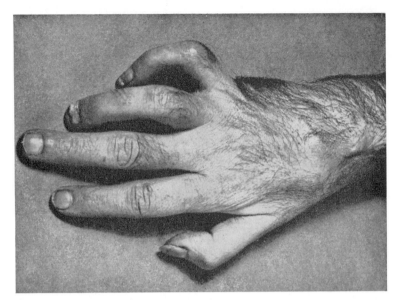

FIGURE 221.   *Ulnar Claw-hand*. Injury of the ulnar was the result of a bullet wound of the wrist. A typical "ulnar claw-hand" has developed. Trophic changes are restricted to the field of the ulnar: the nail of the little finger is furrowed, that of the ring finger atrophic. (B.G.H.)

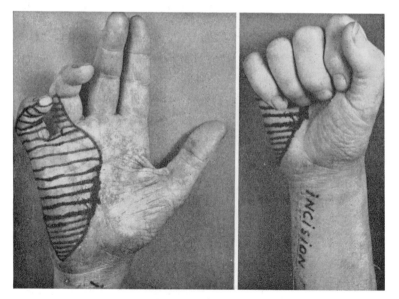

FIGURE 222.   *The Hand in a Case of Ulnar Palsy*. Injury occurred at the wrist when the patient fell down an elevator shaft. When a effort is made to straighten the fingers, the fourth and fifth remain in palmar flexion and the metacarpophalangeal joint of the fifth in extension. In the attempt to make a fist, the ulnar fingers, especially the fifth, fail to close, and the thumb flexes somewhat but does not oppose. The area of sensory loss is indicated. (B.G.H.)

en griffe. Complete claw-hand occurs only in combined ulnar and median palsy, except in those few instances in which all the lumbrical muscles are supplied by the ulnar nerve.

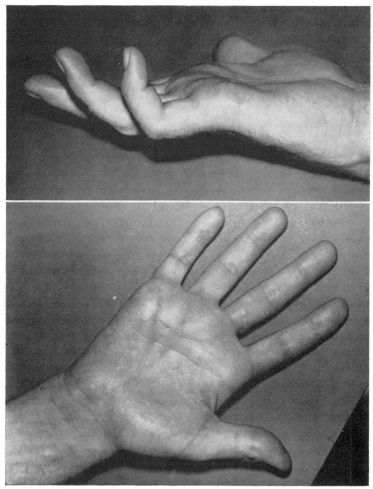

FIGURE 223.   *Trick Movement in Ulnar Palsy.* The patient is able to reduce considerably the degree of flexion of his little and ring fingers when the back of his hand is supported on a flat surface. (Courtesy of Lt. Col. George J. Hayes, M.C., Walter Reed Army Hospital.)

The clawing develops earlier and more obviously when the medial half of the flexor digitorum profundus muscle is spared. It also becomes more pronounced when, through regeneration of the nerve, the previously paralyzed flexor digitorum profundus again assumes its function.

The flexion of the little and ring fingers can to a certain degree be overcome by the patient when the back of his hand is planted firmly on a flat surface (Fig. 223). This is a *trick movement* against which the examiner should be on his guard. Reduction in the *main en griffe* of ulnar palsy is to be seen in Figure 224. (See also pages 88 and 89 for trick movements in ulnar palsy.)

Highet (1942b) has emphasized that the extensor communis exerts powerful extension at the interphalangeal joints when the metacarpophalangeal joints are held in a position of slight flexion, and on the basis of this observation has devised a splint which overcomes clawing by holding the metacarpophalangeal joints in this position. A plaster cast based on this principle had previously been devised by Kendall and Kendall for use in poliomyelitis subjects.

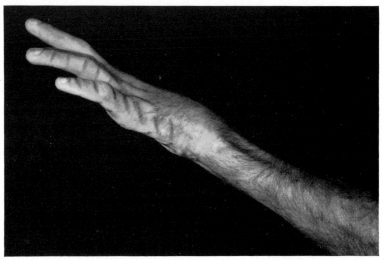

FIGURE 224.   *A Substitute Motor Action Based on Anatomical Variation.* The ulnar nerve was severed in the region of the mid-forearm. The hand is "atavistic" and has hypomobile joints, rather straight strong fingers, and heavy extensor tendinous slips inserted into the lateral bands. Reduction in the characteristic *main en griffe* is brought about by slight hyperextension at the metacarpophalangeal articulations and slight flexion at the wrist. (DUH, D-45050.)

Motor Function

FANNING OF THE FINGERS AND BRINGING THEM TOGETHER AGAIN Fanning of the fingers is weakened because of paralysis of the dorsal interossei, but it can be accomplished to a limited degree by means of the extensor digitorum, which is innervated by the radial. Ability to bring the fingers together, a movement dependent on the palmar interossei, is also reduced, but here again another muscle group, the flexors of the fingers, comes to the aid of the palmar interossei, provided the fingers are slightly flexed. If they are *not* flexed (or actively extended) the movement cannot be performed, except for the index finger which may be adducted by the extensor indicis.

ADDUCTION OF THE THUMB   Although the adductor pollicis is paralyzed in ulnar nerve lesions, the movements of palmar and ulnar adduction of the thumb still can be performed. When the patient attempts to grasp an object, such as a piece of paper, between the thumb and the edge of the palm, the purpose is accomplished by flexing the thumb at the interphalangeal joint by means of the flexor pollicis longus, supplied by the median nerve (*Froment's signe de journal*) (Fig. 225). This pincers movement is aided somewhat by the extensor pollicis longus.

FIGURE 225.   *The "Signe de Journal" (of Froment) in Ulnar Palsy, Right.* In order to grasp a piece of paper between thumb and index finger, the thumb, incapable of adequate adduction because of paralysis of the adductor pollicis, flexes at the phalangeal joint. Flexion of the thumb is accentuated when the attempt is made to pull the paper away. The hollow between first and second metacarpals is due chiefly to atrophy of first dorsal interosseous muscle. (W.R.)

ATTEMPT AT MAKING A FIST   When asked to make a fist, the patient does so more successfully with the radial than with the ulnar fingers, the reason being that the flexors of the radial side are supplied by the median nerve and are therefore intact (Fig. 222). The capacity of the fifth and fourth fingers for limited flexion is due to action of the flexor digitorum sublimis muscle, which also is innervated by the median. The fifth and fourth fingers cannot flex at the distal interphalangeal joints since this movement requires integrity of the medial half of the flexor digitorum profundus. The ability to overcome hyperextension at the metacarpophalangeal joints in making a fist is due to action of the flexor digitorum sublimis.

OPPOSITION   The opponens action of the thumb usually is weakened by reason of paralysis of the adductor pollicis. The capacity of the little finger to oppose is completely lost: flexion at the interphalangeal joints and extension at the metacarpophalangeal joint prevent the little finger from moving forward to meet the advancing thumb (Fig. 226); abduction of the little finger (ordinarily encountered in ulnar palsy) further hinders opposition; loss of power of palmar elevation of the base of the 5th metacarpal (a function chiefly of the opponens digiti quinti) makes it impossible for the base of the little finger to be lifted toward the thumb. The lack of movement of the ulnar portion

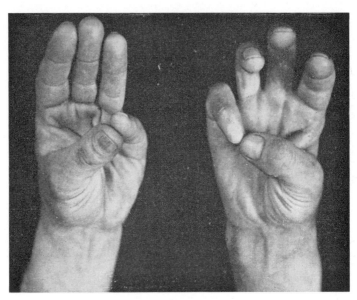

FIGURE 226.   *Attempted Opposition of Thumb and Little Finger in a Case of Ulnar Nerve Palsy, Right.* The thumb rotates and moves fairly adequately across the palm, but owing to loss of power of elevation of the distal ulnar part of the palm the flexed little finger is unable to reciprocate. (W.R.)

of the hand when opposition of the little finger is attempted (Sunderland, 1944a) is most clearly seen when the hand is viewed from the dorsal aspect (Fig. 218).

In slowly progressive ulnar nerve lesions reduced power of opposition may be the earliest sign.

MOVEMENTS AT THE WRIST   The flexor carpi ulnaris both flexes and adducts the hand at the wrist. In ulnar palsy, palmar flexion can still be executed owing to intact flexor carpi radialis and palmaris longus muscles, but when this movement is performed against resistance the hand tends to tilt to the radial side. When a fist is made or when the patient attempts to abduct the little finger against resistance, the examiner no longer is able to feel the tendon of the flexor carpi ulnaris (at the wrist) go taut. It is self-evident that if transection of the ulnar nerve is distal to the level where the branch to the flexor carpi ulnaris comes off (i.e., just below the elbow), wrist movements do not suffer.

Sensibility

The extent of the areas of total anesthesia and of hypesthesia varies somewhat from case to case. A representative example is illustrated in

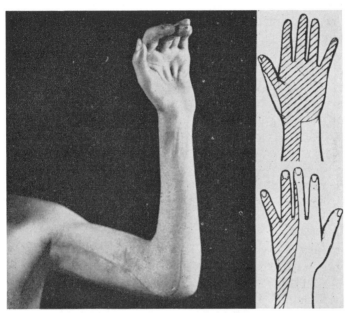

FIGURE 227. *Advanced Atrophy in a Case of Combined Ulnar and Median Palsy.* A gunshot wound of the upper arm was sustained five months previously. The prominence of the flexor tendons is the result of atrophy of interosseous muscles. Both the thenar and the hypothenar eminences are hollowed. The degree of flexion of each of the fingers is about equal. The sensory map indicates injury also of the musculocutaneous nerve and of the medial cutaneous nerve of the the forearm. (W.R.)

Figure 222. It may be taken as a rule that in complete interruption of the ulnar above the junction of the middle and lower thirds of the forearm, the tip of the little finger is devoid of sensibility. Frequently the rest of the little finger and the adjacent ulnar side of the palm are similarly affected. As regards hypalgesia and hypesthesia, their boundary usually approximates that of the area of anatomical distribution of the nerve. Deep sensibility of the joints of the 5th digit usually is lost.

Sensory deficit sometimes includes the ulnar part of the wrist, but when the deficit extends well up the forearm it is due to interruption of the medial cutaneous nerve of the forearm (Fig. 220).

When the ulnar nerve is severed below the level at which the dorsal cutaneous branch is given off (i.e., in the proximal part of the lower fourth of the forearm) (*2* in Fig. 217), the dorsal aspect of the hand is free from sensory change, the sensory deficit being limited to the dorsal aspect of the fourth and fifth fingers. With severance of the ulnar nerve at this level, its palmar branch (*1* in Fig. 217) is also spared, with the result that sensibility of the more proximal part of the ulnar aspect of the hand is normal.

The remarks on sensory changes are subject, of course, to modification, when there are variations in the field of supply of the ulnar nerve (Fig. 209, p. 243).

The Medial Cutaneous Nerve of the Arm and of the Forearm, and the Intercostobrachial Nerve

The medial cutaneous nerves of arm and forearm come off the medial cord of the brachial plexus in close association with the ulnar. The former is derived from spinal segments T1, the latter from segments C8 and T1. They extend downward to supply the areas of skin indicated in Figure 217. Damage to them produces fairly circumscribed zones of decreased sensibility in the respective fields.

The intercostobrachial nerve is composed of branches from the second and third intercostal nerves and from the medial cord of the brachial plexus. The nerve gains the axilla by piercing the serratus anterior muscle. It innervates the skin of the axilla and extends down to supply much the same cutaneous field as does the medial cutaneous nerve of the arm (Figs. 29, 30; pp. 42, 43).

Combined Ulnar and Median Nerve Palsies

Because of their proximity in the axilla and in the proximal three fourths of the upper arm, the ulnar and median nerves are apt to be damaged simultaneously by missiles which penetrate these regions; also vascular injury is a frequent concomitant and when it occurs, the palsy is doubly disabling. In the forearm the involvement of these two nerves is often linked with massive tissue destruction and with fracture of the ulna and/or radius.

In interruption of the ulnar and median nerves, all intrinsic muscles of the hand become atrophied. Combinations of *flat hand* and *claw-hand* result (Figs. 168, 227, 228, 229). In early stages the fingers are slightly flexed because of unopposed action of extensor muscles (supplied by the radial nerve) at the metacarpophalangeal joints. The fingers become progressively more flexed into the hand (i.e., clawed) when anastomotic fibers from the musculocutaneous nerve aid in the re-

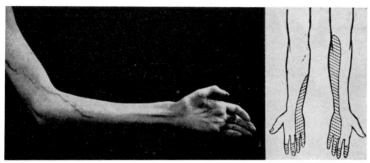

FIGURE 228.   *Combined Ulnar, Median and Radial Palsy.* Multiple penetrating missile wounds of the left arm were incurred fifteen months previously. Muscles of the hand are atrophic. The fingers have assumed the "claw" position. The attitude of the thumb may be attributed to paralysis of abductor and extensor pollicis (radial n.) and of the opponens pollicis (median n.). The sensory examination indicates involvement also of the medial cutaneous nerve of the forearm. (W.R.)

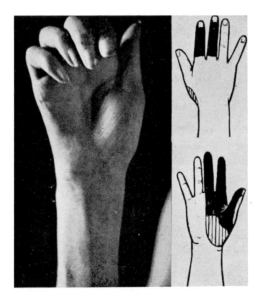

FIGURE 229.   *Combined Median and Ulnar Palsy, Right, with Progressive Flexion of the Fingers.* A bomb fragment penetrated the middle part of the upper arm; seven weeks later a neurolysis of median and ulnar nerves was performed. At that time there were anesthesia (*black*) and hypesthesia (*lined*) in the area indicated (see inset). Subsequently, when regeneration set in and the flexor digitorum profundus became re-innervated, the flexion of the fingers became progressively more marked. Extension and adduction of the thumb remained unaltered. (W.R.)

innervation (as frequently occurs) or when, through ulnar and median nerve regeneration, the flexor digitorum profundus and sublimis muscles again become active (Fig. 229). When regeneration is complete, the profundus and sublimis are no longer unopposed and as a consequence the clawing gradually disappears.

In earlier stages all efforts to make a fist are futile. Some degree of flexion of the fingers is accomplished by dorsiflexing the hand. This flexor action is, however, a *supplementary* one due to the increased tension put on the flexor tendons in the region where they cross the radio-carpal articulation. Flexion at the wrist often meets with a degree of success despite the fact that the flexor carpi radialis, palmaris longus and flexor carpi ulnaris muscles are paralyzed. This is due to the action of the abductor pollicis longus, supplied by the radial nerve. The same applies to adduction of the thumb, which is carried out by the extensor pollicis longus. Since in combined median and ulnar palsy the adductor movement is the only means of grasping, this form of palsy is highly crippling.

When interruption of these two nerves occurs at the level of the upper arm or axilla, the flexors of the hand are also involved, as a consequence of which the corresponding part of the forearm undergoes atrophy.

In combined ulnar and median palsy, trophic disturbances of the skin and fingernails are common.

Sensory Changes

Since overlap from adjacent nerve fields is minor, the zones of complete and partial sensory loss are relatively large. A representative pattern of sensory loss is illustrated in Figure 227.

The Radial Nerve*

ANATOMY

Origin and Course

Components of the radial nerve arise from spinal segments C5, C6, C7, C8 and frequently from T1 (Fig. 230). They traverse the posterior divisions of the trunks to unite in the posterior cord. On emerging from this cord, the radial nerve pursues its course through the axilla, then gains the upper arm where it winds round the back of the humerus (in the spiral groove). It then proceeds downward to the radial aspect of the bend of the elbow.

At the elbow, the radial nerve divides into two terminal branches: (1) the *superficial branch*, of cutaneous distribution, which descends the radial side of the flexor aspect of the forearm, becomes superficial

---

* Known also as the musculospiral nerve.

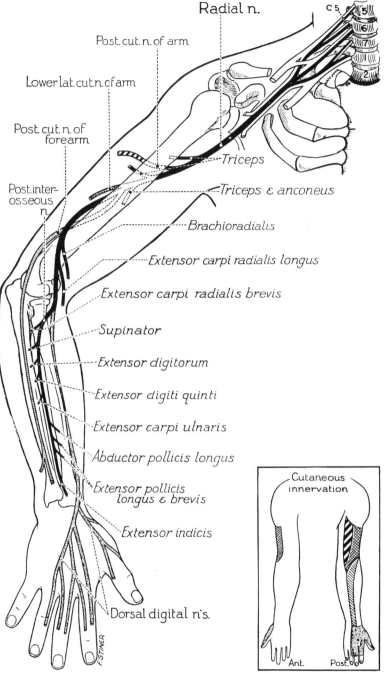

Radial n.

Post. cut. n. of arm

Lower lat. cut. n. of arm

Post. cut. n. of forearm

Post. inter-osseous n.

Triceps

Triceps & anconeus

Brachioradialis

Extensor carpi radialis longus

Extensor carpi radialis brevis

Supinator

Extensor digitorum

Extensor digiti quinti

Extensor carpi ulnaris

Abductor pollicis longus

Extensor pollicis longus & brevis

Extensor indicis

Dorsal digital n's.

Cutaneous innervation

Ant.   Post.

FIGURE 230.   *The Course and Distribution of the Radial Nerve.* **The patterns of the cutaneous nerves are duplicated in the inset. The names of the various muscles supplied by the radial are in italics.**

in the more distal part of the forearm, then bends round the radial border of the forearm to gain the dorsal surface of the wrist and hand; and (2) the *deep branch* (the posterior interosseous nerve), wholly muscular in distribution, which passes round the neck of the radius, traverses the supinator muscle, then extends downward on the dorsal aspect of the forearm to reach and course along the interosseous membrane.

Usual Distribution

Innervation by the radial is limited to muscles of the arm and forearm. The cardinal function of the nerve is that of extension at elbow,

TABLE 9   *Distribution of the Radial Nerve*

MUSCULAR BRANCHES

From Radial Nerve Proper	From Posterior Interosseous Nerve
In Arm	
Triceps	
Anconeus	
Brachioradialis	
Extensor carpi radialis longus	
In Forearm	
	Extensor carpi radialis brevis
	Supinator
	Extensor digitorum
	Extensor digiti quinti
	Extensor carpi ulnaris
	Abductor pollicis longus
	Extensor pollicis longus
	Extensor pollicis brevis
	Extensor indicis

CUTANEOUS BRANCHES

In Arm

Posterior cut. n. of arm
Lower lat. cut. n. of arm
Posterior cut. n. of forearm

In Wrist and Hand

Dorsal digital nerve

wrist, finger and thumb joints. The cutaneous distribution of the radial is to the arm, forearm, and hand.

Variations in Distribution

The chief variation is in the supply of the hand. Figure 230 shows that the dorsal digital nerves are distributed to the thumb and to two and one-half fingers. Frequently these nerves supply the thumb and only one and one-half fingers, the remainder being innervated by the ulnar. Rarely the field of supply of the superficial branch of the radial nerve (i.e., in the region of the hand at the base of the thumb, as in Fig. 231) is supplied by the median nerve (Sittig, 1928). Other variations are indicated in Figure 209.

The radial sometimes sends a twig to the brachialis muscle but this probably is an afferent path.

INJURIES

The radial nerve is among the most commonly affected in the warwounded.

The clinical picture varies in accordance with the site at which the radial nerve has been injured. For paralysis to be complete the nerve

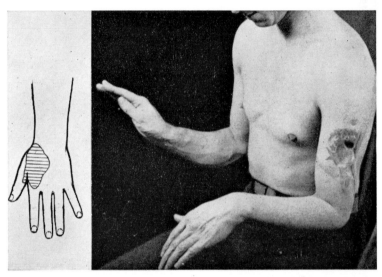

FIGURE 231.   *Wrist-drop in Radial Nerve Palsy, Left.* Fracture of the humerus (middle third) together with partial interruption of the radial nerve occurred nine months previously when the upper arm was penetrated by shell fragments. The attempt to dorsiflex both hands is successful only on the right. Triceps function is preserved. Only the radial side of the dorsum of the hand shows sensory loss. (W.R.)

must be interrupted in its axillary course, for at the lower border of the axilla the nerve gives off its tricipital branches. The radial nerve is most subject to injury in the mid-humeral region: i.e., at a level below the site where branches are given off to the triceps.

Appearance of the Arm and Hand

In cases of complete radial nerve palsy nothing unusual in the attitude of the arm meets the eye. When, however, the pronated forearm is flexed at the elbow, a wrist-drop becomes apparent (Figs. 231, 232): the hand hangs down, the fingers are moderately flexed, and the thumb is adducted. Hyperextension of the fingers, due to contractural shortening of the extensor digitorum, is seen in long-standing radial nerve palsy.

Motor Function

In Total Paralysis   Extensors both at the elbow and wrist are powerless. If, however, wrist-drop is not in excess of an angle of 120 degrees, moderate dorsiflexion at the wrist may be performed by fully flexing the fingers. In this *supplementary movement* the extensor ten-

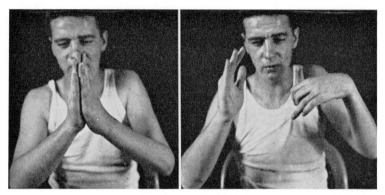

FIGURE 232.   *Palm-to-Palm Test in Radial Nerve Palsy.* When the palms are brought together the only conspicuous defect is in the angle between hand and forearm. In separation, the hand of the affected side drops at the wrist. (W.R.)

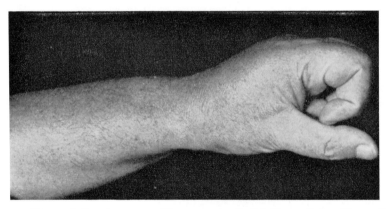

FIGURE 233.   *A Supplementary Movement in Radial Nerve Palsy.* The radial nerve was severed in connection with fracture of the humerus. Wrist-drop is being overcome by forced flexion of the fingers (DUH, D-25177.)

dons are shortened by reason of changes in the direction of leverage occasioned by the flexion. The power of extension at the metacarpophalangeal joints is nullified in radial nerve palsy, but the movement may be brought about by fully flexing at the wrist: this tightens the tendon of the extensor digitorum, thereby pulling the fingers into extension at the metacarpophalangeal joints. Extension at the interphalangeal joints is not affected, since the muscles on which this movement depends, the lumbricals and interossei, are intact. Ability to perform this movement should not be construed as evidence that the extensor digitorum is contracting. *Supplementary extension at the wrist* through forced flexion of the fingers is illustrated in Figure 233. In some cases,

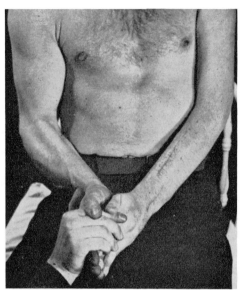

FIGURE 234.   *Paralysis of the Brachioradialis Muscle in a Case of Interruption of the Posterior Cord of the Brachial Plexus.* Injury of the posterior cord followed a gunshot wound of the left supraclavicular region. When flexion of the forearms is resisted, the brachioradialis of the affected side fails to contract. The biceps brachii also is atrophic. (W.R.)

however, palmar flexion of the hand increases as the patient attempts to tighten his grip.

Ability to extend the thumb is ostensibly lost, but by carrying out certain maneuvers a limited degree of extension at the interphalangeal and metacarpophalangeal joints can almost always be induced.

Thus, when the ulnar border of the flexed thumb is brought in contact with the palm of the hand and then palmar abduction of the thumb is performed, the thumb simultaneously extends at both its joints. This extension is executed by the slip from the abductor pollicis brevis which passes round the radial aspect of the thumb to blend with the tendon of the extensor pollicis longus (Sunderland, 1944b).

Palmar abduction of the thumb is weakened but opposition is well performed.

Supination cannot be carried out unless the forearm is in such a position that the biceps muscle comes into play. Even then the action is limited. Flexion at the elbow is weakened by reason of brachioradialis paralysis; when this movement is attempted against resistance, the brachioradialis (known also as the "supinator longus") no longer springs up to bridge the angle between arm and forearm (Fig. 234).

Attempts to make a fist are unavailing. Flexion of the fingers is possible only when the patient's hand is dorsiflexed.

IN INTERRUPTION SLIGHTLY ABOVE THE SITE WHERE THE BRANCH TO THE BRACHIORADIALIS IS GIVEN OFF   This is the site of most frequent

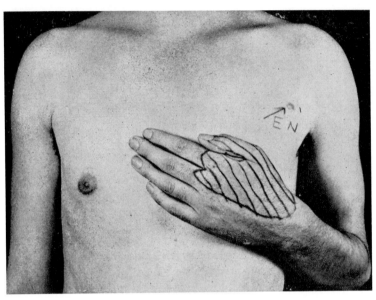

FIGURE 235.   *The Area of Sensory Deficit in a Case of Radial Nerve Palsy.* The injury occurred seven months previously. The site of entrance of a bullet (EN) is indicated. (R.G.H.)

injury to the radial nerve. The picture is the same as that described for total paralysis except that extension at the elbow can be performed by the intact triceps.

OTHER DISSOCIATED PARALYSES   Sparing of some of the extensor muscles of the forearm indicates partial interruption of the radial nerve in its course through the proximal one half of the upper arm. The nerve bundle supplying the extensor of the third finger seems to be the one most commonly spared. When the radial nerve is totally interrupted below the level of the branch to the extensor carpi radialis longus, the hand deviates rather strikingly to the radial side when it is dorsiflexed. On interruption of the radial nerve below the level where the branch to the extensor carpi radialis brevis is given off, the patient can extend his hand so that its dorsum comes to lie parallel to the dorsum of the forearm. This movement cannot, however, be performed against resistance.

When the radial nerve is interrupted at a level below the branch to the extensor digitorum, the hand can be dorsiflexed and the fingers extended, but the hand deviates toward the radial side because of paralysis of the extensor carpi ulnaris. The thumb extensors are totally paralyzed.

Sensibility

It will be noted in Figure 230 that four cutaneous branches are given off by the radial nerve. The two distributed to the skin of the upper

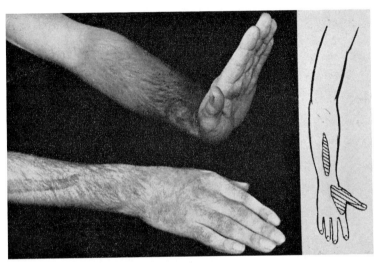

FIGURE 236.   *Radial Nerve Palsy, Right.* The palsy followed penetration of the lower third of the arm by a bomb fragment. The patient is unable to dorsiflex the hand of the affected side. The areas of sensory deficit are indicated. (F.G.H.)

arm have little clinical import because their fields of supply usually are adequately shared by branches of the medial cutaneous nerve of the arm and the musculocutaneous.

When the radial nerve is divided above the level where the posterior cutaneous nerve of the forearm is given off, there frequently is a small area of total anesthesia on the dorsal surface of the hand between the bases of the first and second metacarpals; surrounding hypesthesia occupies a somewhat greater area and not infrequently extends on to the dorsum of the forearm (Figs. 231, 235, 236). Thus, the sensory deficit in radial nerve palsies is surprisingly small, and may be altogether absent. Injury confined to the posterior interosseus nerve seldom gives rise to sensory deficit. Sensory changes in radial nerve palsy may, however, be more widespread in the presence of certain variations in radial nerve distribution (Fig. 209).

In *compression injury* of the radial nerve, when of first degree (p. 123), motor and proprioceptive functions are most affected, and touch and pain sensibilities may also be implicated. The sparing of the *posterior cutaneous nerve of the forearm* under such conditions has been ascribed to the protection afforded its fibers within a separate funiculus of the radial nerve at the level compressed.

CHAPTER 13

Injuries of the Peripheral Nerves Derived from the Lumbar Plexus

The Lumbar Plexus

ANATOMY

THE LUMBAR plexus, situated in the substance of the psoas major muscle, is formed by the union of anterior primary rami L1, L2, L3 and

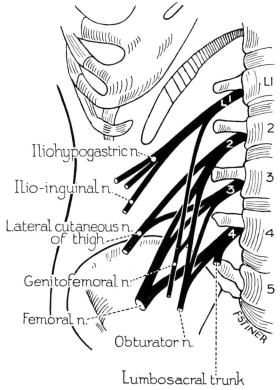

FIGURE 237. *Diagram of the Constituents of the Lumbar Plexus.* The lumbosacral trunk is the liaison between lumbar and sacral plexuses.

L4 (Fig. 237). Its uppermost ramus frequently receives a communicating branch from ramus T12 (the *subcostal nerve*) while its lowermost ramus gives off a sizeable branch (the lumbosacral trunk, or *n. furcalis*) to the sacral plexus.

The lumbar plexus has a much simpler pattern than the brachial plexus in that it consists solely of undivided anterior primary rami and their two divisions, anterior and posterior. The *undivided anterior primary rami* give off branches to the quadratus lumborum and the psoas. The *anterior divisions* continue distally as the iliohypogastric (anterior

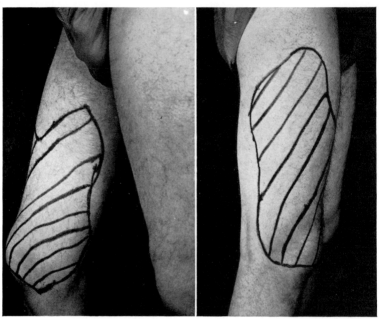

FIGURE 238.   *Missile Wound of the Lumbar Plexus.* A rifle bullet penetrated the posterior axillary line of the right chest wall at the level of the tenth rib and came to lodge in the region of the right lumbar plexus. The right kidney was lacerated. The photographs were taken three and one-half months after injury. At that time there was moderate weakness of the iliopsoas and quadriceps femoris and complete anesthesia, chiefly in the field of L3. (W.G.H.)

branch), the ilio-inguinal, the genitofemoral and the obturator nerves; and the *posterior divisions* as the iliohypogastric nerve (lateral branch), the lateral cutaneous nerve of the thigh, and the femoral nerve.

As is true of the other plexuses, all the anterior primary rami of the lumbar plexus receive grey rami communicantes from the sympathetic ganglionated chain. Only rami L1 and L2 of the plexus give off white rami communicantes to the chain.

INJURIES

Injuries of the lumbar plexus are seldom seen in battle wounds, as implication of adjacent structures frequently is fatal. Spinal roots of the upper part of the cauda equina and anterior primary rami are most commonly affected, their involvement being indicated by the segmental pattern of the disability. Irritation of posterior roots or rami (by pressure or other factors) usually leads to pain in the corresponding dermatomes or sclerotomes; complete interruption of anterior roots or rami is manifested by weakness or paralysis of the constituent muscles of the corresponding myotomes. The sites of the dermatomes are indicated in Figures 20 to 22, those of the sclerotomes in Figures 32 and 33. The various myotomes are listed in Tables 3 and 4 (pp. 36, 37). Figures 25 and 26 indicate the spinal roots most likely to be injured by a depressed fracture of a spinous process.

An example of missile wound of the lumbar plexus, in which dermatome L3 was chiefly implicated, is illustrated in Figure 238.

The Iliohypogastric Nerve

The iliohypogastric nerve is uppermost in the lumbar plexus. Its fibers spring from the undivided anterior primary ramus of segment L1 (Fig. 237). The nerve traverses the psoas major, courses in front of the quadratus lumborum muscle and, reaching the region above the iliac crest, takes a position between the transverse and internal oblique muscles. A little above the anterior superior spine of the ilium it pierces the internal oblique muscle and, further along, the aponeurosis of the external oblique to terminate in the region above the pubis.

Elements of the iliohypogastric nerve are distributed both to muscle and skin. The muscular branches are given off to the internal oblique and transverse of the abdominal wall. The sensory branches are (1) the *lateral cutaneous branch*, which extends to the upper and lateral aspect of the gluteal region (it corresponds to the lateral branch of the anterior primary division of an intercostal nerve), and (2) the *anterior cutaneous branch*, which reaches an area of skin of the anterior abdominal wall a short distance above the pubis (Fig. 30).

Injuries of this nerve lead either to pain or to a limited sensory deficit in the anatomical field of the nerve.

The Ilio-inguinal Nerve

The ilio-inguinal nerve has the earmarks of a typical thoracic nerve: it is segmental in distribution, it is a continuation of an undivided anterior primary ramus (L1), and en route it gives off filaments to muscles (internal oblique and transverse). It differs from an intercostal, however, in that it has no true lateral branch.

The ilio-inguinal nerve circles the trunk at a level somewhat below that of the iliohypogastric (Figs. 239, 240). It travels between trans-

verse and internal oblique muscles and, after piercing the latter and
the external oblique (somewhat ventral to and below the anterior superior spine of the ilium), it courses along the inguinal ligament within
the inguinal canal. The ilio-inguinal nerve comes to the surface by
traversing the superficial inguinal ring and by penetrating the adjoining
external spermatic fascia.

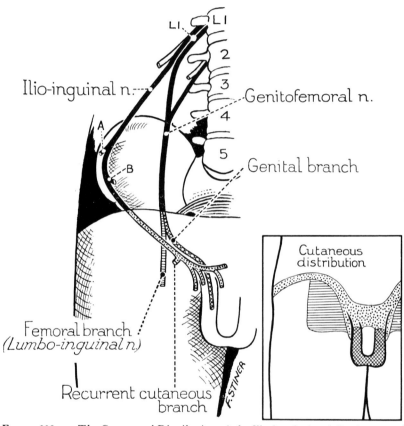

FIGURE 239.   *The Course and Distribution of the Ilio-inguinal and Genitofemoral
Nerves.* As the ilio-inguinal nerve courses along the crest of the
ilium it gives off branches (*A, B*) to abdominal muscles. The cutaneous distribution of each of the nerves is indicated in the inset.

Both muscles and skin are supplied by the ilio-inguinal nerve. The
muscular branches go to the internal oblique and the transverse. The
cutaneous branches emanate from the more medial part of the inguinal
canal. *Anterior branches* extend to (1) the anterior abdominal wall
overlying the symphysis of the pubis, (2) the root and dorsum of the
penis, (3) the upper part of the scrotum, and (4) the part of the thigh
medial to the femoral triangle. Usually a *lateral recurrent branch* inner-

vates a strip of skin of the thigh adjacent to the inguinal ligament (Figs. 30, 239).

Injury of the ilio-inguinal nerve is manifested either by pain or by sensory loss in the anatomical field of distribution (Fig. 240). Owing

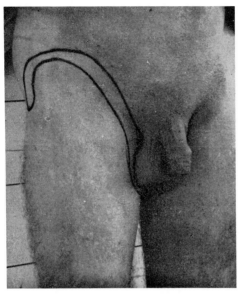

FIGURE 240.   *Area of Anesthesia Following Surgical Section of Ilio-inguinal Nerve in the Inguinal Canal.* The patient had neuralgia in this region subsequent to herniorrhaphy. The photograph was taken one week after operation. (C.H.)

to paralysis of the internal oblique an indirect inguinal hernia may ultimately develop.

The Genitofemoral Nerve

Formed by the union of two roots from the undivided anterior primary rami of segments of L1 and L2, the genitofemoral nerve (known also as the "genitocrural nerve") traverses the psoas major and courses downward into the pelvis in company with the common and external iliac arteries (Figs. 237, 239). Reaching the level of the inguinal ligament, it divides into two branches: (1) the *genital branch* (or "external spermatic nerve") (L1), which enters the deep inguinal ring, traverses the inguinal canal to terminate in the cremaster muscle and the skin of the scrotum and the adjacent part of the thigh; and (2) the *femoral branch* (the "lumbo-inguinal nerve") (L2), which passes into the thigh behind the middle of the inguinal ligament and penetrates the fascia lata to supply an area of skin over the femoral triangle.

Injury of this nerve may lead to neuralgia. In one such instance, a surgical section of the lumbo-inguinal nerve behind the inguinal liga-

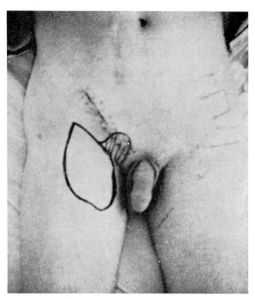

FIGURE 241.   *Area of Altered Sensibility Following Surgical Section of the Lumbo-inguinal Nerve.* The nerve was sectioned because of neuralgia. The photograph was taken one week after the operation. The lined part of the area is hyperesthetic, the unshaded portion analgesic and anesthetic. (C.H.)

ment was followed by sensory change in the region indicated in Figure 241.

The Lateral Cutaneous Nerve of the Thigh

The lateral cutaneous nerve of the thigh is formed by the union of a pair of roots from undivided primary rami L2 and L3 (Figs. 237, 242). The nerve penetrates the psoas major muscle, crosses the iliacus, extends to the region of the anterior superior spine of the ilium and in passing downward into the thigh it courses between the two prongs of the attachment of the lateral part of the inguinal ligament. The nerve continues its downward course, first deep to the fascia lata, then superficial to it. About 10 cm. beneath the anterior superior iliac spine it divides into two branches: the *anterior branch*, which supplies the lateral part of the anterior aspect of the thigh as far down as the knee, and the *posterior branch*, which is distributed to the upper two thirds of the lateral side of the thigh as well as to the lateral aspect of the buttock below the great trochanter.

The nerve is most subject to injury at the site where it passes between the two prongs of the inguinal ligament. Following injury to this region, the nerve tends to become constricted by scar tissue. As a con-

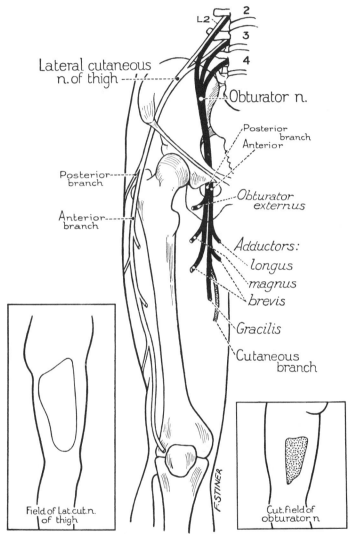

FIGURE 242.   *The Origin and Distribution of the Lateral Cutaneous Nerve of the Thigh and the Obturator Nerve.* The names of the muscles supplied are in italics. The cutaneous fields of each of the nerves are indicated.

sequence a condition known as *meralgia paresthetica* may develop. This consists of paresthesias, numbness and pain in the area of cutaneous distribution. Sometimes anesthesia ensues. Injuries elsewhere in the course of the nerve may produce the same symptoms.

The Obturator Nerve

ANATOMY

Origin and Course

The obturator arises from undivided anterior primary rami L3 and L4 and usually also from L2 (Figs. 237, 242). Its proximal part is in the substance of the psoas major. Taking a vertical course, the obturator emerges from the inner border of the psoas major, dips down into the pelvis (behind the common iliac vessels), proceeds forward and traverses the obturator foramen to reach the thigh. At the level of the obturator foramen it divides into two branches, anterior and posterior, which descend the medial side of the thigh.

Distribution

The obturator innervates muscles and skin of the thigh. No branches are given off in the pelvis. The distribution is as follows:

TABLE 10   *Distribution of the Obturator Nerve*

MUSCULAR BRANCHES

Anterior (Superficial) Branch	*Posterior (Deep) Branch*
Adductor longus	Obturator externus
Gracilis	Adductor magnus
Adductor brevis (frequently)	Adductor brevis (usually)
Pectineus (on occasion)	

CUTANEOUS BRANCH

To medial aspect of thigh

INJURIES

The chief function of the muscles supplied by the obturator is that of adduction of the thigh. The gracilis assists in flexion of the knee and in medial rotation of the tibia; the obturator externus aids in rotating the thigh outward. The adductors have the added function of flexing at the hip.

Interruption of the obturator is manifested chiefly by weakness of adduction of the thigh. Complete atrophy of this muscle group does not ensue since the adductor magnus also receives innervation from the sciatic and the adductor longus sometimes is supplied by the femoral nerve. In walking, the affected leg tends to swing outward because of the unopposed action of the abductors of the thigh. Sensory loss usually is encountered in only a part of the anatomical field. A case of combined palsy of the obturator, femoral and posterior cutaneous nerve of the thigh is illustrated in Figure 243.

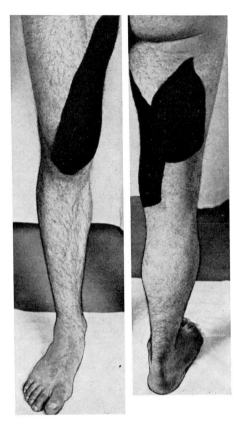

FIGURE 243.   *Sensory Loss of Medial and Posterior Aspects of the Thigh Following Multiple Gunshot Wounds.* The location of the sensory loss indicates interruption of the obturator and of branches of the femoral nerve and of the posterior cutaneous nerve of the thigh. (B.G.H.)

The Femoral Nerve

ANATOMY

Origin and Course

This nerve arises from undivided primary rami L2, L3 and L4 (Figs. 237, 244). In its early course the nerve penetrates the psoas major muscle. It then extends downward and, on passing deep to the inguinal ligament and lateral to the femoral artery, it enters the thigh. Just below the inguinal ligament it divides into a number of branches, one of which, the saphenous nerve (the "long," or "internal," saphenous nerve) extends from the region of the femoral triangle downward, in company with femoral vessels, to the subsartorial canal. Leaving the canal it becomes cutaneous on the medial malleolus and terminates at the middle of the medial border of the foot.

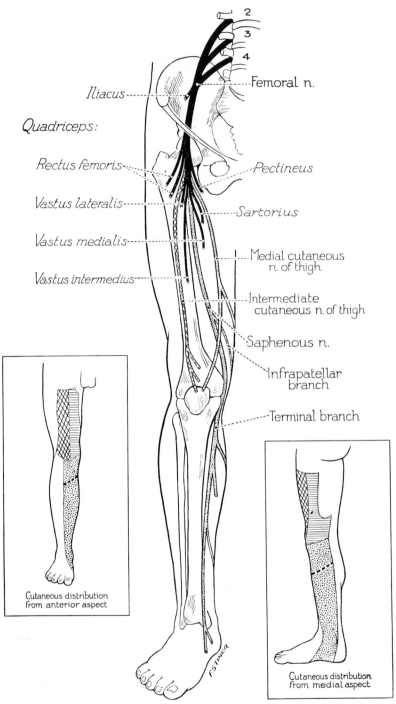

- 2
- 3
- 4
- Femoral n.
- Iliacus
- Quadriceps:
- Rectus femoris
- Pectineus
- Vastus lateralis
- Sartorius
- Vastus medialis
- Medial cutaneous n. of thigh
- Vastus intermedius
- Intermediate cutaneous n. of thigh
- Saphenous n.
- Infrapatellar branch
- Terminal branch
- Cutaneous distribution from anterior aspect
- Cutaneous distribution from medial aspect

F. STINER

FIGURE 244. *The Course and Distribution of the Femoral Nerve.* The names of the muscles supplied by this nerve are in italics. The patterns of the cutaneous nerves are duplicated in the insets. In the field of the saphenous nerve the broken line represents the boundary between the fields of the infrapatellar and terminal branches.

Distribution

The femoral nerve supplies muscles and skin of the front of the thigh. One of its cutaneous branches, the saphenous, is distributed to the medial side of the leg and foot (Fig. 244).

TABLE 11   *Distribution of the Femoral Nerve*

MUSCULAR BRANCHES

In Abdomen

Iliacus

In Thigh

Pectineus
Sartorius
Quadriceps femoris
Adductor longus (sometimes)

CUTANEOUS BRANCHES

In Thigh	*In Leg and Foot*
Intermediate cutaneous n.	Saphenous n.
Medial cutaneous n.	Infrapatellar branch
	Terminal branches

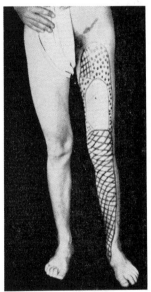

FIGURE 245.   *Femoral Nerve Palsy.* The patient received a missile wound in the left inguinal region and subsequently the femoral nerve became constricted by scar tissue. The photograph was taken six months after the injury. Moderate atrophy of the muscles of the anterior part of the thigh is visible. The *crosshatching* indicates hyperesthesia, the *dots* hypesthesia, and the *unmarked field* of the thigh, total anesthesia. The lumbo-inguinal nerve also is affected. (W.R.)

INJURIES

The muscles supplied by the femoral nerve function chiefly as extensors at the knee and as an aid in flexion of the thigh at the hip. Extension at the knee is initiated by the rectus femoris and is continued in collaboration with the vasti. The pectineus helps in adducting the thigh. The sartorius (the "tailor's muscle") takes part in flexion at the hip and the knee joint and in fixing the flexed hip; it also assists in lateral rotation of the thigh.

Injuries of the femoral trunk are seldom seen clinically since wounds in this region, by lacerating blood vessels, tend to be fatal. In femoral

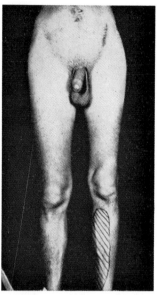

FIGURE 246.   *Partial Interruption of Femoral Nerve.* Nerve damage resulted when a bullet penetrated the lower left quadrant of the abdomen. Laparotomy was performed and perforations of the ileum repaired. Later a neurolysis of the left femoral nerve was carried out. Six months after injury there is still some atrophy of the quadriceps and an area of sensory deficit over the region of the saphenous nerve. (R.G.H.)

palsy, a wasting of the anterior part of the thigh is evident (Figs. 245, 246). There is a failure of the quadriceps to contract when the attempt is made to tighten the knee-cap and to elevate the foot from the bed. The patient is able to stand and to walk even though he cannot actively extend the leg at the knee or adequately flex at the hip. Level surfaces can be negotiated without much trouble even though the affected foot is planted insecurely and the knee overextended (by tensor fasciae latae and gracilis), but great difficulty is experienced in going uphill or upstairs.

Sensory deficit usually is encountered in most of the area within the anatomical limits of the field. Interruption involving the *saphenous nerve* usually produces anesthesia of the inner side of the leg from knee to ankle (Figs. 245, 246, 247).

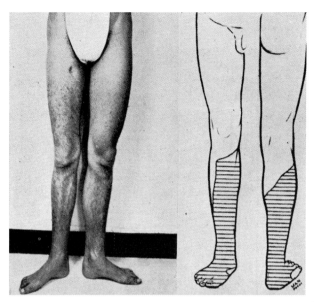

FIGURE 247.   *Partial Interruption of the Femoral and Sciatic Nerves in the Middle
Third of the Thigh, Right.* A shell fragment entered the lateral surface of the thigh midway between hip joint and knee and emerged
from the anteromedial surface of the thigh (note scar). Atrophy of
muscles of the thigh and the calf is visible. Among other movements,
lateral (external) rotation at the hip is defective. The sensory map
indicates involvement of saphenous as well as of tibial and common
peroneal nerves. The bottom of the foot was hyperesthetic.
(Rh.G.H.)

CHAPTER 14

Injuries of the Sacral Plexus and Its Constituent Nerves

The Sacral Plexus

THE SACRAL plexus is situated within the true pelvis. It is formed by the union of undivided primary rami L4, L5, S1, S2 and S3 and is sup-

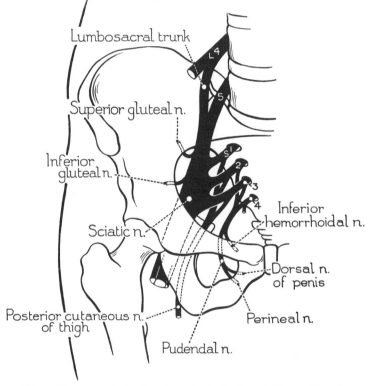

FIGURE 248. *Diagram of the Constituents of the Sacral Plexus.* The three divisions of the sciatic nerve are indicated. Not illustrated is the inferior medial clunical nerve, which arises from anterior primary rami S2 and S3 and courses downward between the posterior cutaneous nerve of the thigh and the pudendal nerve.

plemented by a part of S4 (Fig. 248). Ramus L4 also enters into the constitution of the lumbar plexus, while ramus S4 gives off a root to the coccygeal plexus. Like the lumbar plexus, it is composed of two parts: undivided anterior primary rami and divisions. Posterior divisions extend distally as superior gluteal, inferior gluteal, and common peroneal nerves; anterior divisions comprise the tibial nerve, the nerve to the hamstrings, the posterior cutaneous nerve of thigh, and the pudendal nerve.

Each undivided anterior primary ramus of the plexus receives postganglionic sympathetic fibers which pursue their course distally in the respective nerve trunks to reach blood vessels, sweat glands and piloerector muscles. In addition, undivided anterior primary rami S2, S3'and usually S4 give off parasympathetic fibers destined for the urinary bladder and anal sphincters.

Injuries of the sacral plexus are uncommon. Lesions of roots or undivided primary rami give rise to disabilities of segmental distribution.

Owing to the physical rigors of combat training and of actual warfare, *rupture of a lumbar intervertebral disc* is relatively frequent among troops. The clinical syndrome must also be differentiated from lesions of the lumbosacral plexus. The most common sites of disc protrusion are between the vertebrae L4 and L5 and between L5 and S1 where the nerve roots of L5 and S1 respectively may be compressed. In general, patients with lumbar disc lesions show alterations in the normal lumbar symmetry, with loss of the normal lumbar lordosis and scoliosis, paravertebral muscle spasm, restriction in flexion, and localized tenderness over the point of disc protrusion. The neurological changes in the lower extremity will include unilateral, bilateral or crossed leg raising restriction, loss or diminution of knee and ankle tendon reflexes, dermatome sensory alterations, and highly characteristic, minimal motor weakness (Spurling, 1953) (Figs. 15, 16).

The Sciatic Nerve and Its Branches

ANATOMY

The Sciatic Nerve Proper

The sciatic nerve takes origin from undivided primary rami L4, L5, S1, S2 and S3 (Fig. 248). As a single trunk (although even here it is divisible into component parts: tibial, common peroneal and nerve to the hamstring muscles) it leaves the pelvis by traversing the greater sciatic foramen. After emerging in the gluteal region it courses laterally and then downward, coming to lie in the hollow midway between the ischial tuberosity and the greater trochanter. In this region it is under cover of the gluteus maximus muscle. On reaching the thigh, where, at the inferior aspect of the buttock, it occupies a superficial position, the nerve descends in the plane between the adductor magnus and the hamstring muscles. At a variable distance above the popliteal fossa, the sciatic nerve terminates by dividing into two branches: the tibial and common peroneal.

Incorporated in the medial side of the sciatic trunk, or independent of it, is the *nerve to the hamstrings* (indicated but unlabeled in Fig. 248). It supplies adductor magnus, semimembranosus, semitendinosus, and the long head of the biceps femoris. The short head of the biceps is

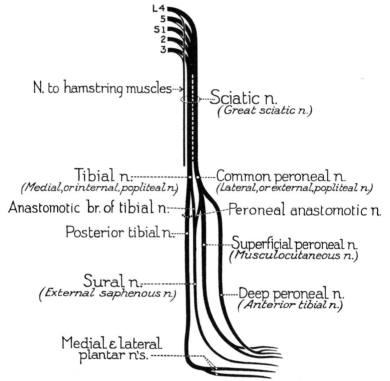

FIGURE 249.   *Diagram of the Divisions and Branches of the Sciatic Nerve.* The nerve to the hamstring muscles is incorporated in the sciatic trunk. The tibial nerve becomes the posterior tibial at the upper border of the soleus muscle (indicated by broken lines). Synonyms for the various nerves are included.

innervated by another component of the sciatic, the common peroneal. Other branches associated with the intrapelvic part of the sciatic are the *nerve to the quadratus femoris and inferior gemellus* (L4, L5, S1) and the *nerve to the obturator internus and superior gemellus* (L5, S1, S2). Neither is of clinical significance. (Twigs to the *piriformis muscle* come from rami S1 and S2).

The various branches derived from the sciatic nerve are shown diagrammatically in Figure 249. Seen as a whole, the pattern of distribution of sciatic branches is relatively simple. The *tibial nerve* gives off an anastomotic branch which joins the peroneal anastomotic nerve (p. 291) to form the *sural nerve*, the latter extending down the back of the leg to the outer side of the foot. At the upper level of the soleus muscle the tibial goes over into the *posterior tibial nerve*, which, on reaching the sole of the foot, divides into *medial* and *lateral plantar nerves*. The *common peroneal nerve* divides into the *superficial peroneal* and *deep peroneal nerves*, both of which ultimately reach the dorsum of the foot.

The Tibial Nerve (Fig. 250)

The tibial nerve is derived from all the undivided anterior primary rami of the sacral plexus. It becomes separated from its fellow, the common peroneal, at a variable distance above the popliteal fossa. The nerve extends downward in the middle of this fossa to the upper level of the soleus muscle. En route it gives off branches to the following muscles: gastrocnemius (both heads), plantaris, soleus, popliteus and usually the tibialis posterior. Moreover, as stated above, it contributes to the formation of the *sural nerve*. The latter nerve reaches the skin by piercing the deep fascia in the middle third of the back of the leg. It continues downward and, on reaching the ankle, gives off the *lateral calcanean nerve* to the heel; it then rounds the back of the lateral malleolus to enter the foot. The cutaneous distribution of this nerve is shown in Figure 250.

The Posterior Tibial Nerve (Fig. 250)

As stated in the section on Anatomy the posterior tibial nerve is a continuation of the tibial nerve. It starts at the level of the fibrous arch of the soleus. In its course downward, the nerve rests on the tibialis posterior muscle as well as on the tibia, then continues between flexor digitorum longus and flexor hallucis longus. The nerve terminates under the flexor retinaculum (behind and inferior to the medial malleolus) by dividing into the lateral and medial plantar nerves. The nerve supplies soleus, tibialis posterior, flexor digitorum longus, and flexor hallucis longus. The only cutaneous branch is the *medial calcanean nerve*, which supplies the corresponding part of the heel.

The Lateral and Medial Plantar Nerves (Fig. 250)

The terminals of the posterior tibial nerve are the lateral plantar nerve, which is the homologue of the ulnar nerve, and the medial plantar which corresponds to the median. Their muscular and cutaneous supplies are indicated in the legend of Figure 250. It will be noted in Figure 29 that these nerves also supply the distal part of the dorsal surfaces of the toes.

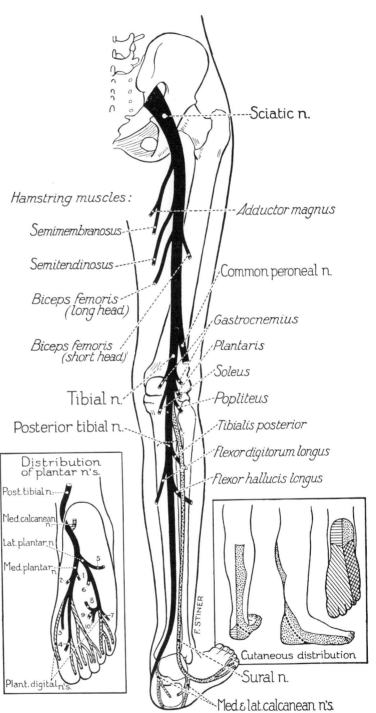

Sciatic n.

Hamstring muscles :

Adductor magnus

Semimembranosus

Semitendinosus

Common peroneal n.

Biceps femoris
(long head)

Gastrocnemius

Plantaris

Biceps femoris
(short head)

Soleus

Tibial n.

Popliteus

Posterior tibial n.

Tibialis posterior

Flexor digitorum longus

Flexor hallucis longus

Distribution
of plantar n's.

Post. tibial n.

Med. calcanean
n.

Lat. plantar n.

Med. plantar
n.

F. STINER

Cutaneous distribution

Sural n.

Plant. digital n's.

Med. & lat. calcanean n's.

FIGURE 250.   *The Course and Distribution of the Sciatic, Tibial, Posterior Tibial
and Plantar Nerves. A dotted line marks the transition between*

The Common Peroneal Nerve (Figs. 250 and 251)

Incorporated in the common peroneal, a nerve which is comparatively short, are fibers of spinal segments L4, L5, S1 and S2. Commencing in the lower part of the thigh, it courses downward along the lateral border of the popliteal fossa to reach the back of the head of the fibula. It winds round the neck of the fibula, whereupon it divides into superficial and deep peroneal nerves.

As the common peroneal nerve passes through the popliteal fossa it gives off two branches. One of these is the *lateral cutaneous nerve of the calf*, the distribution of which is indicated in Figure 251. The other is the *peroneal anastomotic nerve*, which after passing over the lateral head of the gastrocnemius muscle (beneath the deep fascia) extends to the middle third of the leg, where it joins the anastomotic (communicating) branch of the tibial nerve to form the *sural nerve* (Fig. 249). In the many instances in which the two anastomotic nerves fail to unite, the peroneal anastomotic nerve may supply the field of the sural nerve or be distributed only to the skin of the lateral side of the leg, heel, and ankle.

The Superficial Peroneal Nerve (Fig. 251)

The superficial peroneal nerve begins at the level of bifurcation of the common peroneal, i.e., just below the neck of the fibula. It descends the leg in front of the fibula, coursing between peronei and extensor digitorum longus. In the lower third of the leg it divides into two branches which become cutaneous by piercing the deep fascia. Both run downward to supply the skin of the front and side of the leg and the dorsum of the foot—in the areas indicated in Figure 251. En route the nerve gives off branches to the peroneus longus and brevis muscles.

The cutaneous nerve supply of the dorsum of the foot is subject to considerable variation. Frequently the superficial peroneal innervates all toes except the lateral half of the fifth. In some instances the sural nerve takes over much of the field of the lateral cutaneous branch of the superficial peroneal nerve.

---

tibial and posterior tibial nerves. The cutaneous fields of the medial calcanean and medial plantar nerves are indicated in the inset by *lines;* the field of the sural nerve and its lateral calcanean branch by *dots;* and that of the lateral plantar nerve, by *crosshatch.* The names of the muscles supplied are italicized. The numbered branches of the plantar nerves are as follows: 1, flexor digitorum brevis; 2, abductor hallucis; 3, flexor hallucis brevis; 4, 1st lumbrical; 5, abductor digiti quinti; 6, flexor digitorum accessorius; 7, flexor digiti quinti brevis; 8, adductor hallucis; 9, interossei; 10, 2d, 3d and 4th lumbricals. In order to simplify, the sural nerve is indicated as arising solely from the tibial nerve; actually it usually receives an anastomotic branch from the common peroneal nerve, as illustrated in Figure 249.

The Deep Peroneal Nerve (Fig. 252)

This nerve begins just below the head of the fibula. It winds round
the neck of the fibula, gaining the front of the leg, where it pursues its

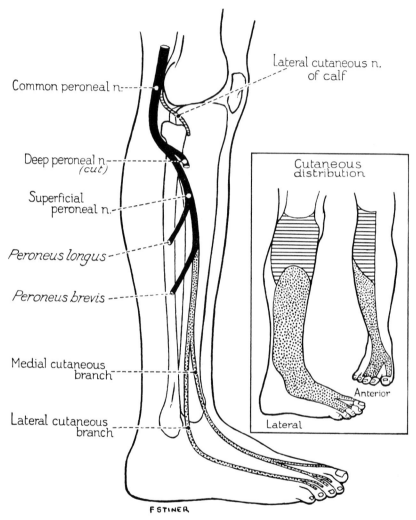

Common peroneal n.

Lateral cutaneous n.
of calf

Deep peroneal n.
(cut)

Superficial
peroneal n.

Peroneus longus

Peroneus brevis

Medial cutaneous
branch

Lateral cutaneous
branch

Cutaneous
distribution

Anterior

Lateral

F STINER

FIGURE 251.   *The Course and Distribution of the Superficial Peroneal Nerve.* The
names of the muscles innervated are in italics. The dotted pattern in
the inset indicates the cutaneous field of the superficial peroneal
nerve, the lined pattern that of a branch of the common peroneal
nerve, the lateral cutaneous nerve of the calf.

course on the interosseous membrane and on the distal part of the tibia.
Reaching the ankle it passes under the superior extensor retinaculum;
and on gaining the foot it divides into medial and lateral branches: the

former extends to the skin of the lateral side of the great toe, the medial side of the second toe and ends in the first dorsal interosseous muscle, while the latter reaches the extensor digitorum brevis. The deep per-

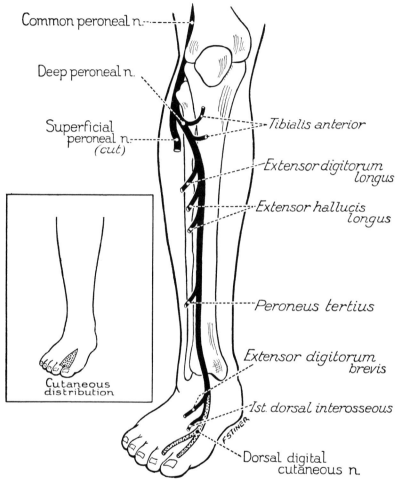

Common peroneal n.

Deep peroneal n.

Superficial
    peroneal n.
        (cut)

Tibialis anterior

Extensor digitorum
                longus

Extensor hallucis
                longus

Peroneus tertius

Extensor digitorum
                brevis

1st. dorsal interosseous

Cutaneous
distribution

Dorsal digital
        cutaneous n.

FIGURE 252.   *The Course and Distribution of the Deep Peroneal Nerve.* The muscles supplied are indicated in italics. The cutaneous distribution of the nerve is shown in the inset.

oneal nerve and its branches supply the following muscles: tibialis anterior, extensor hallucis longus, extensor digitorum longus, peroneus tertius, first dorsal interosseous muscle, and extensor digitorum brevis.

INJURIES

Injuries of the Common Peroneal Nerve and Its Branches

Of all the sciatic branches, the common peroneal is most liable to injury. Even when there is direct trauma to the sciatic trunk the common peroneal usually is affected more than the tibial. The nerve may be seriously injured not only by missiles but also by stretching subsequent to fracture of the head of the fibula and by rupture of the lateral collateral ligament (Platt, 1940; Highet and Holmes, 1943); moreover it is susceptible to pressure exerted in the region of the head of the fibula, for instance by a tightly applied plaster cast (Fig. 151).

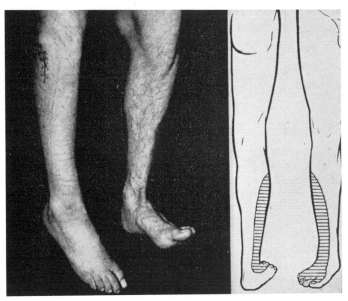

FIGURE 253.   *Common Peroneal Nerve Palsy, Right.* Fracture of the neck of the fibula and "stretch" injury to the common peroneal nerve occurred when this soldier fell into a gulley to avoid strafing. Among other movements, dorsiflexion of the foot and toes cannot be performed. The sensory deficit is in the fields of the superficial and deep peroneal nerves. Sural, plantar nerves and other branches of the tibial have escaped damage. (W.R.)

The *deep peroneal nerve* (anterior tibial) is commonly affected by pressure exerted in the popliteal fossa and in the region of the head of the fibula as well as by undue stretching and even by crossing the legs (Eaton, 1937). The deep peroneal nerve supplies the dorsiflexors of the foot and the extensors of the toes. Consequently, interruption of this nerve leads to foot-drop; efforts to raise the foot or to elevate the toes are unavailing (Fig. 253). "Steppage gait" is apparent, and an examination of the dorsum of the foot will reveal that the tendons no longer stand out prominently as they do under normal circumstances. When nerve involvement is incomplete the play, or dance, of the various tendons will differ as the foot is put in such a position as to stretch them, for instance by having the patient stand on his heels. Because of atrophy of the muscles which extend the foot, the tibia stands out sharply like a keel. In determining the strength of dorsi-flexion at the ankle it is important that the foot first be lifted into a dorsal position before the testing is done, for although the foot is in-capable of dorsiflexion from the plantar position it may retain its dorsal position against gravity. When tapped, the toes may exhibit rebound dorsiflexion when their extensor muscles are paralyzed.

If the superficial peroneal nerve is intact and its muscles (peroneus longus and brevis) are working unopposed, the foot tends to evert when the patient walks. In time pes valgus may develop.

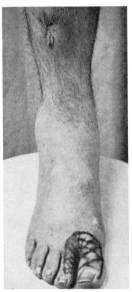

FIGURE 254.   *Interruption of the More Distal Part of the Deep Peroneal Nerve.*
Multiple missile wounds of the leg were incurred. Sensory loss is confined to the field of the deep peroneal nerve. There is no motor disability. (B.G.H.)

When the deep peroneal nerve is divided below the point where branches are given off to the tibialis anterior and the extensor digitorum longus, the patient can perform all movements adequately except ele-vation of the great toe. Implication of the extensor digitorum brevis may be detected by electrical tests. Sensory deficit often occurs in the region between the great and second toe (Fig. 254).

The *superficial peroneal nerve* supplies the muscles of the side of the leg, the peroneus longus and brevis, which evert the foot. After inter-ruption of this nerve, eversion can no longer be performed. Dorsiflexion is possible, but in the course of the movement the foot tends to become inverted. In longstanding cases the foot may acquire an equinovarus position.

Sensory loss is usually confined to the more medial part of the dorsum of the foot, leaving the cutaneous fields of deep peroneal and sural intact, but it may also be detected on the lateral aspect of the lower leg (Figs. 255, 256).

In *injuries of the common peroneal nerve* (lateral, or external, popliteal nerve), the clinical picture is the sum of those which follow injuries to deep and superficial peroneal nerves. Owing to loss of dorsi-

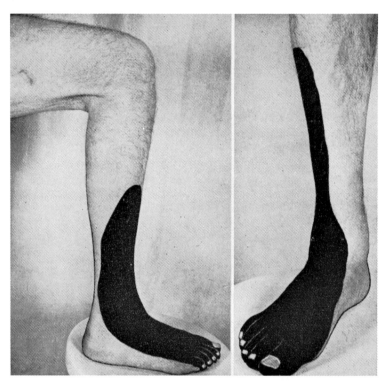

FIGURE 255.   *Common Peroneal Nerve Palsy Following Injury of the Sciatic Nerve.* The site of exit of the missile is visible. Sensory loss is present only in the field of the common peroneal nerve. (B.G.H.)

flexion and eversion at the ankle, the foot hangs down, often assuming the equinovarus position: the inversion, which is due chiefly to the unopposed action of the tibialis posterior, is not to be construed as evidence that the tibialis anterior is contracting. This possibility may be easily ruled out by noting the loss of ability to dorsiflex at the ankle, which under normal conditions is induced by contraction of the tibialis anterior. Another feature of palsy of the common peroneal nerve is that of loss of power to straighten or elevate the toes. What is known as "steppage" gait results: the distal part of the foot and its outer margin drag, and at the end of the excursion the foot tends to strike the ground with an audible "clop." *Delayed common peroneal palsies* are illustrated in Figures 150 and 256.

Sensory deficit usually is encountered in the dorsum of the foot and outer side of the leg. Examples are shown in Figures 150, 255, and 256.

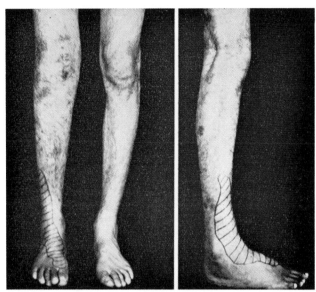

FIGURE 256.   *Delayed Palsy of the Common Peroneal Nerve, Right.* The right knee was crushed between two trucks. Involvement of the common peroneal nerve was not apparent until one week later. Subsequently, the wound broke down and sequestra were removed. The sensory deficit is in the region of the common peroneal nerve. (R.G.H.)

Injuries of the Tibial Nerve and Its Branches

Since the tibial nerve supplies muscles of the back of the leg and the sole of the foot, an interruption of the nerve makes plantar flexion of the foot and toes impossible (Fig. 257).

Complete posterior tibial nerve palsy entails the loss of function of flexor digitorum longus and flexor hallucis longus and of muscles of the plantar surface of the foot. Usually the most striking finding in early cases is that of sensory loss over the plantar surface of the foot (Fig. 258). In time the small muscles of the foot undergo atrophy, increasing the concavity of the plantar arch (pes cavus) and otherwise altering pedal contours.

When interruption of the posterior tibial nerve occurs distal to the level where muscular branches are given off, changes usually are encountered only on the sole of the foot (Fig. 259). These changes consist of complete sensory loss and anhidrosis. On occasion claw-foot may develop; distal toe joints are plantarflexed (by the flexor digitorum

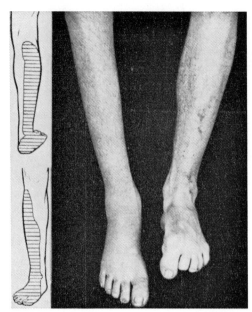

FIGURE 257. *Combined Tibial and Common Peroneal Palsy, Right, Due to Gunshot Wound of the Lower Thigh.* There is atrophy of the muscles of the anterior and lateral aspects of the calf of the leg. The foot-drop and inability to plantarflex the toes are due to interruption of common peroneal and tibial nerves, respectively. (W.R.)

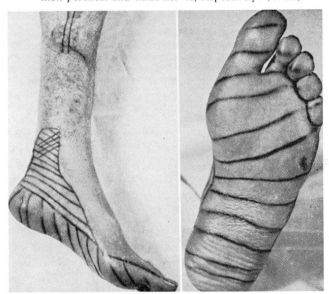

FIGURE 258. *The Region of Sensory Loss in a Case of Interruption of the Posterior Tibial Nerve.* A machine gun bullet penetrated the lowermost region of the calf. Subsequent causalgia was relieved by sympathectomy. One year after the injury the predominant sensory loss is in the fields of the plantar nerves. Note the characteristic pressure, or trophic, ulcer over the head of the fifth metatarsal bone. (B.G.H.)

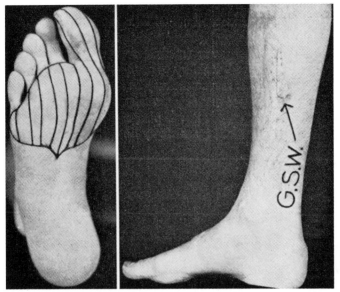

FIGURE 259.   *Partial Interruption of the Posterior Tibial Nerve Below the Level Where Muscular Branches Are Given Off.* The site of entrance of a bullet (G.S.W.) is indicated. Muscle power is normal. Anesthesia of the entire plantar surface of the foot gradually receded until only the ball of the foot and great toe were hypesthetic. (R.G.H.)

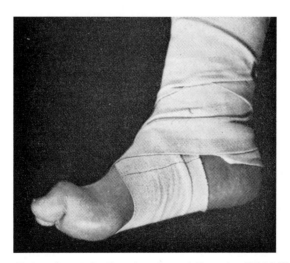

FIGURE 260.   *Deformity of the Toes in a Case of Posterior Tibial Nerve Injury.* The toes are dorsiflexed at the metacarpophalangeal joints and plantarflexed at the phalangeals. The attitude of the great toe is due to unopposed action of the extensor hallucis longus and brevis. Injury to the uppermost part of the posterior tibial nerve occurred seven months previously. Compare with Figure 152 in which deformity of the toes is lacking. (W.R.)

longus) while the metatarsophalangeal ones are dorsiflexed (unopposed action of the extensors in conjunction with paralysis of the interossei) (Fig. 260).

In *palsy of the tibial nerve* (medial, or internal, popliteal) similar changes may be observed. Inability to plantarflex the foot also is noted, though on occasion this movement may be performed by means of the peroneus longus (*a supplementary movement*). Another characteristic of tibial nerve palsy is that of loss of plantar flexion of the toes but this movement may be induced by strongly dorsiflexing the foot, thereby

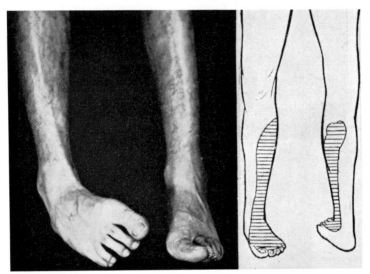

FIGURE 261.   *Interruption of the Tibial (Below the Level Where the Sural Nerve Is Given Off) and Common Peroneal Nerves.* The left popliteal region was severely contused in a motorcycle accident. At operation the distal part of the tibial and the common peroneal were found encompassed by scar tissue. Among movements lost is inversion of the foot—an action dependent chiefly on the tibial nerve. Sensory deficit involves also the entire sole of the foot. (W.R.)

stretching the flexor tendons. Inversion at the ankle is merely impaired (paralysis of the tibialis posterior muscle) since in this movement the anterior tibial muscle participates. In combined tibial and common peroneal palsy the ability to invert the foot is lost (Fig. 261).

The patient experiences difficulty in getting his heel off the ground in walking. The gait is shuffling and the steps devoid of spring. Injuries of the more proximal part of the tibial nerve tend to involve certain elements of the nerve more than others: the small muscles of the foot, the flexor digitorum longus and the tibialis posterior are likely to be affected, in that order (Foerster, 1937).

If the lesion is below the point where the sural (external saphenous)

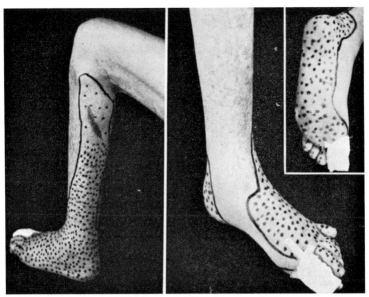

FIGURE 262.   *Complete Interruption of the Common Peroneal and Sural Nerves Together with Partial Interruption of the Tibial.* Shell fragments penetrated the popliteal space. The scar in the upper third of the calf is from another wound which caused no significant nerve damage. The distal extension of Hoffmann-Tinel's sign in this case is illustrated in Figure 169. (W.R.)

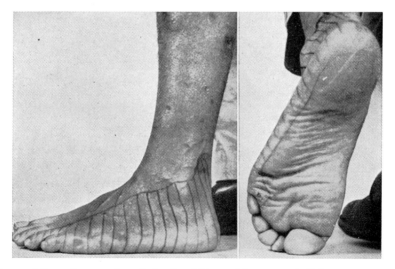

FIGURE 263.   *Interruption of the Sural Nerve.* Numerous shell fragments penetrated the leg several months previously. The only remaining sensory deficit is in the field of the sural nerve. (R.G.H.)

nerve is given off, sensory loss usually is encountered over the more medial part of the plantar surface of the foot and over the distal third of the side of the leg (Fig. 261); if above this level, sensory loss will encompass the lateral edge of the foot as well (Fig. 262). Occasionally the sural nerve bears the brunt of an injury (Fig. 263).

Injuries of the Sciatic Nerve

Injuries of the sciatic nerve are frequent in combat and are often due to the passage of a missile through the nerve. Sciatic nerve paralysis may also occur in association with fracture of the femur or posterior dislo-

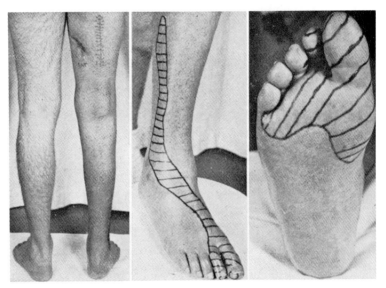

FIGURE 264.   *Incomplete Interruption of the Sciatic Nerve in the Region of the Thigh.* The site of the exit of a missile is indicated. The calf muscles are markedly atrophied. Sensory loss is in the fields of the common peroneal and the tibial. (B.G.H.)

cation of the hip. Regardless of the type of trauma, the peroneal component of the sciatic usually suffers more damage than the tibial (Figs. 150, 255, 264). Sometimes they are affected equally (Figs. 265, 266), and occasionally only tibial elements are involved (Fig. 267). In acute injury of the sciatic nerve, the leg is for a time completely paralyzed; hence, precise localization of the lesion is not possible until a week or two after the injury.

TOTAL INTERRUPTION   Total interruption of the sciatic in missile wounds is uncommon. When it occurs much of the leg becomes useless. Ability to flex and extend at ankle and toe joints and power of eversion and inversion of the foot are lost. The position of talipes equinus

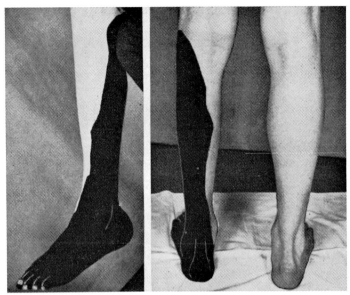

FIGURE 265.   *Interruption of Distal Portion of Sciatic Nerve, Left.* Both the tibial and the common peroneal nerves have been interrupted. The muscles of the calf are atrophied. The area of anesthesia includes also the sole of the foot. (B.G.H.)

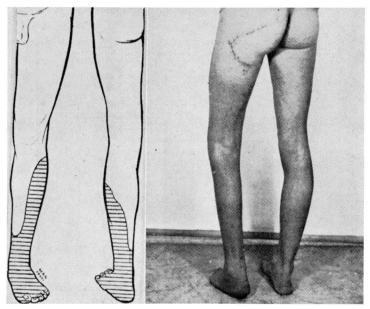

FIGURE 266.   *The Area of Sensory Loss in a Case of Sciatic Nerve Palsy, Left.* A bullet penetrated the region of the left buttock. Thigh and lower leg muscles are atrophic. The sensory loss is in the areas of distribution of tibial and common peroneal nerves. (H.G.H.)

303

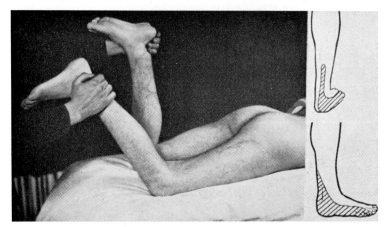

FIGURE 267.   *Partial Interruption of Sciatic Nerve, Right.* A bullet traversed the lower aspect of the buttock. Flexion at the knee is considerably weakened. The tendon of the semitendinosus (on the medial side of the knee) is visible but not the tendon of the long head of the biceps femoris (on the lateral side). The sensory deficit is in the fields of distribution of the sural and posterior tibial nerves. Previously the cutaneous field of the superficial peroneal nerve also had been affected. (W.R.)

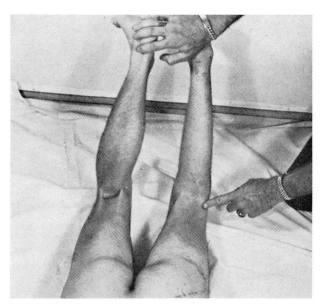

FIGURE 268.   *Sciatic Nerve Palsy, Left.* A bullet penetrated the left gluteal region four months previously. There is atrophy of certain of the hamstring muscles (especially the long head of the biceps where the examiner's finger points) as well as those of the lower leg. (H.G.H.)

inevitably is assumed and frequently a "flail movement" can be produced at the ankle. Flexion at the knee is usually greatly impaired, but despite paralysis of the biceps femoris, semitendinosus and semimembranosus the movement may be fairly well performed by the sartorius (femoral nerve) and gracilis (obturator nerve). Cases in which the hamstring muscles were partially damaged are illustrated in Figures 267 and 268.

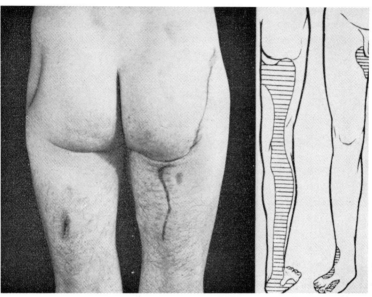

FIGURE 269.   *Partial Paralysis of the Gluteus Maximus, Right.* Mortar shell fragments penetrated the right infragluteal region eleven months previously. The belly of the muscle hangs down, the infragluteal fold is of diminished depth, and the hollow between buttock and trochanter is unduly shallow. Sensory defects are in the region of distribution of the sciatic (sole of the foot included) and of the posterior cutaneous nerve of the thigh. (W.R.)

Extension at the knee is unimpaired by interruption of the sciatic nerve. Thigh movements are unaffected except for extension at the hip, which may be slightly weakened. The ensuing atrophy leads to "spindle-leg." The patient is able to stand, but when he walks his gait is peculiar in that he flexes unduly at the hip in order to bring the dropped foot clear of the ground. If the Achilles tendon is palpated while the patient is standing, it will be found much softer than that of the sound side. (Where sciatic nerve injury is in question this palpation test is a valuable aid in assessing the degree of hypotonia of the calf muscles; Wartenberg, 1953.)

Sensibility below the knee is lost except along the inner side of the leg and ankle, which is innervated by the saphenous nerve (Figs. 262, 266).

INTERRUPTION OF THE TIBIAL AND PERONEAL COMPONENTS OF THE SCIATIC NERVE WITH PRESERVATION OF THE NERVE TO THE HAMSTRINGS Simultaneous loss of function of these two sciatic components as a consequence of war wounds is common. In such cases flexion at the knee is, for all practical purposes, preserved.

THE ASSOCIATION OF SCIATIC WITH OTHER PALSIES   Wounds of the buttock which involve the sciatic may injure adjacent nerves as well. Thus, in associated inferior gluteal nerve palsy the buttock is flaccid and is displaced downward, the cutaneous fold between buttock and thigh losing in depth (Fig. 269). The power of extension at the hip is impaired or lost (Fig. 272.) When the posterior cutaneous nerve of the thigh is included in the injury, the back of the thigh is either hypesthetic or anesthetic (Fig. 269).

The Superior and Inferior Gluteal Nerves

The superior and inferior gluteal nerves supply muscles of the buttock. They arise from the posterior surface of the plexus: the superior gluteal from rami L4, L5 and S1, and the inferior gluteal from rami L5, S1 and S2 (Fig. 248).

The *superior gluteal nerve* takes a lateral course, leaving the pelvis via the greater sciatic foramen (Fig. 270). It enters the buttock by passing above the piriformis muscle, and as it proceeds laterally it gives off branches to the gluteus medius and gluteus minimus. These two muscles have an important role in abduction and in medial rotation of the thigh. The nerve also supplies the tensor fasciae latae.

Paralysis of the gluteus medius is readily detectable. When the patient is recumbent the affected leg is rotated outward. In walking, the trunk bends somewhat toward the affected side. When the patient stands on the affected leg, the contralateral part of the pelvis drops, as may be easily recognized when the examiner places a finger on each of the anterior superior spines of the ilium. Another test of value is that of having the patient stand with the side to be tested close against a wall. When the weight is placed on the leg next to the wall the patient will fall or turn sharply away from the wall owing to the pelvic tilt.

The *inferior gluteal nerve* gains the buttock in company with the sciatic and the posterior cutaneous nerve of the thigh (Fig. 270). On reaching the lower border of the piriformis it divides into a number of branches which supply the gluteus maximus.

Interruption of the inferior gluteal nerve paralyzes the gluteus maximus, thus seriously interfering with extension at the hip; as a consequence there is difficulty in rising from a sitting position, in going up stairs, and the like. The belly of the muscle sags, the infragluteal fold

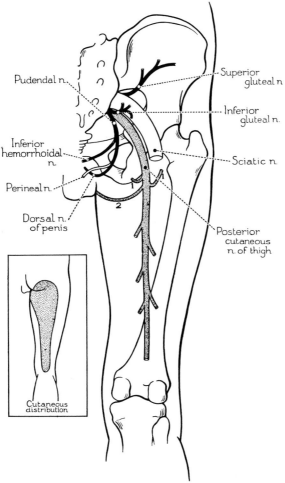

FIGURE 270.   *The Course of Nerves Derived from the Sacral Plexus.* The respective courses of the superior and inferior gluteals, the pudendal and the posterior cutaneous nerve of the thigh, as well as their relation to the sciatic, are indicated. The two most proximal branches of the posterior cutaneous nerve of the thigh extend on to the buttock; the third reaches the lateral aspect of the scrotum (see inset). The distribution of the perineal nerve is indicated in the inset and in Figure 31.

is all but erased and the hollow adjacent to the greater trochanter disappears (Fig. 269). Eventually, atrophy of the buttock becomes obvious.

The Posterior Cutaneous Nerve of the Thigh

The posterior cutaneous nerve of the thigh is derived from anterior primary rami S2 and S3, and usually also that of S1. It reaches the but-

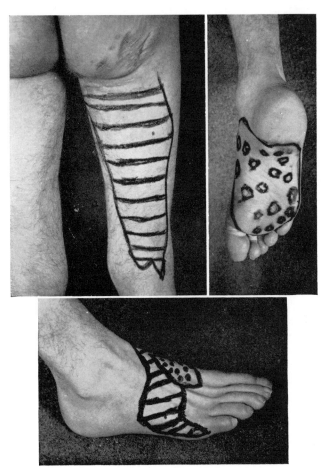

FIGURE 271.   *Interruption of the Posterior Cutaneous Nerve of the Thigh (Complete) and of the Sciatic Nerve (Partial).* The sites of entrance of machine gun bullets and shell fragments in the gluteal region are visible. The sensory maps indicate involvement of the posterior cutaneous nerve of the thigh and of the superficial peroneal and posterior tibial components of the sciatic nerve. The *lines* indicate anesthesia and analgesia, the *dots* hypesthesia, and the *circles* hyperesthesia. The wounds were received in July, 1944, and the photographs were taken in May, 1945. By that time considerable improvement had occurred in both motor and sensory function. (W.R.)

tock by passing through the greater sciatic foramen and then courses downward into the buttock on the medial side of the sciatic nerve (Fig.

270). Its close association with this nerve has gained for the posterior cutaneous nerve the name "lesser sciatic nerve."

Reaching the inferior border of the gluteus maximus, the nerve extends downward under the fascia lata in the groove between the biceps femoris and semitendinosus to reach the popliteal fossa, giving off, en route, branches to the skin of the posterior aspect of the thigh and popliteal fossa (Fig. 270). The main branches of this nerve are: ·(1) the *inferior lateral clunical nerves*, which pass round the medial border of the gluteus maximus to supply the more lateral part of the inferior

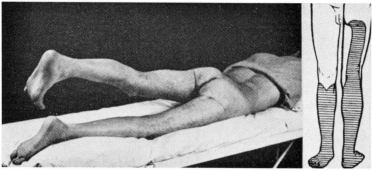

FIGURE 272.   *Interruption of the Sciatic and of the Posterior Cutaneous Nerve of the Thigh, Right.* The nerves in the region of the sciatic notch were injured by a bullet which entered the lower part of the right buttock and emerged from the lateral aspect of the left buttock. All muscles supplied by the sciatic are paralytic. The patient is able to extend the left leg at the hip but not the right one. Other movements depending on the sciatic also cannot be performed. Loss of sensibility is complete. The sensory map indicates also that the posterior nerve of the thigh is completely functionless. (W.R.)

aspect of the buttock, and (2) the *perineal branches*, which extend medially below the ischial tuberosity to supply the more lateral part of the perineum, a small lateral area of the adjoining part of the scrotum, and the root of the penis.

Interruption of the nerve gives rise to sensory deficit of variable extent on the back of the thigh, the lateral part of the perineum, and the lower lateral part of the buttock (Figs. 269, 271, 272).

Closely associated with the posterior cutaneous nerve of the thigh is the *inferior medial clunical nerve*, which arises independently from anterior primary rami S2 and S3 and extends downward by piercing the sacrotuberous ligament; it then winds round the lower border of the gluteus maximus and becomes cutaneous near the coccyx, and supplies the more medial part of the inferior aspect of the buttock (Figs. 28, 31). In Cunningham's textbook this nerve is referred to simply as the "perforating cutaneous nerve." Sometimes this nerve is incorporated as a gluteal branch of the posterior cutaneous nerve of the thigh or it may be a branch of the pudendal nerve.

The Pudendal and Associated Nerves

The pudendal and other nerves of the lower sacral plexus, being protected by the bony pelvis, do not figure significantly in peripheral nerve injuries. Their involvement is indicated by loss of perineal and scrotal sensibility, and when bilaterally damaged there are disturbances in function of the bladder, rectum and external genitalia, the most striking of which consists of urinary retention, followed by overflow (dribbling) incontinence and in due time, if severe bladder infection has not supervened, by bladder automaticity. Such disabilities occurring in the wounded are more commonly due to lesions involving the cauda equina and/or conus medullaris.

The bladder and rectum are supplied by pudendal, sympathetic and parasympathetic nerves. Afferent fibers from the bladder and rectum utilize the same routes as pursued by the sympathetic and parasympathetic fibers.

THE PUDENDAL (OR PUDIC) NERVE

The pudendal nerve is the chief source of supply of the perineum, scrotum, and penis. Through its branches to the external sphincter of the bladder come impulses which are concerned with the voluntary control of urination. The nerve takes origin from undivided anterior primary rami S, S3 and S4, and extends into the gluteal region via the greater sciatic foramen (Fig. 270). In this part of its course the nerve is medial and inferior to the sciatic. Reaching the gluteal region it bends downward and passes through the lesser sciatic foramen to reach the perineum. While in the pudendal canal (situated in the lateral wall of the ischiorectal fossa) it divides into terminal branches: the *inferior hemorrhoidal nerves*, which supply the sphincter ani externus and the skin encircling the anus; the *perineal nerve*, which, after giving off scrotal nerves, supplies various perineal muscles, the bulb and the corpus spongiosus of the penis as well as the mucous membrane of most of the urethra; and the *dorsal nerve of the penis*, which, after sending branches to the crus and corpus cavernosum of the penis, continues on to innervate the skin of the distal two thirds of the penis (Fig. 30).

SYMPATHETIC NERVES

The sympathetic nerves to the bladder arise in spinal segments T12, L1 and L2. The preganglionic fibers course downward in the sympathetic chain, emerge as splanchnic nerves which extend to the inferior mesenteric and more distal ganglia of the pelvic plexus. Postganglionic fibers, passing through the hypogastric plexus, go to the detrusor and the internal sphincter of the bladder. By inhibiting the former and contracting the latter, the sympathetic fibers are concerned in the filling of the bladder. Filling and evacuation are, however, not dependent on the integrity of the sympathetic innervation for, as a rule, both proceed in a normal manner after hypogastric sympathectomy. In regard to the rectum, the sympathetic system also plays a subsidiary role, its main action being that of inducing the accumulation of the bowel contents by exerting an inhibitory action on the bowel wall. Here, too, section of the hypogastric nerves has little functional consequence.

SACRAL PARASYMPATHETIC NERVES

The sacral parasympathetic nerves are instrumental in evacuation of the bladder and in defecation. The preganglionic fibers arise from spinal segments S2, S3 and usually S4, course out the corresponding anterior roots to gain undivided anterior primary rami (Fig. 10). Emerging from these rami, the fibers extend distally via the pelvic plexus to reach postganglionic cell stations adjacent to and within the outer wall of the bladder and rectum. Postganglionic fibers gaining the bladder innervate the detrusor and internal sphincter. Evacuation is dependent largely on the rhythmic contractions of the bladder, which increase in intensity as the bladder becomes more and more distended. When, under normal conditions, these contractions are sufficiently intense, the internal sphincter relaxes and the urine escapes into the urethra; then, unless successfully opposed voluntarily, the external sphincter relaxes and bladder evacuation proceeds. The rhythmic contractions and the relaxation of the internal sphincter are dependent on the parasympathetic innervation, though the postganglionic neurons are capable of considerable independent action when separated from the spinal cord by interruption of the preganglionic neurons; the relaxation of the external sphincter is dependent, as mentioned, on inhibitory action exercised through the pudendal nerve. Acute injury to either set of nerves results in paralysis of the evacuation mechanism and thus leads to urinary retention.

In the presence of injury of the cauda equina, automatic defecation usually occurs through the action of the anal plexus. Since under such conditions the pudendal nerve is also interrupted, voluntary control over defecation can no longer be exercised. Acute damage of sacral or higher levels of the spinal cord has a greater tendency to lead to fecal incontinence for paralysis of rectum and internal sphincter is more pronounced.

Bibliography

Abbott, L. C., and Saunders, J. B. deC. M.: Injuries of the Median Nerve in Fractures of the Lower End of the Radius. Surg., Gynec. & Obst. *57*:507–516, 1933.

Albert, M., and Mitchell, W. R. D.: Volkmann's Ischaemia of the Leg. Lancet *1*:519–522, 1943.

Appleton, A. B.: A Case of Abnormal Distribution of the N. Musculocutaneous, with Complete Absence of the Ramus Cutaneous N. Radialis. J. Anat. & Physiol. *46*:89–94, 1911.

Athanassio-Bénisty: Traitement et restauration des lésions des nerfs. Paris, Masson et Cie., 1917.

Bauwens, P.: Electro-Diagnosis and Electrotherapy in Peripheral Nerve Lesions. Proc. Roy. Soc. Med. *34*:459–468, 1941.

Bénisty, A.: Treatment and Repair of Nerve Lesions. London, University of London Press, 1918.

Bing, R.: Compendium of Regional Diagnosis in Lesions of the Brain and Spinal Cord. Ed. 11, transl. and edited by W. Haymaker. St. Louis, The C. V. Mosby Co., 1940.

Black, A. N., Burns, B. D., and Zuckerman, S.: An Experimental Study of the Wounding Mechanism of High-Velocity Missiles. Brit. M. J. *2*:872–874, 1941.

Bodechtel, G., Krautzun, K., and Kazmeier, F.: Grundriss der traumatischen peripheren Nervenschädigungen. Mit Berücksichtigung der Berufskrankheiten. (Vom neurologischen Standpunkt aus gesehen). 2. Aufl., Stuttgart, Georg Thieme, 1951.

Bolk, L.: Die Segmentaldifferenzierung des menschlichen Rumpfes und seiner Extremitäten. II. Beiträge zur Anatomie und Morphogenese des menschlichen Körpers. Morphol. Jahrb. *26*:91–211, 1898.

Bowden, R. E. M., and Gutmann, E.: Denervation and Re-innervation of Human Voluntary Muscle. Brain *67*:273–313, 1944.

Bradley, K. C.: Personal communication to the authors, 1953.

Callender, G. R.: Wound Ballistics. Mechanism of Production of Wounds by Small Arms Bullets and Shell Fragments. War Med. *3*:337–350, 1943.

Creutz, W.: Arthropathie aus peripherer Nervenschädigung. Ztschr. f. d. ges. Neurol. u. Psychiat. *138*:140–148, 1932.

Cunningham's Text-book of Anatomy. Ed. 9, edited by J. C. Brash. London, Oxford University Press, 1951.

Dejerine, J.: Sémiologie des affections du système nerveux. Paris, Masson et Cie., 1914.

——— and Schwartz, E.: Déformations articulaires analogues à celles du rhumatisme chronique avec troubles trophiques cutanés et hyperidrose relevant d'une lésion irritative du nerf médian. Rev. neurol. 27:414–417, 1915.

Denny-Brown, D., and Brenner, C.: The Effects of Percussion of Nerve. J. Neurol., Neurosurg. & Psychiat. *7*:76–95, 1944a.

———, and ———: Lesion in Peripheral Nerve Resulting from Compression by Spring Clip. Arch. Neurol. & Psychiat. *52*:1–19, 1944b.

Denny-Brown, D., and Brenner, C.: Paralysis of Nerve Induced by Direct Pressure and by Tourniquet. Arch. Neurol. & Psychiat. *51*:1–26, 1944c.

———, and Pennybacker, J. B.: Fibrillation and Fasciculation in Voluntary Muscle. Brain *61*:311–334, 1938.

Doupe, J., Cullen, C. H., and Chance, G. Q.: Post-traumatic Pain and the Causalgic Syndrome. J. Neurol., Neurosurg. & Psychiat. *7*:33–48, 1944.

Eaton, L. M.: Paralysis of the Peroneal Nerve Caused by Crossing the Legs: Report of a Case. Proc. Staff Meet. Mayo Clin. *12*:206–208, 1937.

Echlin, F., Owens, Jr., F. M., and Wells, W. L.: Observations on "Major" and "Minor" Causalgia. Arch. Neurol. & Psychiat. *62*:183–203, 1949.

Elkin, D. C.: The Treatment of Aneurysms and Arteriovenous Fistulas. Bull. N. Y. Acad. Med. *22*:81–87, 1946.

———, and Woodhall, B.: Combined Vascular and Nerve Injuries of Warfare. Ann. Surg. *119*:411–431, 1944.

Foerster, O.: Die Symptomatologie und Therapie der Kriegsverletzungen der peripheren Nerven. Deutsche Ztschr. f. Nervenh. *59*:32–172, 1918.

———: Die Symptomatologie der Schussverletzungen der peripheren Nerven. In Lewandowsky, M.: Handbuch der Neurologie, Ergänzungsbd., 2. Teil. 1929, pp. 975–1508.

———: The Dermatomes in Man. Brain *56*:1–39, 1933.

———: Symptomatologie der Erkrankungen des Rückenmarks und seiner Wurzeln. In Bumke, O., and Foerster, O.: Handbuch der Neurologie *5*:1–403, 1936.

———: Spezielle Physiologie und spezielle functionelle Pathologie der quergestreiften Muskeln. In Bumke, O., and Foerster, O., Handbuch der Neurologie *3*:1–639, 1937.

———: Operativ-experimentelle Erfahrungen beim Menschen über den Einfluss des Nervensystems auf den Kreislauf. Ztschr. f. d. ges. Neurol. u. Psychiat. *167*:439–461, 1939.

Frazier, C. H., and Silbert, S.: Observations in Five Hundred Cases of Injuries of the Peripheral Nerves at U. S. A. General Hospital No. 11. Surg., Gynec. & Obst. *30*:50–63, 1920.

Freeman, N. E.: The Treatment of Causalgia Arising from Gunshot Wounds of the Peripheral Nerves. Surgery *22*:68–82, 1947.

Fulton, J. F.: Physiology of the Nervous System. Ed. 3. New York, Oxford University Press, 1949.

Gerard, R. W.: The Physiology of Pain: Abnormal Neuron States in Causalgia and Related Phenomena. Anesthesiology *12*:1–13, 1951.

Girard, P. M., and Childress, H. M.: Sciatic Nerve Pressure Following Rupture and Fibrosis of a Hamstring Muscle. J.A.M.A. *113*:2412–2413, 1939.

Golseth, J. G., and Fizzell, J. A.: An Instrument for Direct Nerve Stimulation. J. Neurosurg. *4*:393–396, 1947.

Götze, W.: Über die Leistungssteigerung der Muskulatur nach peripheren Nervenverletzungen durch Prostigmingaben. Zentralbl. f. Neurochir. *7*:55–59, 1942.

Granit, R., Leksell, L., and Skoglund, C. R.: Fibre Interaction in Injured or Compressed Region of Nerve. Brain *67*:125–140, 1944.

Griffiths, D. L.: Volkmann's Ischaemic Contracture (Hunterian Lecture). Brit. J. Surg. *28*:239–260, 1940.

Gurdjian, E. S., and Smothers, H. M.: Peripheral Nerve Injuries in Fractures and Dislocations of Long Bones. J. Neurosurg. *2*:202–219, 1945.

Guttmann, L.: Topographic Studies of Disturbances of Sweat Secretion after Complete Lesions of Peripheral Nerves. J. Neurol. & Psychiat. *3*:197–210, 1940.

Harris, H. A.: Peripheral Nerve Injuries. Lancet *1*:220, 1943.

Harris, W.: The Morphology of the Brachial Plexus. London, Oxford University Press, 1939.

Harvey, A. M., and Kuffler, S. W.: Motor Nerve Function with Lesions of the Peripheral Nerves. A Quantitative Study. Arch. Neurol. & Psychiat. *52*:317–322, 1944.

Head, H.: Studies in Neurology. Vol. 2. London, Oxford University Press, 1920.

Henderson, W. R.: Clinical Assessment of Peripheral Nerve Injuries; Tinel's Test. Lancet 2:801, 1948.

Herz, E., Glaser, G. H., Moldaver, J., and Hoen, T. I.: Electrical Skin Resistance Test in Evaluation of Peripheral Nerve Injuries. Arch. Neurol. & Psychiat. *56:* 365–380, 1946.

Highet, W. B.: Procaine Nerve Block in the Investigation of Peripheral Nerve Injuries. J. Neurol., Neurosurg. & Psychiat. *5:*101–116, 1942a.

———: Splintage of Peripheral Nerve Injuries. Lancet *1:*555–558, 1942b.

———: Innervation and Function of the Thenar Muscles. Lancet *1:*227–230, 1943a.

———: Peripheral Nerve Injuries. In Maingot, R., Slesinger, E. G., and Fletcher, E., War Wounds and Injuries, ed. 2. Baltimore, Williams & Wilkins Co., 1943b, pp. 61–140.

———, and Holmes, W.: Traction Injuries to the Lateral Popliteal Nerve and Traction Injuries to Peripheral Nerves after Suture. Brit. J. Surg. *30:*212–233, 1943.

Hirschmann, J.: Über den Fusssohlenschmerz und dessen Behandlung bei Verletzung des Nervus tibialis. Nervenarzt *16:*25–30, 1943a.

———: Schon- und Gewohnheitslähmungen bei Nervenschussverletzungen. Ztschr. f. d. ges. Neurol. u. Psychiat. *175:*688–698, 1943b.

Hoffmann, P.: Über eine Methode, den Erfolg einer Nervennaht zu beurteilen. Med. Klin. *11:*359–361, 856–858, 1915a.

———: Weiteres über das Verhalten frisch regenerierter Nerven und über die Methode den Erfolg einer Nervennaht frühzeitig zu beurteilen. Med. Klin. *11:* 856–858, 1915b.

Holmes, W., Highet, W. B., and Seddon, H. J.: Ischaemic Nerve Lesions Occurring in Volkmann's Contracture. Brit. J. Surg., *32:*259–275, 1944.

Homans, J.: Minor Causalgia: A Hyperesthetic Neurovascular Syndrome. New England J. Med. *222:*870–874, 1940.

Horner, F.: Ueber eine Form von Ptosis. Klin. Monatsbl. f. Augenh. 7:193–196, 1869.

Hutton, W. K.: Remarks on the Innervation of the Dorsum Manus, with Special Reference to Certain Rare Abnormalities. J. Anat. & Physiol. *40:*326–331, 1906.

Inman, V. T., and Saunders, J. B. deC. M.: The Clinico-anatomical Aspects of the Lumbosacral Region. Radiology *38:*669–678, 1942.

———, and ———: Referred Pain from Skeletal Structures. J. Nerv. & Ment. Dis. *99:*660–667, 1944.

———, ———, and Abbott, L. C.: Observations on the Function of the Shoulder Joint. J. Bone & Joint Surg. *26:*1–30, 1944.

Jones, F. W.: The Principles of Anatomy as Seen in the Hand. Ed. 2. Baltimore, Williams & Wilkins Co., 1942.

Jones, R. (ed.): Orthopaedic Surgery of Injuries. Vol. 2. London, Oxford Univ. Press, 1921, p. 555.

Jung, R.: Die allgemeine Symptomatologie der Nervenverletzungen und ihre physiologischen Grundlagen. Nervenarzt *14:*493–516, 1941.

———: In Lexer, E., Lehrbuch der Allgemeinen Chirurgie, neugearbeitet von E. Rehn. Vol. 2. 1952, pp. 284–286.

Keegan, J. J., and Garrett, F. D.: The Segmental Distribution of the Cutaneous Nerves in the Limbs of Man. Anat. Rec. *102:*409–438, 1948.

Kelly, M.: Spread of Sensory and Motor Loss after Nerve Injury. Neurology *2:*36–45, 1952.

Kendall, H. O., and Kendall, F. P.: Muscles. Testing and Function. Baltimore, Williams & Wilkins, 1949.

Krambach, R.: Über einen Fall von Athetose nach peripherer Schussverletzungen. Ztschr. f. d. ges. Neurol. u. Psychiat. *53:*230–234, 1920a.

———: Über Störungen der Tiefensensibilität bei peripheren Schädigungen. Ztschr. f. d. ges. Neurol. u. Psychiat. *59:*272–280, 1920b.

Kramer, F.: Allgemeine Symptomatologie der Rückenmarksnerven und der Plexus. In Bumke, O., and Foerster, O.: Handbuch der Neurologie *3:*640–700, 1937.

Kraus, W. M.: The Cutaneous Distribution of the Trigeminal Nerve. Ann. Surg. *101:*212–221, 1935.

Learmonth, J.: A Variation in the Distribution of the Radial Branch of the Musculo-Spiral Nerve. J. Anat. *53:*371–372, 1919.

———: Personal communication to the authors, 1950.

316 BIBLIOGRAPHY

Lehmann, W.: Die Störungen der Lage und Bewegungsempfindungen in Zehen und Fingergelenken nach Nervenschüssen. Münch. med. Wchnschr. *63*(3): 1597–1600, 1916.

Leriche, R.: Étude critique des mécanismes de la douleur chez les amputés. (Nouvelles orientations de son traitement. Prophylaxie.) J. Chir. *66:5*–21, 1950.

Lewey, F. H., Kuhn, Jr., W. G., and Juditski, J. T.: A Standardized Method for Assessing the Strength of Hand and Foot Muscles. Surg., Gynec. & Obst. *85:* 785–793, 1947.

Lewis, D.: Nerve Injuries Complicating Fractures. S. Clin. N. America *16:*1401–1413, 1936.

Lewis, T.: Experiments Relating to Cutaneous Hyperalgesia and Its Spread through Somatic Nerves. Clin. Sc. *2:*373–423, 1936.

———: Pain. New York, The Macmillan Co., 1942.

Livingston, W. K., Davis, E. W., and Livingston, K. E.: "Delayed Recovery" in Peripheral Nerve Lesions Caused by High Velocity Projectile Wounding. J. Neurosurg. *2:*170–179, 1945.

Lyons, W. R., and Woodhall, B.: Atlas of Peripheral Nerve Injuries. Philadelphia, W. B. Saunders Co., 1949.

Makins, G. H.: On Gunshot Injuries to the Blood-Vessels: Founded on Experience Gained in France during the Great War, 1914–1918. Bristol, John Wright & Sons, 1919, pp. 94–96.

Marinesco: Sur les lésions des centres nerveux consécutives à l'élongation des nerfs périphériques et craniens. Compt. rend. Soc. biol. *11:*324–326, 1901.

Mayfield, F. H.: Causalgia. Springfield, Ill., Charles C Thomas, 1951.

Meyerding, H. W.: Volkmann's Ischemic Contracture. J.A.M.A. *94:*394–400, 1930.

Mitchell, S. W.: Injuries of Nerves and Their Consequences. Philadelphia, J. B. Lippincott & Co., 1872; Chap. XIV, Neural Maladies of Stumps.

———, Moorehouse, G. R., and Keen, W. W.: Gunshot Wounds and Other Injuries of Nerves. Philadelphia, J. B. Lippincott & Co., 1864.

Mutch, J. R.: The Pupil after Cervico-Thoracic Sympathetic Ganglionectomy: Photographic Observations in Man. Edinburgh M. J. *43*(2): 743–746, 1936.

Napier, J. R.: The Significance of Tinel's Sign in Peripheral Nerve Injuries. Brain *72:*63–82, 1949.

Nathan, P. W.: On the Pathogenesis of Causalgia in Peripheral Nerve Injuries. Brain *70:*145–170, 1947.

Nerve Injuries Committee, Medical Research Council: Aids to Investigation of Peripheral Nerve Injuries. M. R. C. War Memorandum No. 7, London, His Majesty's Stationery Office, 1942.

Newman, L. B.: A New Device for Measuring Muscle Strength. The Myometer. Arch. Phys. Med. *30:*234–237, 1949.

Nordén, Å.: Peripheral Injuries of the Spinal Accessory Nerve. Acta chir. scand. *94:*515–532, 1946.

Nulsen, F. E., and Lewey, F. H.: Intraneural Bipolar Stimulation: A New Aid in the Assessment of Nerve Injuries. Science *106:*301–302, 1947.

Oppenheim, H.: Text-Book of Nervous Diseases. Ed. 5, vol. 1, trans. by A. Bruce. London & Edinburgh, T. N. Foulis, 1911.

Parkes, A. R.: Traumatic Ischaemia of Peripheral Nerves With Some Observations on Volkmann's Ischaemic Paralysis. Brit. J. Surg. *32:*403–414, 1945.

Perthes: Ueber Fernschädigungen peripherischer Nerven durch Schuss und über die sogenannten Kommotionslähmungen der Nerven bei Schussverletzungen. Württ. Medic. Corresp. Blatt, 1916.

Philippides. D.: Die Prüfung der Vasomotorenfunktion bei peripheren Nervenläsionen. Chirurg *14:*385–389, 1942a.

———: Das Wesen und die Behandlung der Kausalgie. Chirurg *14:*481–489, 1942b.

Platt, H.: Traction Lesions of the External Popliteal Nerve. Lancet *2:*612–614, 1940.

Pollock, L. J.: Overlap of So-called Protopathic Sensibility as Seen in Peripheral Nerve Lesions. Arch. Neurol. & Psychiat. *2:*667–700, 1919a.

Pollock, L. J.: Supplementary Muscle Movements in Peripheral Nerve Lesions. Arch. Neurol. & Psychiat. *2:*518–531, 1919b.

———: Extracranial Injuries of Multiple Cranial Nerves. Arch. Neurol. & Psychiat. *4:*517–528, 1920.

———: Nerve Overlap as Related to the Relatively Early Return of Pain Sense Following Injury to the Peripheral Nerves. J. Comp. Neurol. *32:*357–378, 1921.

———: The Pattern of Sensory Recovery in Peripheral Nerve Lesions. Surg., Gynec. & Obst. *49:*160–166, 1929.

———: Peripheral-Nerve Injuries. In Solomon, H. C., and Yakovlev, P. I.: Manual of Military Neuropsychiatry. Philadelphia, W. B. Saunders Co., 1944.

———, and Davis, L.: Peripheral Nerve Injuries. New York, Paul B. Hoeber, Inc., 1933.

———, Golseth, J. G., Mayfield, F., Arieff, A. J., and Oester, Y. T.: Electrodiagnosis of Lesions of Peripheral Nerves in Man. Arch. Neurol. & Psychiat. *60:*1–19, 1949.

Puckett, W. O., Grundfest, H., McElroy, W. D., and McMillen, J. H.: Damage to Peripheral Nerves by High Velocity Missiles Without a Direct Hit. J. Neurosurg. *3:*294–305, 1946.

Rasmussen, T. B., and Freedman, H.: Treatment of Causalgia: An Analysis of 100 Cases. J. Neurosurg. *3:*165–173, 1946.

Redlich, E.: Über Störungen des Vibrationsgefühls bei Schussverletzungen der peripherischen Nerven. Jahrb. f. Psychiat. u. Neurol. *37:*92–107, 1917.

Richards, R. L.: Traumatic Ulnar Neuritis. The Results of Anterior Transposition of the Ulnar Nerve. Edinburgh M. J. *52:*14–21, 1945.

Richter, C. P.: Instructions for Using the Cutaneous Resistance Recorder, or "Dermometer," on Peripheral Nerve Injuries, Sympathectomies, and Paravertebral Nerve Blocks. J. Neurosurg. *3:*181–191, 1946.

———: Personal communication to the authors, 1953.

———, and Katz, D. T.: Peripheral Nerve Injuries Determined by the Electrical Skin Resistance Method. I. Ulnar Nerve. J.A.M.A. *122:*648–651, 1943.

———, and Woodruff, B. G.: Facial Patterns of Electrical Skin Resistance. Their Relation to Sleep, External Temperature, Hair Distribution, Sensory Dermatomes and Skin Disease. Bull. Johns Hopkins Hosp. *70:*442–459, 1942.

———, and ———: Lumbar Dermatomes in Man Determined by the Electrical Skin Resistance Method. J. Neurophysiol. *8:*323–338, 1945.

Ritchie, A. E.: The Electrical Diagnosis of Peripheral Nerve Injury. Brain *67:*314–330, 1944.

Russell, W. R., and Harrington, A. B.: Early Diagnosis of Peripheral Nerve Injuries in Battle Casualties. Brit. M. J. *2:*4–8, 1944.

———, and Spalding, J. M. K.: Treatment of Painful Amputation Stumps. Brit. M. J. *2:*68–73, 1950.

Seddon, H. J.: Three Types of Nerve Injury. Brain *66:*237–288, 1943.

Sherman, I. C.: Contractures Following Experimentally Produced Peripheral-Nerve Lesions. J. Bone & Joint Surg. *30:*474–488, 1948.

Shumacker, Jr., H. B.: Causalgia. III. A General Discussion. Surgery *24:*485–504, 1948.

Sittig, O.: Atypische Ausbreitung des sensiblen Radialisgebietes an der Hand. Monatsschr. f. Psychiat. u. Neurol. *67:*229–233, 1928.

Smithwick, R. H.: Modified Dorsal Sympathectomy for Vascular Spasm (Raynaud's Disease) of the Upper Extremity. A Preliminary Report. Ann. Surg. *104:*339–350, 1936.

———, Freeman, N. E., and White, J. C.: Effect of Epinephrine on the Sympathectomized Human Extremity. An Additional Cause of Failure of Operations for Raynaud's Disease. Arch. Surg. *29:*759–767, 1934.

Spalteholz, W.: Handatlas der Anatomie des Menschen. 5. Aufl., III. Bd. Leipzig, S. Hirzel, 1909.

Speidel, C. C.: Studies of Living Nerves. III. Phenomena of Nerve Irritation and Recovery, Degeneration and Repair. J. Comp. Neurol. *61:*1–80, 1935.

Spielmeyer, W.: Zur Klinik und Anatomie der Nervenschussverletzungen. Berlin, Springer, 1915, pp. 32, 33.

Spurling, R. G.: Early Treatment of Combined Bone and Nerve Lesions. Bull. U. S. Army M. Dept. *4:*444–446, 1945.

———, and Matson, D. D.: Simple Tests of Nerve Trunk Injuries. Bull. U. S. Army Med. Dept. *75:*71–76, 1944.

———, and Woodhall, B.: Experiences with Early Nerve Surgery in Peripheral Nerve Injuries. Ann. Surg. *123:*731–748, 1946.

Stone, T. T.: Phantom Limb Pain and Central Pain. Relief by Ablation of a Portion of Posterior Central Cerebral Convolution. Arch. Neurol. & Psychiat. *63:*739–748, 1950.

Stookey, B. P.: Surgical and Mechanical Treatment of Peripheral Nerves. Philadelphia, W. B. Saunders Co., 1922.

Strotzka, H.: Die sog. Fernschädigung bei Nervenschüssen und ihre konservative Therapie. Ztschr. f. d. ges. Neurol. u. Psychiat. *175:*304–312, 1942.

Subcommittee on Neurosurgery, Division of Medical Sciences of the National Research Council: Neurosurgery and Thoracic Surgery. Philadelphia, W. B. Saunders Co., 1943.

Sunderland, S.: The Significance of Hypothenar Elevation in Movements of Opposition of the Thumb. Australian & New Zealand J. Surg. *13:*155–156, 1944a.

———: Flexion of the Distal Phalanx of the Thumb in Lesions of the Median Nerve. Australian & New Zealand J. Surg. *13:*157–159, 1944b.

———: Voluntary Movements and the Deceptive Action of Muscles in Peripheral Nerve Lesions. Australian & New Zealand J. Surg *13:*160–184, 1944c.

———: Blood Supply of Peripheral Nerves. Practical Considerations. Arch. Neurol. & Psychiat. *54:*280–282, 1945; see also *53:*91, 1945, and *54:*283, 1945.

———: Rate of Regeneration in Human Peripheral Nerves. Analysis of the Interval Between Injury and Onset of Recovery. Arch. Neurol. & Psychiat. *58:*251–295, 1947.

———: A Classification of Peripheral Nerve Injuries Producing Loss of Function. Brain *74:*491–516, 1952a.

———: Factors Influencing the Course of Regeneration and the Quality of the Recovery after Nerve Suture. Brain *75:*19–54, 1952b.

———, and Bedbrook, G. M.: The Relative Sympathetic Contribution to Individual Roots of the Brachial Plexus in Man. Brain *72:*297–301, 1949.

———, and Bradley, K. C.: The Cross-Sectional Area of Peripheral Nerve Trunks Devoted to Nerve Fibers. Brain *72:*428–449, 1949.

———, and ———: Denervation Atrophy of the Distal Stump of a Severed Nerve. J. Comp. Neurol. *93:*401–420, 1950.

——— and ———: Rate of Advance of Hoffmann-Tinel Sign in Regenerating Nerves. Further Observations. Arch. Neurol. & Psychiat. *67:*650–654, 1952.

———, and Ray, L. J.: The Intraneural Topography of the Sciatic Nerve and Its Popliteal Divisions in Man. Brain *71:*242–273, 1948.

———, and ———: Denervation Changes in Mammalian Striated Muscle. J. Neurol., Neurosurg. & Psychiat. *13:*159–177, 1950.

———, and ———: The Effect of Denervation on Nail Growth. J. Neurol., Neurosurg. & Psychiat. *15:*50–53, 1952.

de Takáts, G.: Nature of Painful Vasodilatation in Causalgic State. Arch. Neurol. & Psychiat. *50:*318–326, 1943.

Tilney, F., and Riley, H. A.: The Form and Functions of the Central Nervous System. An Introduction to the Study of Nervous Diseases. Ed. 3. New York, Paul B. Hoeber. Inc., 1938, pp. 162–164.

Tinel, J.: Le signe du "fourmillement" dans les lésions des nerfs périphériques. Presse méd. *23:*388–389, 1915.

———: Nerve Wounds. Symptomatology of Peripheral Nerve Lesions Caused by War Wounds. Transl. by F. Rothwell; rev. and edited by C. A. Joll. London, Baillière. Tindall & Cox, 1917.

Trotter, W.: The Insulation of the Nervous System (Victor Horsley Memorial Lecture). Brit. M. J. *2:*103–107, 1926.

Turel, R.: La Douleur en Neurologie. Paris, Masson et Cie, 1951, p. 72.

Ulmer, J., and Mayfield, F.: Causalgia. A Study of 75 Cases. Surg., Gynec. & Obst. *83:*789–796, 1946.

Vogel, P.: Über Verletzungen des axillaren Gefässnervenstranges. Ein Beitrag zur Klinik der Plexuslähmungen des Armes. Nervenarzt *14:*484–493, 1941.

Walshe, F. R. M.: The Anatomy and Physiology of Cutaneous Sensibility: A Critical Review. Brain *65:*48–112, 1942.

Wartenberg, R.: A Sign of Ulnar Palsy. J.A.M.A. *112:*1688, 1939.

———: A Test for Median Nerve Function. Surg., Gynec. & Obst. *73:*872–873, 1941.

———: Diagnostic Tests in Neurology; A Selection for Office Use. Chicago, Year Book Publ., 1953.

Weddell, G., Guttmann, L., and Gutman, E.: The Local Extension of Nerve Fibers into Denervated Areas of Skin. J. Neurol. & Psychiat. *4:*206–225, 1941.

Wexberg, E.: Kriegsverletzungen der peripheren Nerven. Ztschr. f. d. ges. Neurol. u. Psychiat. *36:*345–399, 1917.

———: Kriegsverletzungen der peripheren Nerven. Ztschr. f. d. ges. Neurol. u. Psychiat. (Referatenteil) *18:*257–365, 1919.

———: Traumatische Erkrankungen der peripheren Nerven und des Plexus. In Bumke, O., and Foerster, O.: Handbuch der Neurologie *9:*23–68, 1935.

White, J. C.: Pain after Amputation and Its Treatment. J.A.M.A. 1030–1035, 1944.

———, Heroy, W. W., and Goodman, E. N.: Causalgia Following Gunshot Injuries of Nerves. Role of Emotional Stimuli and Surgical Cure through Interruption of Diencephalic Efferent Discharge by Sympathectomy. Ann. Surg. *128:*161–183, 1948.

———, Smithwick, R. H., and Simeone, F. I.: The Autonomic Nervous System. Anatomy, Physiology and Surgical Application. Ed. 3. New York, The Macmillan Co., 1952, pp. 153–156.

Wilson, S. A. K.: Neurology. Edited by A. N. Bruce. Vol. 1. Baltimore, Williams & Wilkins Co., 1940.

Woodhall, B.: Discussion in a Symposium on the Intervertebral Disc. J. Bone & Joint Surg. *29:*370–475, 1947.

———: The Surgical Repair of Acute Peripheral Nerve Injury. S. Clin. N. America *5:*1369–1390, 1951.

———: Trapezius Paralysis Following Minor Surgical Procedures in the Posterior Cervical Triangle. Results Following Cranial Nerve Suture. Ann. Surg. *136:*375–380, 1952a.

——— (Chairman): Preliminary Report: Peripheral Nerve Regeneration Study Centers (not published), 1952b.

———, and Lyons, W. R.: Peripheral Nerve Injuries. I. The Results of "Early" Nerve Suture: A Preliminary Report. Surgery *19:*757–789, 1946.

Woods, A. H.: Misleading Motor Symptoms in the Diagnosis of Nerve Wounds. Arch. Neurol. & Psychiat. *2:*532–538, 1919.

Zülch, K. J.: Kriegsverletzungen der peripheren Nerven, ihre Diagnostik und chirurgische Behandlung. Med. Klin. *38:*985–989, 1942a.

———: Die Nervenschussschmerz. Ztschr. f. d. ges. Neurol. u. Psychiat. *175:*188–224 1942b.

Index